Classification and Cataloguing in Digital Libraries

CLASSIFICATION AND CATALOGUING IN DIGITAL LIBRARIES

Edited by
S.P. Singh

OMEGA PUBLICATIONS
NEW DELHI-110 002 (INDIA)

OMEGA PUBLICATIONS
4378/4B, G-4 JMD House
Gali Murari Lal, Ansari Road
Daryaganj, New Delhi - 110 002
Phone : 65901906 (Off.)
e-mail : omega_publications@yahoo.com

Head Office :
78/3, Laxmi Garden
Near Satya Jyoti School,
Gurgaon (Haryana)
Mob : 9811787417

Classification and Cataloguing in Digital Libraries

First Published : 2009

ISBN : 978–81–8455–152–5

PRINTED IN INDIA

Published by Mahendra Garg for Omega Publications, New Delhi-110002 and Printed at Tarun Offset Press, Delhi-110053

Preface

Classification is a tool for organizing the document stores or library. A document is the physical carrier of a message. A document may be in various forms like book, films, slides, periodicals, newspapers, cards bearing the names and addresses of local organizations in a reference library files and machine readable media. The messages that documents bear may be simple facts, views, interpretations of events or works of art. For example Gita is message, just as Yojna is periodical, The Hindu is newspaper or name and address record is directory. When the number of documents become too much for a person seeking a particular information to scan through all those, it becomes necessary to organize them. When these tasks become too great to be performed informally, it is institutionalized. Specialists are appointed to carry out the task. These specialists are librarians and other information workers, whose function is to mediate between their clients and the documents containing the message.

Librarian's contribution to society is very precisely. He enables clients to find any required subject of documents from the total set as quickly and easily as possible. He selects and collects documents, organizes his collection, cooperates with other librarians and information workers, and he helps as well as encourages his readers to use documents. The main task on which the user depends, is the organization of collection which means the arrangement of documents in some helpful order and the provision of catalogues and indexes which act as both-keys and complements to that order. We call the techniques developed to bring about this organization 'fixing'.

The major issues described in this book are : *Process of Classification; Collection and Classification in Library; Theory of Classification Schedule; Library Computerisation; Digital Cataloguing Resources; Cataloguing by Multimedia; On-line Cataloguing; Challenges to Traditional Cataloguing; Digital Library Topical Area; Textual Material and Digital Library; Preservation of Digital Information; etc.*

No doubt, these will serve the purpose of trainees and trainers, professionals and policy planners in the field. Since the sources of information are all secondary, we express our gratitude to the scholars whose works are cited or substantially made use of. We are thankful to all those who rendered ready help and cooperation while working on this project.

—Editor

Contents

1

Process of Classification

The process of classification, in an enumerative scheme achieved first by consulting the index and then by proceeding location pinpointed in the schedules. Although the index lists subjects rather than concepts one should never classify of index alone as this can lead to error. The relevant schedules examined in order to find the correct number. To take a example, if a book which deals with the work of famous such as Shakespeare, Dinkar and Nehru were to be classified, index entry for 'Literature' might be referred to and the class obtained. However after proceeding to in the schedules it apparent immediately that 'Literature' is divided by language the question whether all the authors dealt with are English authors must then be classified. Thus the structure classification scheme itself acts are as classifying.

If the classification of machine bolts were copied in a hierarchical scheme, dividing first by material, then by thread shape and head shape and finally by finish, it would begin to the following, appearance: brass bolts stainless steel machine bolts steel.

Round

Unifinished Chromium

plated Zinc plated Painted

Flat

Unfinished Chromium

plated Zinc plated Painted

Hexagonal

Unfinished Chromium

plated Zinc plated Painted

Square

Unfinished Chromium

plated Zinc plated Painted

1 BA

Round

Unfinished Chromium

plated Zinc plated Painted

Flat

Unfinished Chromium

plated Zinc plated Painted

Hexagonal

Unfinished Chromium

plated Zinc plated Painted

Square

Unfinished Chromium

plated Zinc plated Painted

2BA

Round Unfinished Chromium

plated Zinc plated Painted

Flat

Unfinished Chromium

plated Zinc plated Painted and

so on. Several problems are apparent:

The extract from the scheme shown here has only progressed as far as the subject 'Painted flat 2 BA stainless steel bolts', yet already it is far longer than the faceted scheme.

As subjects, and not concepts, are being listed, constituent concept, such as 'unfinished' have to be repeated every time that they occur in a complex subject. However, it is still only possible to classify a subject if it is listed. For example, the subject 'Chromium plated stainless steel bolts' (that is, omitting the size) cannot be classified nor can the subject 'chromium plated bolts',

Because of the problems (1) and (2), a hierarchical, enumerative scheme'tends to become a compromise, and enumeration is not carried to its logical conclusion. Therefore the finished scheme it often very complex in nature and the basic principles of constructior are difficult to identify.

CLASSIFICATION FOR OFFICE ORGANIZATION

The following are illustrative extracts from a possible enumerative classification for the organization, by subject, of off in files,

16 TRAINING

16.1 MATERIALS

16.11 Visual aids Supplies

16.12 COURSES

16.2 Clerical

16.2.2 Management

16.2.3 Engineering

The index entries to the above schedule would be:

Clerical courses	16.2.1
Courses	16.2
Engineering courses	16.2.3
Management courses	16.2.2
Materials	16.1
Supplies	16.1.2
Training	16
Visual aids	16.1.1

A system might be suitable for the products, supplies, services and functions of an organization. As an advantage the flexibility which the system offers, in that it is easy to subdivide and add topics, but, a disadvantage is the fact that an index is essential. Therefore a combination of systems for storing and retrieving information in the office and recommends 'direct filing', that is, alphabetical sequences by name, subject, and so on, where an index is not required.

A hierarchical enumerative scheme has the further problem that a subject can only be classified if it is enumerated, or listed. To take a simple example from the above scheme, the subject 'Visual aids for clerical courses', cannot be classified. A choice would have to made between 'Visual aids' (16.1.1) and 'Clerical courses' (16.2.1).

DEWEY DECIMAL CLASSIFICATION

This is a classification which covers the whole of knowledge was devised over a hundred years ago for shelf arrangement libraries. It has simple decimal, expansible notation. Here, is example, are some parts of the Literature class, which the reader see equate closely to the scheme shown above although the notations different:

800	Literature
810	American literature in English
811	Poetry
812	Drama
813	Fiction
829	Literature of English and Anglo-Saxon languages
821	English poetry
822	English drama
823	English fiction
830	Litnature of Germanic (Teutonic) languages
831	German poetry
832	German drama
833	German fiction
840	Literature of Roman languages. French literature
841	French poetry
842	French drama
843	French fiction

With a decimal notation each subject is capable of division into nine subsidiary subjects, for example 821, 822, 823, 829, all of which are theoretically co-equal. As very few subject divide into nine parts naturally distortion is bound to occur, nevertheless this is an easily understood system and offers hospitality and expansibility. The Dewey scheme utilizes a three figure 'minimum' base, a illustrated above; further division continues after the decimal period for example:

822.3 English drama of the Elizabethan period where the '3' represents 'elizabe than period'. A fifth digit may then indicate a particular dramatist within this period, for example:

822.3 Shakespeare

If an item which deals with a work such as 'A criticism of Shakespeare's Macbeth' were classified by the above scheme, the classification is by subject, but if the actual text of Macbeth were to be defined, classification in this case would be by form, that is, literary form, it will be necessary in general classification to cater for this classes.

641.5 Cookery

641.52 For breakfast

641.53 For luncheon, brunch, elevenses, tea, supper, snacks

641.54 For dinner

641.55 Time and money-saving cookery

641.552 Money-saving cookery

641.555 Tune-saving cookery

641.56 For special situations

641.561 For one or two persons

641.562 For persons of specific ages

641.5622 Infants and children

641.5627 Adults aged 65 and over

641.563 For health, appearancepersonal reasons

641.5631	For persons with heart diseases
641.56311	For sick persons
641.56314	For persons with diabetes
641.5632	Cookery with specified vitamin and mineral content
641.5634	High-calorie cookery
641.5635	Low-calorie cookery
641.5636	Vegetarian cookery
641.5637	Health-food cookery
641.5638	Protein, fat, carbohydrate cookery
641.504	For various specific times of year
641.506	For Christian church limitations and observances
641.507	For religious limitations and observances
641.508	For special occasions. Holidays, birthdays, etc.

The above extract illustrates the great detail of this scheme but it is also somewhat confusing and illustrates the problems of enumeration A compromise has had to be reached and hierarchical process of division has not been continued at each step. For example, division by 'Meal' is not further subdivided by'Special situations' and then by 'Health, etc.', but division by each of the characteristics is carried out separately. Thus it is impossible classify the subject 'Cooking dinner for one' or 'Cooking for aged 65 and over who suffer from heart disease'. A choice has to made in these instances between 'Cooking for dinner' or 'Cooking for one' and 'Cooking for adults aged 65 and over, or 'Cooking persons with heart disease'.

What is known as 'cross-classification' also occurs. This happens when different characteristics are applied at the one point division. For example, 'For special situations' is divided by characteristics of 'number of people' and 'age' at the one step.

The index to the Dewey decimal classification is a very detailed often praised indeed and its relative nature, which was devised all lauded by Melvil Dewey (the scheme's creator), has had considerable influence on many other indexes. Here is an illustrative example:

Sadism

Gen. med.	616.85835
geriatrics	618.97685835
pediatrics	618.9285835
psychology	157.7
statistics	312.385835

other aspects were see Sexual deviations

This indicates that various aspects of the subject 'Sadism' can be found in five different places in the schedules, and the cross reference informs the user that additional aspects may be found bconsulting 'Sexual deviations'.

Dewey classification numbers can become quite lengthy and the digits after the decimal point are sometimes split into groups of the for greater convenience and ease of use.

Library of Congress Classification

This classification was constructed at the turn of the century for the US Library of Congress and it reflects knowledge as represented in the books which are included in this great library's stock. The following extracts are taken from Class T 'Technology', Classes published in separate volumes and Class currently contains close 01 400 pages. This is only one of upwards of thirty volumes in the complete scheme, which gives some indication of the vast size that a classification which attempts to enumerate all subjects can reach.

Within Class T, Class This 'Building construction', and The 6000 onwards is concerned with 'Building fittings and their installation'. Here is a brief outline of this section of the scheme:

Building Fittings and their Classification

6010- GENERAL WORKS

6100- PLUMBING AND PIPEFITIING

7000- HEATING AND VENTILATION

7700- ILLUMINATION LIGHTING

8000- DECORATION AND DECORATIVE FURNISHINGS

9000- PROTECTION OF BUILDINGS

Each of these divisions is further subdivided, for example:

PROTECTION OF BUILDINGS

6488 6489 6490

9025 General works

9031 Against damage from natural causes 9100- x Protection against fire

9700 Protection from burglary, sabotage, etc.,

The above extracts illustrate the hierarchical nature of the scheme but fail to do the scheme justice in that Class TH from division 6000 onwards actually takes up 21 pages of complex schedules and the principles of construction become hidden in a wealth of enumerative detail. Here, for instance, are the divisions of one very small section, 'Plumbing of the bathroom':

Plumbing of bathrooms, Toilet rooms, Lavatories

6485 General works

6486 General special. Specifications, etc.

6487 Systems

Details Fixtures

6488 General works

6489 Catalogues of bathroom fixtures

6490 Basins Baths

6491 General works

6492 Shower baths, Sprays

6493 Tubs

6494 Foot baths

6495 Sintz baths

6496 Bidets

6497 Soil fixtures

6498 Water closets. Toilets

6499 Urinals

6500 Flush tanks and auxiliary valves, etc.

The subject 'Plumbing of a bidet', for example, would have the class number TH6496. Despite the detail displayed here, the true nature of the Library of Congress scheme is still not fully revealed. Here is a further extract from 'Heating of buildings':

Heating of buildings

7201 Periodicals, societies, etc.

7205 Congresses

7207 Collected works (non-serial)

7209 Dictionaries and encyclopedias Directories

7212 General works

7216 Special localities

7215 History

7216 Country divisions, A-Z General works

7221 Early to 1860

7222 1869

Utility of Scheme

The process of classification in an enumerative scheme, achieved first by consulting the index and then by proceeding to the location pinpointed in the schedules. Although the index lists subjects rather than concepts, one should never classify from the index alone as this can lead to error. The relevant schedules must be examined in order to find the correct number. To take a simple example, if a book which deals with the work of famous authors such as Shakespeare, Dinkar and Nehru were to be classified, the index entry for 'Literature' might be referred to and the class number obtained. However after proceeding to 1 in the schedules it will be apparent immediately that 'Literature' is divided by language and the question whether all the authors dealt with are English language authors must then be classified.

It is possible to introduce an element of synthesis, or 'number building into a hierarchical enumerative scheme, in several different ways. This helps to reduce the length of the schedules but improves efficiency.

One method is to provide auxiliary tables of terms which may be applicable throughout the schedules. These tables may include, for example: Common subdivisions, such as those of form of presentation, for example 'Encyclopaedia' or 'Serial'. Geographical tables for specifying 'place', for example 'United States' or 'United Kingdom'.

Permit tables for specifying 'time', for example 'Twentieth century' .

Another method is to include instructions within the schedules themselves for dividing one classification number in the same manner as answer. All plants, for instance, may suffer from 'injuries', 'disease' and 'pests'. Instead of enumerating each of these concepts under every individual plant, they can be listed once and instructions given for the division of each plant in, the same way.

BIBLIOGRAPHIC CLASSIFICATION

The 1940-53 edition of this general classification scheme for library materials by HE. Bliss is essentially enumerative but a certain amount of synthesis is provided for by 'systematic schedules', some of which may be applied throughout the scheme but others are applicable only in specific classes. Below are shown extracts from two schedules of the former variety:

Numerical Divisions of Any Class or Section

1. Reference books (including dictionaries, glossaries, encyclopedias, indexes, handbooks)
2. Bibliography....
3. History....
4. Biography....

Geographical Division

a	America
aa	North America
ed	Europe
ea	Great Britain

'Education', in the Bibliographic classification, is J, and by use of the above schedules: A history of education in Great Britain == J3ea

This number has been derived in a very similar way to the way in which classification is achieved in a faceted scheme. The subject is analyzed into its constituent concepts and a notation assigned to each:

History = 3 Education = J Great Britain= ea

The instructions for citation order and method of combination given in the scheme must now be followed. Usually, classification would be first by subject then by 'place' and then by 'form', but when 'form' is 'history', as in this case, 'place' is cited last. As different symbols are used, a linking device is not required.

Bliss was a firm believer in brevity of notation. He thought that the economic limit should be three or four letters or digits. Perhaps because of this, he did not emphasize sufficiently what he refers to as 'composite notation', a general method of number building for complex subjects which he admitted might be necessary for specialist classification. He advocated the possible use of a hyphen to link numbers. Using this method, the classification number for the subject. 'The influence of politics upon the history of education in Great Britain', could therefore be:

J3ea-R where R is 'Politics'.

DEWEY DECIMAL CLASSIFICATION

Like the Bibliographic classification, the Dewey scheme makes use of generally applicable special tables for standard subdivisions, areas, and so on. In addition, in more recent editions, there is a great deal of provision for synthesis, or number building, in many specific places throughout the scheme. The instructions at 636.8 'Cats', for instance, are:

636.8 Cats

636.8003-78009 Standard subdivisions Notations from Table

General principles

636.801-.808 Add to base number 636.80 the numbers following 636.0 in 636.01636.08, *e.g.*, breeding cats.

From Table = 'Encyclopedias' and therefore, following the first instruction above:

An encyclopaedia of cats = 636.8003

Referring to 636.0, which is the general number for 'Animal husbandry' :

636.801-.808

636	Animal husbandry
636.081	Selection and acquisition
636.0812	Judging
636.0811	Ownership makrs
636.082	Breeding
636.084	Feeding

It can be ascertained that the classification number for:

Feeding cats = 636.8084

The above number is derived as follows:

Base number for cats	=	636.80
Add numbers following	=	636.0
Number for feeding	=	636.084
Add '84' to '636.80'	=	636.8084

The example given in the scheme, 'Breeding cats', is obtained in similar fashion.

Two Major Examples

There are two major examples of synthesis being grafted on to an enumerative scheme.

The first dates back to the turn of the century when the Universal decimal classification was formulated. This scheme, which has been issued in a number of different languages and has progressed through a number of editions, was based upon the every decimal classification but a number of signs of combination and abbreviation were introduced to allow for number building. The second scheme is of much more recent origin and is the ongoing mission of the Bibliographic classification.

Universal Decimal Classification (UDC)

General number building is allowed for by signs of combination, for example:

+ Addition

/ Extension (used for consecutive numbers)

= Relation

Here are some examples of UDC classification numbers. They are the same as their counterparts in the Dewey decimal classification except that the figure minimum is abolished, therefore

310 in Dewey becomes 31 in UDC

31 Statistics

51 Mathematics

53 Physics

54 Chemistry

63 Agriculture

Applying the sings of combination to the above numbers in order to build up numbers for composite subjects would achieve results as illustrated in the following examples:

Mathematics and physics	= 51 + 53
Physics and chemistry	= 53/54
Statistics relating to agriculture	= 63:31
	or 31:63

There is no stipulated citation order in UDC, hence the possible alternative for the last number. This provides for great flexibility, if necessary, a double colon may be used to 'fix' the order of the constituent elements of a compound number, especially when UDC is used in a computer-based information system, for example:

Statistics relating to agriculture = 63:31

Unfortunately UOC retains a great deal of enumeration and this can result in conflict with the synthetic facilities. For example, a common auxiliary table for 'persons' (Table l(k)—05) is applicable throughout the main schedules:

-05 Persons

-053 Persons according to age or age groups

.2 Children and infants

6 Young persons. Adolescents. Teenagers'

.8 Adults. Grown ups

.9 Old persons. Persons in old age

-55 Persons according to sex and kinship

.1 Male persons. Men

.15 Boys

.2 Female persons. Women

.25 Girls

The subject Accident statistics' is classified at 313.12 and therefore, by applying the above table:

Accident statistics relating to women= 313.12-055.2

However, the table is not used consistently but is sometimes replaced by enumeration, for example:

343.91 Kinds of criminal

343.914 Women as criminals

362.8 Care of young persons

362.86 Care ahd welfare of girls and young women

However, that the number listed, or enumerated, in the schedule is shorter than the number that would have been obtained through the use of synthesis, for example:

343.91-055.2 Women as criminals

Bibliographic Classification Revised Edition

A new revision of the Bibliographic classification based upon facet analysis, began to appear in 1977 and is still in progress. It is the work of Jack Mills and his colleagues at the Polytechnic of North London. Within Class U Arts/ Useful arts, UVE in both the original scheme and the revision is 'Clothing industries'. Given below (some extracts from this class, on the left the original and on the right the revision, which illustrate the difference between the two.

UVC CLOTHING INDUSTRIES

Original Scheme	*Revision*
UVD Men's and 'boys' clothing	UVD Products
UVDN Men's and boys' neckties,	By mode of manufacture, *e.g.*
gloves, hats, caps	UVDC Knitwear
	By material, *e.g.*
UVE Children's clothing	UVD E Textile
(No enumeration)	By occasion when worn, *e.g.*
UVF Women's and girls' clothing	UVDKL Industrial
UVFL Women's and girls	'By sex, *e.g.*
underwear, lingerie	UVDQ Unisex.
hosiery, gloves	UVDS Female
	By sex, *e.g.*
	UVDV Child
	By part of body covered, *e.g.*
	(Trunk and arm)

Two Classifications

Faceted. A faceted scheme lists concepts only-classification numbers for complex subjects are built up by means of synthesis.

Advantages. Because complex subjects are not listed, such schemes are easier to compile.

The schedules are shorter for the same reason but, despite their brevity, they permit the classification of both very simple and very complex subjects.

New subjects can very often be catered for by the combination of already existing concepts.

Disadvantages. The notation can become long and complex and why be unsuitable for the arrangement of documents on shelves as in a library. The problem of citation order can cause difficulty.

Enumerative. An enumerative scheme attempts to list all possible subjects, both simple and complex, within the defined subject field or fields.

Advantages. Such scheme have been generally accepted and widely used with considerable success throughout the world for a long period of time. A fairly short and uncomplicated notation can be used. 'Notationally', it is easier to display the structure of the scheme.

Disadvantages. It is impossible to list every conceivable subject.

There can be a lack of accommodation for even simple subject.

New subjects cannot be accommodated and regular revision may be required.

In relation to the use of general enumerative schemes in libraries, standardization is facilitated because classification numbers may be included in centralized records. For example, Dewey decimal classification and Library of Congress classification numbers, are included in eye-readable and machine-readable records supplied by the Library of Congress and the British Library. With schemes such as the Dewey decimal classification there is also the possibility of 'integrity of numbers', that is the stabilizing of existing numbers, a policy initiated by Dewey.

However, general schemes may be unsuitable for certain purposes. For example, in libraries and information services which specialize in particular subject fields, they are not detailed enough specific areas. Special classification schemes, restricted by subject are therefore required. Although these may be enumerative faceted, the latter is now more common. Special schemes are useful for the manual filing of office papers and for the coding entities in computerized systems.

Policies of Notation

Each concept within the classification scheme must be allocated a notational symbol which will enable the representation of that concept by a 'shorthand' code or classification number. Number digits could perform this function.

A common error is to think that choice of notation is the first in the compilation of a classification scheme. It should now be apparent that this is not so; the allocation of a notation is one of final steps.

Notation is, however, a very important feature. Poor note can reduce the value of even the best constructed scheme. Some of the policies which might be booked.

Uniqueness. There should be taken that one concept or subject cannot be mistaken for another. In a machine-based system, for example could be disirous if the coding for a component, say a ball-bearing were the same as that allocated to a completed product such gear box. A distinction must however be made between unique identification of a subject and identification of an actual item example, in a library the subject 'Use of artificial satellites telecommunication' might have the number XX 007 but there well be a great number of cooks dealing with this subject, all with the same class number. For unique identification of each book some must be added to this number, so that in effect it becomes a book number. This addition could consist of letters and digits could represent author, copy number, volume, and so on. A is situation exists in a computer-based system where a code used as the sole key for identification and location of a data record if several records have the same classification number then further coding must be added.

Simplicity. Notation should be easily comprehensible and must have ordinal value as it reflects and 'fixes' chosen orders, therefore:

1 A

2 or B

3 C

not

$

&

*

Confusion should be avoided, for example the use of both the upper case letter '0' and the digit '0', or the lower case letter 'I' and the digit '1'. It is advantageous if notation is easily memorized, written and spoken.

For classification and coding in industry, 'in order to assist the many functions of manufacture by providing a logical and meaningful system of identification for information, data and components II' the best type of symbolisation is generally considered to be purely numerical and of uniform length'.

Brevity. Notation should be as brief as possible. Note that the longer the base, the shorter the classification numbers. For example, using letters, with a base of 26, it is possible to allocate class numbers no longer than two letters to 676 subjects (that is 26 x 26). Using numerals, with a base of 10, only 100 subjects (that is, 10 x 10) can be allocated numbers no longer than two digits.

Hospitality. Notation should have the ability to accommodate new concepts or subjects as necessary. It should allow for the insertion of both subordinate and coordinate subjects. The former is catered for quite easily by the decimal use of numbers (or the use of letters on the same principle). If 1 represents 'Fiction' and 2 'Poetry' then further expansion is possible in this manner:

1 Fiction

11 Historical fiction

12 Romantic fiction

13 Science fiction

2 Poetry

21 Lyric poetry

The insertion of the coordinate subjects is more difficult but i could be provided for by leaving gaps, for example:

1 Construction

4 Testing

7 Maintenance

but the gaps may not be in appropriate places and therefore could interfere with the required order.

Flexibility. It may be useful to be able to alter citation order according to the needs of a particular set of users. Facet analysis lends itself admirably to variations in preferred citation order.

Expressiveness. This means that the notation reflects the structure of the scheme and such a notation may also be known as 'structural' or 'hierarchical', for example:

I Military ordinance

II Artillery

III Field artillery

Although sometimes considered helpful (the user can understand the systematic order more easily and it can be effective tool in hierarchical computer searching), expressiveness is not essential if it results in longer classification numbers and limits hospitality.

Although the above features may be desirable, it is obviously going to be difficult to incorporate them all into a single scheme. It is particularly difficult in a faceted scheme for synthesis does not lend itself to brevity, simplicity, or expressiveness.

Retroactive Notation. One device which is sometimes used in faceted schemes in an attempt to shorten numbers is 'retroactive' notation. 'Retroactive' simply means 'backwards'. In notational terms a change of facets is indicated by a reversal of alphabetic or numeric direction from forwards to backwards. A classification number such as:

ABCD

shows no change of direction and therefore is derived from one facet only. However the classification number:

CDEBCDABC

shows a change of direction, and therefore a change of facet, between the E and the B, and the D and the A. It could have been written as:

CDE/BCD/ABC

but the '/' is superfluous because of the retroactive nature of the number.

In allocating such a notation, it will be seen that the first letters of the alphabet are used to introduce those facets which are to be cited last and not for the primary facets. The letter A', having been used once, must not be used again in any earlier facet. Similarly 'B', having been used once, must not be used again. Thus the notational base, which is available, is progressively reduced. Care must therefore be taken that when the primary facets are reached, there are still sufficient notational symbols remaining. It is usual to ensure that an adequate amount of the notational base is reserved for the primary facets before allocating a notation to other facets.

Example: Hospitality-from the Library of Congress classification In the fifth edition of Class Q Science will be found:

QD CHEMISTRY

ORGANIC CHEMISTRY 241 Periodicals

243 Yearbooks

245 Collected works

248 History

'Encyclopadeias' are not enumerated or listed, and therefore An encyclopaedia of organic chemistry' cannot be'classified. In the sixth edition of Class Q, however, appears:

246 Dictionaries and encyclopedias

This class number has been neatly slotted into the appropriate place in the scheme by making use of the gap left, for hospitality pruposes, in the notation between 245 and 248.

'An encyclopaedia of organic chemistry' can now be classified, the number being:

QD 246

The notation is 'mixed' comprising upper case letters and digits.

Example. *Flexibility.* From the London education classification. In this scheme the facets are arranged in an order of in CI concreteness, for example:

Lab Teaching methods

Mim Mathematics

Ras Primary schools

The recommended or preferred citation order is there for t:everse of this, for example:

Ras Mim Lab = Teaching mathematics in primary schools

It is pointed out, however, by Foskett, the compiler individual libraries or information services may wish to vat; order: 'One of the greatest advantages of a faceted classification is that...the facets can be arranged in any sequence, to suit particular user'. If it were desired to bring together all items dealing with 'Teaching methods' and to sub-arrange first by subject and by environment, then the citation order could be altered to come to the schedule order and the classification number would become

Lab Mim Ras = Teaching mathematics in primary schools

Note the 'pronounceable' notation. This led to some interesting mnemonic classification numbers, for example:

Bux = Documentation Pil = Sex education Ror = Choir schools

Unfortunately in the second edition four letter notation had I introduced and the pronounceable element was therefore reduced.

A change of facet as consistently indicated by a change from lower to an upper case letter. The upper case letter therefore as a facet indicator.

Example. Expression-from the Colon classification

X	Economics
X7	Public finance
X72	Tax
X724	Income tax
X7244	on salary

Note the way in which the structure of the scheme is reflected in the notation.

Example. Retroactive notation-from the Dewey decimal classification

Perhaps without realizing it. Dewey included a 'flavour' of retroactive notation in his 'History' class:

42	History of England
42.051	History of England in the Tudor period
42.1	History of London
42.105	History of London in the Tudor period

Note that whenever the notation returns to '0', that is goes backwards toT, then the characteristics of division changes from 'Place' to 'Time'.

COLON CLASSIFICATION

The Colon Classification owes its name to the fact that the notational device first used by it to demarcate facets in Class Number was the symbol 1/:1/ (colon). Hereafter the word 'facet' will be used instead of 'dimension' or 'zone' in accordance with the terminology of the Colon Classification.

In the first three editions of the Colon classification, the implied assumption was that the number of facets in a universe of discourse is constant. Of course, among the fixed number of facets several arrangements are possible, some of which may be 'more or less helpful'. Of the 'more or less helpful' arrangements one is forcedly preferred for adoption. To mechanise the arrangement of facets in the preferred order, a rigorous face-formula is given for each universe of discourse called a Main or a Canonical class.

An important contribution of the Colon classification, the Library classification: Fundamentals and procedure (1944) and the Elements of library classification (1946) is the isolation of the concept of Universes with Loose Assemblage. They have introduced the term 'Phase' in describing an existent which is loosely assembled. In the first edition, the Colon classification (1933) prescribed the digit "0" (zero) as the symbol to connect the class numbers corresponding to the constituents of an existent with loose assemblage. Of course the resulting number is itself a class number. It may be called a Phased Class Number. Each constituent of a Phased Class Number is itself a Class Number. The second edition of the Colon classification (1939) recognized two species of phase-relation for which it prescribed zero and colon as the respective connecting symbols. The Fundamentals made an objective analysis of the problem. The Elements isolated one more species of phase-relation. The Agile has indications that the projected work in India includes a thorough analysis of phases, isolation of different species of phase-relations, and prescription of distinctive connecting symbols for them. It is hoped that this investigation will lay down a technique for handling new species of phases as and when they come to be known, though they may be unknown at present.

The Colon Classification is perhaps the first of the analytico-synthetic variety. It is a pure example of that variety. Its preliminary schedules include those of *(1)* Main Classes, *(2)* Common Subdivisions, *(3)* Geographical Divisions, *(4)* Language Divisions, and *(5)* Chronological Divisions.

Then follow one chapter for each 'of the Main Classes. In each chapter, if the Main Class is not broken down in the first instance into Canonical Divisions, there are usually one or two schedules corresponding to the one or two trains of characteristics which are relevant to its classification. In other words, the facets of the Main Class are mentioned and the foci in each of them are enumerated. If the Main Class is broken down into Canonical Divisions in the first instance, such of the Canonical Divisions as admit of them are provided with similar schedules based on the trains of characteristics relevant to their classification. Generally speaking the divisions in each of the above-mentioned schedules are enumerated in a 'more or less helpful' order. There are however regions where alphabetical arrangement is prescribed in the form 'Divide by Alphabetical Device'; and there are definite rules which prescribe the minimum arrangement is prescribed in the form 'Divide by Alphabetical Device'; and there are definite rules which prescribe the minimum arrangement is prescribed in the form number of the initial letters which should be used to secure individualisation. An example of this will be found in the Full Crop Schedule worked out for Agriculture in the Abgila of March 1950. It will be found in the Full Crop Schedule worked out for Agriculture in the Abgila of March 1950. It will be found that the international name of crops is prescribed to be used for Alphabetical Device. The Alphabetical Device is used only when there is strong evidence to show that there is no other arrangement which is at all helpful. The point is that when none of the possible arrangements has more of the element of helpfulness than the purely alphabetical one, the alphabetical arrangement scores because people are more familiar with it.

The first part of Colon classification is entitled 'Rules of classification'. It gives objective definition of Class Number and of most other concepts. In the preliminary chapters it describes various devices by which class numbers should be constructed. What are called Facet-and Phase-Formulae are defined. These formulae enable one to analyse a given specific subject in a systematic manner and rearrange the words in the name of the specific subject filling up ellipses if any, as a preliminary to the construction of the class number. The facet-formula of the main class or canonical division to which the specific subject belongs helps in this analysis and breakdown of the specific subject into its fundamental constituent elements. Connecting symbols are prescribed by the rules and also indicated in the facet-and phase-formulae for synthesizing the fundamental constituent numbers, got by translating the fundamental constituent concept, into the derived composite class number as the translation of the name of the specific subject. It is this process of first analysing the specific subject and at the last stage synthesizing the class number which makes the Colon Classification an analyticos-ynthetic classification.

The potential vocabulary of the Colon Classification is infinite. Its infinity is of a higher order than that of the Decimal Classification. The order of infinity of its potential vocabulary is that of the number of facets and phases its notation can accommodate. To take the example given in section 1521, we saw that it is impossible to get a Decimal Number for the specific subject 'Curriculum in secondary education'. But we can provide a Colon Number. It is T2 :44. Here

T = Education is Main Class

2 = Secondary education is a division in the Education schedule

44 = Curriculum is a number in the Problem schedule is the connecting symbol prescribed

The facet-formula prescribes the order in which the above symbols should be synthesised. Thus we get an individualizing, coextensive number, *i.e.*, a precise translation for the name of the specific subject. To use the old analogy of visitors and chairs, the Colon Classification can produce a greater abundance of chairs than the Decimal Classification. The occasions when two visitors will be obliged to sit on the same chair will be few and far between. Indeed the ideal is to eliminate such an occasion altogether.

There is one danger in an analytico-synthetic classification when viewed as language. Since an enumerative classification gives a ready-made translation (class number) made by the classificationist himself, it is ensured that no two different translations are made for the same original (specific) subject. But it is well known that when different translators translate with the aid of a dictionary, they may produce different translations. This is perhaps a desirable feature in literary translation. But it will be disastrous in classificatory translation. For, translating the name of a given specific subject into two different class numbers will mean inconsistency in arrangement.

That is why it has been stated that an essential quality of a classificatory language is that it must have no synonym and two different translations for the same original passage should not be allowed or possible. It is the facet-formula which protects Colon Classification from this potential danger. It is that formula which gives the necessary rigidity. But we have to beware that the facet formula does not introduce more rigidity than it is absolutely necessary for avoiding synonyms. If it introduces a greater amount of rigidity than it is necessary, to that extent it will restrict the potential vocabulary of the classificatory language.

To get a view of the map of the field of knowledge provided by the Colon Classification one must take into consideration fully worked-out class numbers, past, present and future. If that is done it will be found that a good map is provided. The conscious implementation of Hospitality in Chain and Hospitality in Array in the methodology of the Colon Classification, keeps co-ordinate classes and subordinate classes quite apart as and when new areas (specific subjects) are explored and have to be marked on the map. The facet-notation enables the Colon Classification to carry out these obligations of cartographers even more thoroughly than the Decimal Classification is able to do.

Viewing the problem from the angle of analogy with transformation, the facet and the phase-notation of the Colon Classification enables to avoid the fault of the Decimal Classification described in section 1523. It is not merely the end sub-cell in the multidimensional space of the field of knowledge, which is transformed into the end sub-interval in the linear space of class numbers, which is fully represented. But everyone of the sub-cells in a cluster constituting a compound cell is rightly transformed.

In using the terminology of the Boolean Algebra the field of Colon Nu Numbers is a closed one in the sense that the product of any two sub-fields is contained within the total field. By throwing the search light of Boolean Algebra on the Colon Classification, it is expected that some of the subtler faults which are escaping unnoticed may be brought to light.

The notation or the Colon Classification is even more resourceful in its counter-tactics than that or the Decimal Classification. It has been able to withstand the grosser attacks of the field of knowledge. But in our days the field of knowledge has started, as it were, bacteria warfare. It has begun to play Hanuman's tactics as described in section 1515. It is playing these tactics unendingly. Just as the vocal muscle of the witch in the Ramayana episode became too stiff at a certain stage for the jaws to be easily moved, we have been experiencing that the rigidity of the facet-formula is causing trouble in putting up the necessary counter-tactics. It is to take away this rigidity that the work on Optional Facets is being pursued.

The Colon Classification has virtually no patent medicine. Every mixture has to be compounded according to prescriptions written out by a competent doctor to meet the exact requirement of the disease diagnosed. This does not mean that mixtures in frequent demand should not be compounded and stored in advance to be handed over readily on demand..

Similarly the Colon Classification has virtually no ready-made toys. Every toy should be built up to suit the exact fancy of the child needing it. This does not mean that the toys in frequent demand should not be assembled in advance and kept in readiness, to be handed over readily on demand.

The Colon Classification has closely followed the optical analogue in the design of its terminology, there is no need to elaborate further the statements made in that section. The structure of the Colon Number discloses more fully than any other classification number the structure of the specific subject.

A new feature of the Colon Classification which, however, needs to be mentioned here concerns the method it uses: (1) to secure theoretically infinite Hospitality in Array and in Chain severally.

To secure Infinite Hospitality in Array the Colon Classification uses not only the Octave Notation but also other devices like Subject Device, Alphabetical Device, Geographical Device and Chronological Device. These are all described and illustrated in the Colon Classification. Of these, it is the Chronological Device which has usually facility to provide truly Infinite Hospitality in Array. It has stood the test admirably in accommodating Authors in Literature with neat individualising class numbers, no matter how many they are. It is also showing its capacity in individualising any number of special schools of thought in any region of knowledge. In the former, it consists in representing an author by the year of his birth. This makes classification of the authors belonging to any particular form of literature in any particular language chronological. This arranges the works by and on them in a manner which is not only helpful, in the ordinary sense, but also suggests the evolution of the literary art.

Thus Hospitality in Chain is got by the decimal-fraction-notation which imitates the denudation process by which the links in the chain are successively derived.

When a link begins to throw forth its links of higher order, it often happens that all the links in the array of the next order are not thrown out at one time. If they are, it may be easy to determine a 'more or less helpful' arrangement among them and allot the extra digit or digits needed to represent them according to the octave notation or any of the devices mentioned above. When they are not thrown out at one time, it is difficult to surmise which place the first link which is thrown out should be given in the array which octave and which place in the octave. It is here that the Colon Classification has contributed what has been described in the Prolegomena as Unscheduled Mnemonics. It is a dubtle device and is therefore a powerful one. It gives a greater degree of autonomy to a classifier in sharpening Simple and Dependent Foci. It is difficult to explain it in general terms though it has been attempted in the Philosophy of library classification. Unscheduled Menmonics consists in using an ordinal digit to represent a primordial idea which is not often represented by any term in a natural language, when it is taken in isolation, but is represented by different terms when it is put in the context of the different subjects. For example, the digit 3 represents Physiology in Biological Sciences, Social practices in Sociology, Functions of State in Political Science, Teaching Technique in Education, Distribution in Economics, Contract in Legal System and so on-all at bottom analogous at least in a thin or distant way. This mnemonic quality enable a classifier to form new foci in any facet without reference to the classificationist. What is more he need not wait to give numbers to these foci until all of them have appeared. Even when only one appears, he can number it with a high probability that it need not be changed and that very other classifier and the classificationist himself would be numbering it in the same way. The organisational set up on national and international basis for removing the effect of the small probability for inconsistency in fixing numbers by unscheduled mnemonics, has been described in Library classification and international documentation of the ELD. I have some vague information that there is a tradition of such unscheduled mnemonics current in the Tantric school. I wish something is done to collect, record and study this tradition of unscheduled mnemonics. Even among the common folk in western countries there is some trace of this which is brushed aside as sheer superstition. But scientific outlook requires that we should not brush aside anything on the sole ground that we cannot fit it into the rational matrix which intellect produces. We should be prepared to postulate and even grant trans-intellectual existents, though it is necessary to be on our guard not to become credulous subjects of fraud.

UNIVERSAL DECIMAL CLASSIFICATION

In late 19th century there was an increasing concern for the problems of documentation. In earlier years cataloguers had concentrated on the problems of describing and recording books mostly in a bibliographic tradition, with a wealth of detail but with a corresponding delay in the dissemination of information. In the early 1890s Paul Otlet and Henri La Fontaine, in Belgium, translated the earlier cataloguers' efforts toward a universal catalog into the world of documentation. They proposed a universal index to recorded knowledge which must include non-book materials and ephermera as well as conventional material. In 1895 the First International Conference on Bibliography, for which Otlet and La Fontaine were largely responsible, approved their plans and established the Institute International de Bibliography (IIB). Otlet and La Fontaine had already agreed that such an index, and bibliographies based on it or contributing to it, must be organised systematically rather than alphabetically. They looked to the Dewey Decimal classification as the basis of a truly international scheme.

Otlet and La Fontaine negotiated with Dewey to use his scheme for the IIB's index. They wanted three things: to translate it into French, to expand its subject schedules and make it truly international in scope, and to allow arrangements to include non-book materials. Dewey was impressed and inclined to agree, but his assistants (in particular Dorcas Fellows) could not tolerate such changes to his original plan. Negotiations dragged on until in despair the Belgians went their own way. Without that reluctance of members of Dewey's staff we might now have only one decimal classification, and a realisation of Dewey's plan: a scheme of universal scope for documentation, a scheme for general use (as in DOC now), and an abridged scheme like the abridged DOC.

The adapted scheme was published for the first time in 1905 by the IIB as the Manual due repertoire universal bibliographique and became known in the English speaking world as the "Brussels classification". Even then it had more detail than the contemporary edition of the DOC, and it had most of the synthetic features peculiar to what is now the Universal Decimal Classification. It was quickly adopted by libraries in Europe, particularly special libraries with a scientific and technological orientation where non-book materials are common.

Impact of UDC

Probably the greatest impact of UDC on libraries has been through the abridged editions now published in some 16 languages. The first of these was not an official UDC abridgment but was a version used by S.C. Bradford in the Science Museum Library in London. Bradford was an early and enthusiastic supporter of UDC who attempted an index in English similar to the original index of the lIB. Bradford is the Science museum Library before the British Standards Institution became the official British publishers responsible for organizing UDC revision and communication of changes as well as publication of English versions.

The first scheme with an analytico-synthetic element was the Universal Decimal Classification. Though the Universal Decimal Classification was not accessible at the time when the Colon Classification was designed and consequently it has not been possible to use it as a model in the designing of the Colon Classification, there is no denying that the latter appeared in the field only a generation later. In spite of it, it had been taken first for description because it has developed the features of an analytico-synthetic classification in a more pronounced and fundamental manner and the auxiliary books and writings centering round it have developed a terminology which makes communication easier. It was a good in disguise that the schedules of Universal Decimal Classification were not accessible for several years after the Colon Classification was designed and developed up to the third edition. If it had been, the pressure of its tradition would have inhibited free thought, even as the Decimal Classification had done. Indeed, it is being realised that many of the faults of the Colon Classification are due to the pressure of the tradition of the Decimal Classification.

In 1931 the lIB became the Institue Internationel de Documentation (II D) and in 1937 changed its name again to the Federation International de Documentation (FID) its present name. In the preparation of the 1927-1933 edition, Otlet and La Fontaine were joined by Frists Donker Duyivis of the Dutch Patent Office, who was to look after the natural science schedules. He became secretary of the II B in 1929 and stayed until his retirement in 1959. He was one of the principal influences on the development of UDC as we know it. The offices of the institute moved to the Hague, together with the master card file of the UDC. From these offices is conducted international coordination of the revision and development of the UDC.

The ultimate coordinating body of the UDC is the Central Classification Committee (CCC). Originally this was made up of the editors of UDC and the secretary-general of FIC, but these members were joined in 1964 by representatives from the national committees responsible for publication of native-language editions and for the coordination of the work of special subject committees within each country. In addition there are international subject committees that report directly to the CCC.

Comment and criticism concerning existing schedules and proposals for revision or new classes travel up this committee structure, ultimately to the CCC. It is common for comments or draft schedules to be circulated at each level for future comment, so the process can be lengthy one, but it is also a process that involves the users of the scheme more directly than with any other major scheme. When draft schedules reach the CCC they are considered in the light of the scheme as whole, and after any modification to avoid clashes with any other schedules, they are issued as P-notes. At one time P stood for projects, and there were two kinds: projects provisions that had to be discussed and debated fully before official acceptance, and projects d' extensitions' that would become part of the UDC automatically if no objection was heard within 4 months. After a period of proliferation of different kinds of P-note, the system was simplified to the second of the original projects. After 4 months without objection the contents of P-notes are cumulated in Extensions and Corrections to the UDC published every 6 months and then cumulated triennially.

Revision takes place in three ways. The first is the obvious and natural extension of topics by more detailed subdivision. The second is by minor alternations of existing subdivision notation. The third and most important, since it is almost unique to UDC, is the "starvation policy" introduced by Donker Duyvis. This policy attempts to deal with a problem of particular significance to UDC that it is used mostly in scientific and technical libraries and is strongest in these dynamic and rapidly changing subject areas. It is difficult to apply a policy of changing the internal structure class as it stands as LC has long done and as DDC now does "its II phoenix schedules" since this policy assumes fairly static collections and the opportunity for fairly leisurely reclassification.

UDC is a synthetic scheme, using punctuation marks, auxiliary schedules to link and add to the basic notation derived from the DDC. The content of the schedules derived from UDC changed significantly over the years, but the basic outline is similar enough to DOC to assure anyone who knows the outline of DDC. They are dealing with a familiar scheme, at least for subject content. For most users, however, the characteristic feature of UDC is its wide range of auxiliary signs and schedules, to allow for addition and extension of class numbers and for subdivisions of language form, place, time, etc. However, the main contribution in the auxiliaries is the use of nondecimal punctuation marks to signal use of DOC or DDC based decimal notation.

Auxiliaries. There are two kinds of auxiliaries: general, affecting the whole scheme; and special, affecting only specified parts of the scheme. The general auxiliaries can in turn be divided into two groups: those that are simply signs that join other notational elements together a those that are signs that introduce explicit tables of subdivision.

To the first general group belong the signs of addition, extension and relation. The addition sign + is used to join together two subjects not adjacent in the schedules.

54+66 CHEMISTRY AND CHEMICAL TECHNOLOGY

It is an awkward combination to index and to file (54+66 shot file before 54 since it covers a larger subject area), and UDC does whole heartedly recommend its use. The extension sign / is used join consecutive notational elements, either two adjacent elements the beginning and end of a sequence.

537/538 ELECTRICITY AND MAGNETISM

22/28 THE CHRISTIAN RELIGION

When the extension sign is used with lengthy notation sharing common higher level, the notation for the higher level may omitted.

621.396/.397 THE EFFECT OF HOT-AIR CENTRAL HEATING ON INDOOR PLANTS

635.695:632.38 VIRUS DISEASES OF INDOOR PLANTS

635.695:582.675 INDOOR ANEMONES

The entity 635.695 INDOOR PLANTS, three laments have been added successively: notation from another class to indicate an effect on the entire notation from within the same class to indicate a problem of the entry, and notation from another class to indicate a kind or subclass of the entry. In other words, the colon is performing three separate functions. Notice also that the order listed here is an ideal arrangement for documents on shelves or in index files of general-to-special type. But the use of only the colon as a relational sign means that UDC numbers must be filed by the notation that fellows the colon, thus reversing that order at least in this case; in fact the order will be arbitrary, depending on what notation follows the colon. There are further problems with the use of the colon. A collection on mathematics and its subdivisions written for engineering students might include:

51:62 MATHEMATICS FOR ENGINEERS

511 ARITHMETIC

511:62 ARITHMETIC FOR ENGINEERS

512 ALGEBRA

512:62 ALGEBRA FOR ENGINEERS

making it impossible to keep together all the textbooks for engineering students. For a long time, principally in the English editions of UDC, brackets were used to "intercalate" the related notation:

51 [62]	MATHEMATICS FOR ENGINEERS
51[62]1	ARITHMETIC FOR ENGINEERS
51[62]2	ALGEBRA FOR ENGINEERS
511	ARITHMETIC
512	ALGEBRA

The official use of brackets is now as a grouping device, for example:

54 + 66 (05)

might mean A JOURNAL (05) ON CHEMISTRY AND CHEMICAL TECHNOLOGY or

CHEMISTRY AND JOURNALS ON CHEMICAL TECHNOLOGY

But UDC now offers

[54 + 66](05)

to make it clear that the meaning is JOURNALS ON CHEMISTRY AND CHEMICAL TECHNOLOGY.

A more serious problem with the single colon as a relational all sign is that no order is specified or even recommended in DC for the elements that it joints. Thus using 633.491 POTATOES and 632.3 PARASITIC DISEASES, both 633.491P:632.3 and 632.3:633.491 may mean PARASITIC DISEASES OF POTATOES. UDC recognized the potential conclusion and took away most of the value of the sign by instruction to use both combinations in indexes or catalogue. This instruction effectively limited the relational sign to a link between only two components and prevented the exploration of assemblies of more than two components.

The use of the double colon can resolve the problem, by indicating that only the combination as expressed ::.may be used: 633.491 :: 632.3, but not 632.3:: 633.491.

Even with the later developments of : and :: the problems cited earlier remain the use of the relational sign in whatever form to indicate effects or influences (phases), problems (facets), and kinds can result in confused file order.

The remaining general auxiliaries are all tables of subdivision with distinctive punctuation marks to indicate their function.

Auxiliaries of Form and Language. The first two concern only the physical document: the common form auxiliary (0...) and the language auxiliary. Both are derived from the ADDC but with an interesting development that is echoed in some of the other auxiliaries. In DDC the list of common form subdivisions is a mixture of what Berwick. Sayers described as 'inner' and 'outer form' on the one hand, the internal point of view or approach to the subject an, on the other hand, the physical arrangement or form of the material, for example, the philosophy of a subject and an ENCYCLOPEDIA, respectively. UDC was able to recognise the distinction and to offer. 1 for the PHILOSOPHY of a subject, leaving the common subdivisions mostly for 'outer form'. It then enclosed DDCs 0... in parentheses to give It a clear indicator of its separateness from subject numbers. Such a concentration on 'outer form' freed notation used in DOC for 'inner form' for further expansion in UDC.

A similar development took place with the language auxiliary. DOC had no such facility; UDC included it because of its international and multilingual applications. Detail was taken from DOC's class 400 LANGUAGE and given the equals sign as an indicator of this separateness from the subject schedules. A further refinement took place when UDC ignored DOC's notational structure of three integers followed by a decimal point and decimal fraction notation. Instead, UDC regarded all notation as decimal and used a period after every three digits, breaking up a number in order to make it more mnemonic. This practice, together with the introduction of parentheses to introduction form and other subdivisions, free the 0 from its use in DOC only as an indictor and allowed it to be used as a specifying digit:

=42 THE ENGLISH LANGUAGE GROUP

=420 ENGLISH

Auxiliaries of Place, Time Race, and Persons time, and race found in varying degree in most major classification schemes. Like the group already discussed, the next group of general auxiliaries includes the common subdivisious of place, these too enjoy a development freed from the national constrictions of DOC.

The general auxiliary of place () took what was earlier the 'divide like' device of DOC (employing subdivisions of 940-999 to subdivide any other number) and is now the DOC Area Tables, and used those digits in parentheses. Because the parentheses indicated only place, the hitherto inaccessible 91 GEOGRAPHY and 92 BIOGRAPHY were now available as (1) and (2) for new meaning. UDC used them to indicate geographic or topographic detail not tied to politoco-geographic areas: rivers, mountains, seas, and even ideas like central, bordering, north, and south, rivers, mountains, and seas are listed and named in (2) as:

(237.15) SIERRE MADRE AND MEXICAN PLATEAU

Concepts like central, bordering, north, and south are listed at (1) as : (1-14) SOUTH

The (1) is simply a carrier digit to support the concept (-14) SOUTH; in fact, the concept may be added to any other geographical subdivisions in parentheses;

(468.1) ANDALUSIA

(468.1-14) SOUTH ANDALUSIA

For time subdivision UDC departed from all other traditions and used the date enclosed in quotation marks; "1976" means in 1970. The notation is decimal, so that "197" means the 1970s a "1970.01,.01" means January 1,1970.

Periods of time can also be indicated by the extension sing "196/197" means the 1960s and 1970s , and a negative sign-me, BC:

"-0055" 55 BC

The auxiliary for race is a combination of the auxiliaries of place and language, combining their signs. The language auxiliary sign= inside parentheses 0 indicates the race that speaks that language with form and place, the race auxiliary is able to expand beyond normal limits of the language specification by the freedom from p language numbers. For example, it is able to specify (=94: ESKIMOS, (96) NEGROES, and further, (1.493 = 40) WALLOONS by combining the race and the place specification using the carrier and a further subdivision.

The auxiliary-05 for person originated in class 3 social sciences but was clearly useful for general application:

62-055.2 WOMEN IN ENGINEERING

The only remaining general auxiliaries are the point of numbers .00....", and .000.' The first and original point view auxiliary .00 is used when many compounds joined by colons m; introduce confusion in a file, as in a collection of documents for business concern. It might be easier to organize the collection by the several aspects of the business and then subdivide by variety of subdivisions using colons. For example:

could be rearranged as:

635.965:582.675	INDOOR PLANTS :MARSH MARIGOLD
635.965:632.38	INDOOR PLANTS :VIRUS DISEASE
635.965:697.38	INDOOR PLANTS: EFFECTS OF CENTRAL HEATING
635.965.004:632.38	INDOOR PLANTS: MATERIAL MARSH MARIGOLD
635.965:002.3:582.675	INDOOR PLANTS:DETERIORATION WEAR:EFFECT OF CENTRAL HEATING.

The introduction to the UDC has more examples of these of .00

A fairly recent addition to the point of view auxiliary is one to account for an author's point of view. The notation is .000 and may be used as follows:

635.965.004:632.38	INDOOR PLANTS:USE/CARE:VIRUS DISEASE
162.6.000.335.5	DIALECTICS FROM THE MARXIST POINT OF VIEW
linking 162.6 DIALECTICS	and 335.5 MARXISM

Special Auxiliaries. Special auxiliaries are subdivisions that deal only with limited ranges of subjects. They have the signs-, .0, and. The-and .0 are equivalent and are so used throughout the scheme, occasionally being combined when more than one kind of special subdivision exists for combination, as in class VIII LITERATURE they may be applied anywhere in the area that they cover:

621-77	SAFETY DEVICES
621.0395-77	SAFETY DEVICES IN NUCLEAR REACTORS
7.061	FORGERY IN ART
75.061	FORGERY IN PAINTINGS

There is no consistency in the use of and .0 in the scheme, as Dubuc points out (10), and proposals have been made to use only.

One other form of special auxiliary is the postrophe to indicate combinations of chemical elements :

546.33	SODIUM
546.13	CHLORINE
546.33'13	SODIUM CHLORIDE

Various Classes

The enumerated schedules themselves resemble the familiar decimal structure of the DOC, but the resemblance is more apparent than real. The same major classes are present and for the most part of the same divisions appear within these classes; but from that point onward (or downward) more and more differences can be seen, resulting from revisions within UDC. For example, RADIO ENGINEERING is represented by 621384 in the DOC but by 621.396 in DOC. This seems to be similar because both numbers begin with 621.3, but in fact the notation is distinctly different, as it is therefore for the whole of this large class.

Differences in the schedules are not limited to notational differences of this kind. UDC has also restructured classes from the form used by DOC; for example, the use in 8 LITERATURE of the two special auxiliaries-AND to accommodate the facets of form and of literary science and technique. The facet of period, if necessary, can of course, be represented by the Common auxiliary of time.

To describe in detail the enumerated content of the classes of UDC would be to repeat in large part a description of DOC, which has been laid out elsewhere in many textbooks and is in any case generally well known. Instead, the major differences are described here.

Generalities. UDC accepted most of this class as Dewey had laid it out in DOC. The major exception was in the early development of 00 as a class devoted to fundamentals of knowledge. DOC has now developed this class, but its form remains distinct from UDC, which divides the class as:

001 THE SCIENCES AND KNOWLEDGE IN GENERAL

002 DOCUMENTATION

003 SEMIOTICS, SYNTACTIC'S, SEMANTICS, WRITING, SCRIPTS, NOTATIONS, SIGNS AND SYMBOLS

005 ORGANISATION STUDY, METHODOLOGY, ANALYSIS AND SYSTEMATIZATION GENERALLY.

007 ACTIVITY AND ORGANISING INFORMATION, COMMUNICATION, CONTROL THEORY (CYBERNETICS) INCLUDING 'HUMAN ENGINEERING'.

008 CIVILIZATION CULTURE PROGRESS

009 THE HUMANITIES THE "ARTS" IN GENERAL

Philoshopy. With minor variations of terminology this class reflects the DOC from which it was originally taken, with the exception of the area of psychology. In DOC, 130 and 150 are devoted to the area of the mind; 130 concentrates on the ills of the mind and also on the occult and paranormal phenomena while 150 is concerned with the operations of the mind in its normal state. UDC anticipated DOC's re-organisation of these classes in using 13 for the occult and parapsychology, and 15 for the functions of the mind. Indeed,

UDC introduced a new classification of the subject at 159.9, so as not to interfere with collections classified by the original 15. This new classification has since been reflected in DDC revisions.

Religion. There are few differences here between DDC and UDC The organisation of this class is biased toward Protestant Christianity because of the persuasion of melvil Dewey and his assistants to the extreme point of the absence of a single notation for Christianity itself, on the assumption that religion was Christianity and anything else was either variation or heresy. UDC fares better than DDC because the synthetic nature of UDC allows the construction of detailed notation for concepts and problems in non-Christian religions denied by the more enumerative structure of DDC.

Social Sciences. In many subdivisions of this major class there are minor differences between DDC and UDC occasioned, for example, by the ability of UDC to use the common auxiliary of place () instead of DDC's "add" device, or by the allocation of specific notation for geographical extension, as in 310 STATISTICS. Otherwise the subdivisions of this class are the familiar ones, with the exception of LAW.

Law is always a problem for classification schemes; the library of Congress has yet to publish a complete schedule. DOCs class 340 LAW for many editions was the most confused class in the scheme, though the revised version in DDEC 18 improved beyond measure. UDC adopted some of the early DOC class, changed some, and relied on synthesis to modify the rest sufficiently to solve most problems of subject description. Part of the problem lies in the use of legal literature by lawyers: in the dichotomy of the literature organised by problem (or kind of law) or by legal system.

UDC subdivided 340 LAW as:

340 LAW IN GENERAL

341 INTERNATIONAL LAW

342 PUBLIC LAW; CONSTITUTIONAL LAW

343 CRIMINAL LAW; PENAL OFFENCES; PENOLOGY, CRIMINOLOGY

344 SPECIAL LAW; CRIMINAL LAW.

347 PRIVATE LAW; CIVIL LAW

348 ECCLESIASTICAL AND CANONICAL LAW

This subdivision avoided the DOC inclusion of US and UK STATUTES AND CASES as major subdivisions of the class LAW, and of LAW OF OTHER COUNTRIES. These inclusions violated the fundamental laws of classification and caused severe confusion in the class and its practical application in law libraries.

As in so many cases, this approach by UDC, based on the analytico-synthetic philosophy, resulted in the later modification of DDC's class to a very similar overall organisation.

●●

2

Collection and Classification in Library

The assembling of collections is a matter of practical convenience, a matter of logistics and convenience. A book does not have to be in any particular collection to be useful. Ideally one would have one's own copies of what one needed and hence neither need nor want to use a library. In practice, however, the cost and bulk of books preclude this possibility, with the exception of a limited quantity of the materials which one might expect to use a great deal. Like compiling a bibliography or a catalogue, the building of a collection is a practical device intended to facilitate access to materials. The overwhelming preponderance of libraries' collections, even of research libraries, serve the second, logistic purpose in the sense that most of the materials acquired also exist elsewhere in other copies in other libraries. Imagine how much different, smaller, and more economical libraries would be if only the archival role mattered, and just one or two copies were acquired nationwide or worldwide. Therefore, assembling of a library collection can reasonably be regarded as the first stage of the process of retrieving material for use.

Ordinarily 'retrieval' is thought of only in terms of catalogues, indexes, classification schemes, or other devices that provide pointers to the documents or data that might satisfy the inquiries that arise. Regardless of the terminology used, the archival role of library collections is, in an important sense, a necessary precondition for, or first stage of, retrieval. Material that has not been collected at all is simply not available for retrieval by anyone. Material that has not been added to local collections is not available for convenient retrieval by individuals at that location.

Bibliographic Classification

The Bliss bibliographic classification (or BC for short) is a library classification system that was created by Henry E. Bliss, published in four volumes between 1940 and 1953. Although originally devised in the United States, it was more commonly adopted by British libraries than by American ones. A revised, second edition of this system (BC2) has been developed since 1977 in the United Kingdom.

Bliss was born in New York in 1870, and in 1891 began to work in the library of the College of the City of New York (now known as the City College of the City University of New York). Bliss had a lifelong interest in the organisation, structure and philosophy of knowledge, and was very critical of the library classification systems that were available to him. He believed that because the popular Library of Congress system had been designed for a specific library (the Library of Congress), that it had no use as a standard system outside of that library. He also greatly disliked the Dewey Decimal system.

Bliss wanted a classification system that would provide distinct rules, yet still be adaptable to whatever kind of collection a library might have, since different libraries have different needs. His solution was the concept of "alternative location", in which a particular subject matter could be put in more than one place, as long as the library made a specific choice and used it consistently.

In 1908, Bliss reclassified 60,000 of his library's books, and in 1910 he published an article with a rough scheme of his general ideas. But as he continued to develop his system, he realised that it was going to be a much larger project than he had originally anticipated. The first of his four official volumes appeared in 1940 (the year he retired), and the last in 1953, two years before his death.

Some of the philosophies of the BC system were:

- alternative location
- brief, concise notation
- organising knowledge according to academic expertise
- for subjects to move gradually from topic to topic as they naturally related to One another

Example

GER MN&,S PWWbca,L	Biochemistry of muscles in animals History of Finland in the 19th century The building and equipment of the YWCA in Albany, New York

Bliss deliberately avoided the use of the decimal point because of his hatred of Dewey's system. Instead he used upper and lower-case letters, numbers, and every typographical symbol available on his extensive and somewhat eccentric typewriter (which included both forward and reverse italics).

BC was not used by many North American libraries. The system was not without its flaws (the result of largely being a one-person project), and the layout of Bliss' text was difficult to read. A few library schools sometimes taught the BC system to their students, but only in a minor capacity. The failure of the system to catch on in North America was partially due to its internal deficiencies, but also because the Dewey Decimal and Library of Congress systems were already well established.

The City College library continued to use Bliss' system until 1967, when they reluctantly switched to the Library of Congress system. It had gotten too expensive to train new staff to use BC, and too expensive to maintain in general. The case was different, however, in Britain, BC proved more popular there and spread to other English-speaking allied countries. Part of the reason for its success was because libraries in teacher's colleges liked the way Bliss had organised the subject areas on teaching and education. By the mid-1950s, BC was being used in at least 60 British libraries, and in 100 by the 1970s. In 1967, the Bliss Classification Association was formed. Their first publication was the Abridged Bliss Classification (ABC), intended for school libraries. In 1977 they began to publish and maintain a much-improved, revised version of Bliss' system, referred to as BC2.

COLON CLASSIFICATION

Colon classification (CC) is a system of library classification developed by S. R. Ranganathan. It was the first ever faceted (or analytico-synthetic) classification. It is especially used in libraries in India.

Its name "Colon classification" comes from the use of colons to separate facets in class numbers. However, many other classification schemes, some of which are completely unrelated, also use colons and other punctuation in various functions. They should not be confused with Colon classification.

As an example, the subject "research in the cure of tuberculosis of lungs by x-ray conducted in India in 1950" results in a call number

L,45;421:6;253:f.44'N5

The components of this call number represent.

Medicine,Lungs;Tuberculosis:Treatment;X-ray:Research.India'1950

DEWEY DECIMAL CLASSIFICATION

The Dewey Decimal Classification (DDC, also called the Dewey Decimal System) is a system of library classification developed by Melvil Dewey in 1876, and since greatly modified and expanded in the course of the twenty-two major revisions which have occurred up until 2004.

The DDC attempts to organise all knowledge into ten main classes that, excluding the first class (000 Computers, information and general reference),' proceed from the divine (philosophy & religion) to the mundane (history & geography). DDC's cleverness is in choosing decimals for its categories; this allows it to be both purely numerical and infinitely hierarchical. It also is a faceted classification, combining elements from different parts of the structure to construct a number representing the subject content (often combining two subject elements with linking numbers and geographical and temporal elements) and form of an item rather than drawing upon a list containing each class and its meaning.

Except for general works and fiction, works are classified principally by subject, with extensions for subject relationships, place, time or type of material, producing classification numbers of not less than three digits but otherwise of indeterminate length with a decimal point before the fourth digit, where present (*e.g.* 330 for economy + 94 for Europe = 330.94 European economy; 973 for United States + 005 form division for periodicals = 973.005, periodicals concerning the United States generally); class-marks are to be read as numbers, in the order: 050, 220, 330.973, 331 etc. Any letter should be read as preceding any number that might have occupied the same character position, so "330.94 A" would come before 330.943. The system uses ten main classes, which are then further subdivided. Each main class has ten divisions and each division has ten sections. Hence the system can be neatly summarised in 10 main classes, 100 divisions and 1000 sections. It is a common misconception that all books in the DDC are nonfiction. However, the DDC has a number for all books, including those that generally become their own section of fiction. If DDC rules were strictly followed, American fiction would be classified in 813. Most libraries create a separate fiction section because of the space that would be taken up in the 800s.

Main Classes

The system is made of up ten categories:

- 000 Computers, information and general reference
- 100 Philosophy and psychology
- 200 Religion
- 300 Social sciences
- 400 Language
- 500 Science and mathematics
- 600 Technology
- 700 Arts and recreation
- 800 Literature
- 900 History and geography

Cultural Bias of the DDC

DDC is commonly used in public and school libraries throughout the world. The schedule contains marked geographical biases derived from its 19th century origins: "Northern Africa for instance occupies all of 961-965, the rest of the continent only 966-969. It is still more biased towards Christianity against other religions, the former covering all of 220-289, while all others get only 292-299 to share. Recent versions permit another religion to be placed in 220-289, with

Christianity relegated to 298, but this is mainly used by libraries operated by non-Christian religious groups, especially Jewish ones.

The DDC has also been criticised for its treatment of literature (800). Because primacy is given to language, national literatures get scattered. For example, Canadian literature in English is classed under English & Old English (820) literatures while Canadian literature in French is classed under French literatures (840). The only exception is for American literature (810); a reflection of the Anglo-American bias inherent in the system.

DDC's numbers formed the basis of the more expressive but complex Universal Decimal Classification, which combines the basic Dewey numbers with selected punctuation marks (comma, colon, parentheses etc.). Despite its frequent revision, DDC is widely considered theoretically inferior to other more modern systems which make freer use of alphabetical characters to produce shorter classmarks for concepts of equal complexity, though it continues to offer a more expressive format than the Library of Congress Classification developed shortly afterward.

Ownership

The Online Computer Library Centre acquired the trademark and any copyrights associated with the Dewey Decimal System when it bought Forest Press in 1988. OCLC classifies new books and maintains the classification system. In September 2003, the OCLC sued the Library Hotel for trademark infringement. The settlement was that the OCLC would allow the Library Hotel to use the system in its hotel and marketing. In exchange, the Hotel would acknowledge the Centre's ownership of the trademark "and make a donation to a nonprofit organisation promoting reading and literacy among children.

000 Generalities

010 Bibliography

020 Library & information science

030 General encyclopedias

040 Not used

050 General serial publications

060 Organisations

070 Journalism, publishing, media

080 General collections

090 Manuscripts & rare books

100 Philosophy & Psychology

110 Metaphysics

120 Epistemology, causation, humankind

130 Paranormal phenomenon

140 Specific philosophical schools

150 Psychology

160 Logic

170 Ethics

180 Ancient, medieval, Oriental philosophy

190 Modern western philosophy

200 Religion

210 Philosophy & theory of religion

220 Bible

230 Christianity

240 Christian moral & devotional theology

250 Christian orders & local church

260 Social & ecclesiastical theology

270 History of Christianity & Christian sects

280 Christian denominations

290 Comparative religion & other religions

300 Social Sciences

310 Statistics

320 Political science

330 Economics

340 Law

350 Public administration & military science

360 Social programmes & services

370 Education

380 Commerce

390 Customs, etiquette, folklore

400 Language

410 Linguisitics

420 English & Old English

430 Germanic

440 French

450 Italian, Romanian, Rhaeto-Romanic

460 Spanish & Portuguese

470 Latin

480 Greek

490 Other languages

500 Natural Sciences & Math

510 Math

520 Astronomy

530 Physics

540 Chemistry

550 Earth sciences

560 Paleontology

570 Life sciences

580 Plants

590 Animals

600 Technology & Applied Sciences

610 Medicine

620 Engineering

630 Agriculture

640 Home economics (cooking)

650 Managelpent

660 Chemical engineering

670 Manufacturing

680 Manufacture for specific uses

690 Building

700 Arts, Sports, Recreation

710 Civic & landscape art

720 Architecture

730 Plastic arts (sculpture)

740 Drawing & decorative art

750 Painting

760 Graphic arts

770 Photography

780 Music

790 Recreation, performing arts, sports

800 Literature & Rhetoric

810 American

820 English & Old English

830 Germanic

840 French

850 Italian, Romanian

860 Spanish, Portuguese

870 Latin

880 Greek

890 Other literatures

900 Geography, History, Biography

910 Geography, travel

920 Biography, genealogy, insignia

930 Ancient world

940 Europe

950 Asia

960 Africa

970 North America

980 South America

990 Other areas

Library of Congress Classification

The Library of Congress Classification (LCC) is a system of library classification developed by the Library of Congress. It is used by most research and university libraries in the U.S. and several other countries—most public libraries continue to use the Dewey Decimal Classification (DDC).

The classification was originally developed by Herbert Putnam with the advice of Charles Ammi Cutter in 1897 before he assumed the librarianship of Congress. It was influenced by Cutter Expansive Classification, DDC, and was designed for the use by the Library of Congress. The new system replaced a fixed location system developed by Thomas Jefferson. By the time of Putnam's departure from his post in 1939 all the classes except K (Law) and parts of B (Philosophy and Religion) were well developed. It has been criticised as lacking a sound theoretical basis; many of the classification decisions were driven by the particular practical needs of that library, rather than considerations of epistemological elegance.

Although it divides subjects into broad categories, it is essentially enumerative in nature.

Universal Decimal Classification

The Universal Decimal Classification is a system of library classification developed by the Belgian bibliographers Paul Otlet and Henri la Fontaine at the end of the 19th century. It is based on the Dewey Decimal Classification, but is much more powerful. It uses auxiliary signs to indicate various special aspects of a subject and relationships between subjects. It thus contains a significant faceted or analytico-synthetic element, and is used especially in specialist libraries. UDC has been modified and extended over many years to cope with the increasing output in all disciplines of human knowledge, and is still under continuous review to take account of new developments.

The documents classified by UOC may be in any form. They will often be literature, i.e. written documents, but may also be in other media such as films, video and sound recordings, illustrations, maps, and realia such as museum pieces. UDC classifications use Arabic numerals and are based on the decimal system. Every number is thought of as a decimal fraction with the initial decimal point omitted, which determines filing order. For ease of reading, a UDC identifier is usually punctuated after every third digit.

Thus, after 61 "Medical sciences" come the subdivisions 611 to 619; under 611 "Anatomy" come its subdivisions 611.1 to 611.9; under 611.1 come all of its subdivisions before 611.2 occurs, and so on; after 619 comes 62. An advantage of this system is that it is infinitely extensible, and when new subdivisions are introduced, they need not disturb the existing allocation of numbers. A document may be classified under a combination of different categories through the use of additional symbols. For example:

+	plus	Addition	*e.g.* 59+636 Zoology and animal breeding
/	stroke	Extension	*e.g.* 592/599 Systematic zoology (everything from 592 to 399 inclusive)
:	colon	Relation	*e.g.* 17:7 Relation of ethics to art
[]	square brackets	Algebraic subgrouping	*e.g.* 31:[622+669](485) statistics of mining and metallurgy in Sweden (the auxiliary qualifies 622+669 considered as a unit)
=	equals	Language	*e.g.* =20 in English; 59=20 Zoology, in English

UDC works extremely well with computers, as it did with earlier automatic sorting devices. A core version of UDC with 60,000 subdivisions, is now available in database format, and is called the Master Reference File (MRF). The current full version of UDC has 220,000 subdivisions.

Library collections, although ordinarily thought of in terms of books and serials, actually contain a very broad range of materials: manuscripts, archives, photographs, recordings, moves, and much else. Not only will a particular collection include different sorts of objects, but some objects combine textual, visual, audio, and artifactual aspects. Further, the same object can be of interest for quite diverse reasons. Collections of library matenals support the purposes of the community served and that those served use the materials in the collections. In a significant sense library materials are used as evidence in learning—as the basis for understanding.

Textbooks and encyclopedias provide material for an introduction to a subject; literary texts and commentaries provide sources for the study of language and literature;

arrays of statistical data provide input for calculations, and inference; statutes and law reports indicate the law; photographs show what people, places, and events looked like; citations and sources are verified; etc. In each case it is reasonable to view library materials as evidence, though without implying that what was read, viewed, listened to, or otherwise used was necessarily accurate, useful, or even pertinent to the user's purposes.

Nor need it be assumed that the user did believe or agree with what was read. In this view collections are regarded as selections of material of actual or potential usefulness in meeting the sorts of inquiries regarded as appropriate for the people for whom library service is provided. Viewing library materials as selections of potential or putative evidence enables us to examine library use more deeply. When faced with evidence people sift, excerpt, evaluate, summarise, and may well add to the cumulation of evidence. Someone inquiring into the role of women in eighteenth-century England could benefit from a very wide range of materials: helpful evidence might be found in literature, diaries, sermons, pictures, in contemporary materials of almost any kind, and in commentaries of many sorts written in the centuries since. Much of the evidence is likely to be indirect, in the implications of texts and images created for quite other purposes. Excerpting and summarising permit copying and condensing of evidence for the convenience of the inquirer, whether by hand, photocopier, or computer. Evaluation of and inference from the texts, images, and objects in the collections leads to understanding, insights, and new ideas. These, in turn, may lead to new material in new articles or books, which may include commentary on the old, thereby increasing the accumulation for the future.

Microfilms

Microfilms and other microforms represented a significant departure from paper materials, yet they differ on only one of the characteristics noted above—special equipment is needed to read them. This adds a requirement for libraries to maintain a new sort of equipment: microform readers and printers. The first major programmes of microfilming library materials began with newspapers in the 1930s. Use of microforms increased greatly in the 1960s as microfiche were used for the dissemination of technical reports by government agencies. Microforms are even more localised than paper materials: not only must the would—be reader and the microform be in the same place, there must also be a usable machine on which to read it at that place. Furthermore, copies are less convenient to make and cannot, like paper, be annotated. They are even less suitable for correction or revision.

There needs to be, therefore, a significant perceived benefit in the accumulation of the collection if there is to be any degree of rationality. A benefit, however, implies a value. Hence, discussion of the scope ought to be related to the choice of values. The collection of books for their own sake—bibliophilia—could be such a value, but it is more likely to be the increase in knowledge of one sort or another within a particular group of people that the library is expected to serve. If the growth of knowledge is to be the determining value and if resources are limited, the only rational procedure is to relate the scope of the retrieval system to those items likely to facilitate the growth of knowledge in the most cost-beneficial way, insofar as one can.

For example, if a copy of a book were never to be used, it is difficult to see how it could have facilitated the growth of knowledge; and, since it took resources to acquire, to process, and to store it, its acquisition was not merely not beneficial, but counterproductive, since those resources might have been used in some other way to foster those values. The library exists in a political and cultural environment. In this environment the funders, the users, and the librarians have social values that form part of the context of the library's mission. Library collections are constrained to be compatible with those social values. It is for this reason that a library's collection will not always contain the most informative material even where it can be afforded. Funders, librarians, and users would probably prefer their library not to include material that facilitates or encourages topics deemed socially undesirable, such as poisoning public water supplies, dangerous drugs, pederasty, or how to make bombs.

MANAGEMENT OF DIGITAL COLLECTION

Collection management involved a range of processes made more efficient by computing and communications technologies—gathering information, coordinating communications, formulating policy, evaluating and planning. While these processes still form the basis of collection management activities, the specific activities which comprise collection management in the year 2000 have evolved during the past decade, and now include assessment of user needs; inter- and intra-library communication; policy development; budgeting and allocation of resources; contract negotiations; macro-evaluation of collections; micro-evaluation for selection, relegation, preservation or withdrawal of stock; and system evaluation. To create an intellectual work, an author undertakes research, draws on personal experience, engages in a creative process, or is involved in a combination of these activities. The task also requires the author to record the results of the foregoing activities in an intellectual work as, for example, a paper for a scholarly journal, an article for a popular magazine or a novel. After recording an intellectual work the author sends it to a publisher, and, if selected for publication, it is demarcated as an intellectual work by the tangible information package in which it is published. This means that all manifestations of a work are clearly identifiable as a mono-graphic edition, a journal article, a chapter of an edited monograph, or even as an adaptation such as a film production.

If the original intellectual work were altered in any way, the outcome would be recognisable either as a new manifestation such as a revised edition or, if the alteration were significant, as a new work in its own right. To create new knowledge an author must still perform research, draw on personal experience, engage in a creative process, or be involved in a combination of these activities and record the results in an intellectual work. The intellectual work, however, is no longer clearly delineated in a tangible information package. The nature of digital information allows it to be interactive and to be altered or linked to other works.

The lack of a physical presence and the very nature of digital media have several consequences. Intellectual works are not captured in a form that ensures their preservation. A work in digital form is easily altered—text can be added, purged, exchanged, amalgamated; that is, an author can easily create a new manifestation of a work, or another author can easily alter a work subtly or indeed in a major way. When a publisher creates both print and digital versions of a work, the digital version may contain interactive data that can be downloaded and manipulated, as well as video and audio items. Libraries are striving to respond to the pervasive and persistent growth of global networking and manage the demand for access to this dynamic medium. Working in the trenches of the digital revolution, librarians and information professionals are beginning to offer internet services to patrons; their work marks the beginning of the grassroots implementation of the public digital library. Such efforts do not come without their attendant risks, and it is extremely important that those who are becoming network service and resource providers and content producers clearly understand what is involved in their participation in the digital revolution from an issues and policy-oriented perspective. The concept of the digital or virhlal library describes a new organisational form that is expected to be linked in some way to physical libraries. Although at best an elusive concept, the digital library has acquired the cachet of a powerful memo, driving research and thinking throughout this decade. In fact, the definition of a digital library is by no means clear; despite the awarding of millions of dollars to develop components of digital libraries and several conferences devoted to the topic, there does not seem to be a consensus on the meaning of the term.

The emerging field of digital libraries brings together participants from many existing areas of research, Currently, the field lacks a clear agenda independent of these other areas. It is tempting for researchers to think that the field of digital libraries is a natural outgrowth of an already known field. It will be limited if viewed only as a subfield of prior research interests. Throughout the past few decades, librarians and information professionals have moved to the front lines of the digital revolution as a consequence of their interests and in response to increasing customer demand, providing internet services to a wide range of patrons in a wide variety of settings. Libraries complement both research and education. Predictably, most of the well-publicised work that has been done on digital libraries has occurred in academic settings and has focused on the technical issues involved in digitising, storing, organising, and providing access to the content of these libraries.

Public and school librarians are working typically without a blueprint, under time and economic constraints and, with a few exceptions, with little assistance from the research community. Their efforts do not come without their attendant risks, and it is extremely important that public and school librarians who are becoming network service and resource providers clearly understand what is involved in their participation in the digital revolution from an issues and policy-oriented perspective. Academic, special, and public/school libraries operate under varying institutional, social, and economic constraints and it is reasonable to expect that researchers and practitioners exploring the possibilities of digital libraries will have access to different resources and will face different problems in their work. One key difference is that the academic digital library projects are taking place under the aegis of the university and the major funding agencies; these projects may allow the public access to their services and resources, but they are not really public. On the other hand, many of the efforts of public and school librarians take place without the same kind of institutional safety net and are intended for immediate public use. They are creating a new organisational form—the public digital library. As the media continues to define the internet as the broadcast television of the 1990s, the general public discovers the vast world of resources and services on the internet, and politicians attempt to impose a regulatory framework on the internet, public and school librarians find themselves on the front lines of provision of access to the net.

As librarians and information professionals begin to offer internet services to patrons, they are in the trenches of the digital revolution and their work marks the beginning of the grassroots implementation of the public digital library. The complexity of the technical challenges that must be faced and overcome in these settings is neither trivial nor easily managed. However, there is an equally challenging set of issues focused loosely around the concept of intellectual freedom which also must be faced and managed. The collection managers' consideration of the authors of works is primarily in the micro-evaluation component of both the selection and withdrawal activities of the collection management function.

In general, however, new works or new manifestations of a work are rarely selected based solely on an author's reputation, since in relation to the overall number of authors there are very few who are well known. Evaluation is more often based on the publisher's reputation which is derived over time from the value adding activities undertaken by the publisher in relation to the intellectual works of many authors. In many large libraries, selection of information packages for purchase is semi-automatic, such as when blanket orders are established or when selection is outsourced to distributors who create profiles based on disciplinary areas. The collection managers in these situations have made macro-evaluation decisions for ongoing bulk selection in which the publishers or the topic areas, or a combination of both, are considered to be more important as variables than are the individual authors or the individual intellectual works. In publishing distributors for example, have acted as intermediaries between publishers and libraries in the sale and distribution of monographs.

The collection manager's role was to establish and monitor the relationship with the distributors, evaluating the performance and ensuring that the services provided by the distributors met the needs of the users and were cost-effective for the library. The e-book publisher, net-Library, has already formed relationships with many publishers of paper-based works with a view to providing customers with an extensive selection of scholarly, reference and professional books in digital format.

When the content is moved to digital format, tile distribution component can be done by the publishers or within another type of publisher/distributor relationship, as is now occurring with many electronic journal titles. Serial publications in paper format have resulted in a distinctive style of publisher/distributor relationship with libraries. The serials vendor or 'Subscription agent has long acted as a middleman between the publishers and the libraries. The vendor's service to the publishers has involved selling subscriptions, aggregating them and maintaining control over them by collecting payments from the subscribers and sending renewal notices at the appropriate times. How does the blurring of boundaries in the publisher/distributor relationship with libraries affect the role of collection management staff? First, there are many new products and services from publishers and distributors which collection management staff must evaluate. In same instances there are clearly distinguishable variations between products which make them easy to evaluate, whereas in other instances the mixing and matching of products and services makes the evaluation task more difficult. The second important impact on the roles of collection managers is that they must now deal with many more types of licensing options which are becoming available for the new types of digital information packages and products. Because of the rapid pace with which these new products are entering the market, the groups involved in licensing e journals have so far had little opportunity to address licensing issues.

In the digital environment, collection managers will have to understand licensing arrangements to ensure that they obtain appropriate access to the products their' clients require. While the model agreements will save the library staff and publishers time in their negotiations, they have nothing to do with prices, so collection managers will still have to determine the best prices and decide whether they should be involved in a consortium to obtain the best product at the best price. Information products and library collections are already changing, and we see this increasingly in the shift away from the sale of print based resources to the licensing of digital information resources by commercial publishers and in the change in thinking by library managers from ownership of library resources to the provision of access to them. Many librarians believe there is a relationship between providing access to online periodical databases and recent reductions in book circulation statistics. If publishers eventually market information products directly to end-users, libraries will be left with only those patrons who have no access other than the library, those for whom the convenience of atmosphere of the library environment is attractive, or those dependent upon print resources that are inimical to being digitised.

The digital publishing of historical documents held in an academic library collection requires a three-way partnership between the library, the computing centre and the academic staff. User studies should be undertaken to determine whether there is sufficient academic need to warrant product development. If there is sufficient need, a collection development plan should be created which would establish a policy for selection of appropriate texts and provide a clear framework for producing and maintaining the digital resources and evaluating the project. The plan should also identify the standards required for creating texts that can be networked, and establish the basis for quality control.

The boundaries between libraries have distinguished individual libraries as unique institutions with their own governance as well as unique collections of resources acquired for specific groups of intended users or for specific purposes. However, we are now in an era during which a global library and information infrastructure is evolving. The growing importance of library consortia is evident by the numerous descriptive articles which have been appearing in the recent literature. Even those writers who highlight the lack of success in cooperative collection development for consortia in the past suggest that the circumstances are right for consortia to perform better. Content management does not suggest that the format of an information package is irrelevant—it affects the way the content is communicated, and content managers need to select the format most appropriate to the user. By focusing on content in conjunction with user needs, collection managers will identify the resources most important for their users, and will ensure that their users can obtain access to those resources in the most suitable format. Managing content requires cooperation and coordination across multiple institutions and includes acquiring and providing access to paper-based resources, signing collective contracts and ensuring appropriate technology to provide access to digital resources, creating and managing e-texts, and a host of other activities which span the boundaries between libraries.

For collection management staff the blurring of boundaries at all levels of the information chain leads to the blurring of boundaries between their roles and responsibilities in collection management and those of other librarians, and even those of individuals working in other fields. Changes to work practices in collection management are already evident. The team approach to selecting information resources in digital form is a clear case in point. With electronic resources there are concerns about the greater expenses incurred through subscriptions, associated hardware and software interfaces with other online systems, printing costs, changes to strategies for providing technical and public service support, and training programmes for both staff and users.

For example, the selection of resources will move from collection development librarians to the users themselves, and collection managers will become 'managers of electronic rights' who ensure that the institution's users have open avenues to the information they need. He contends that in the digital world selection for the local collection is likely to decrease in importance as the primary work of collection development librarians, who are the largest group of subject experts in research libraries. In the digital environment delivery services will, through 'disintermediation', begin to assume or replace some mediation services. One of the most important conceptual goals that academic libraries need to pursue as information becomes increasingly online should be the elimination of the distinction between academic library collection building and specialised scholarly publication. This distinction is eliminated in the digital environment because academic staff members will select the intellectual works for inclusion in the control zone, thus bestowing the prestige on selected works which was formerly conferred by the publishers of scholarly communication.

The libraries' role will be to ensure that this subset of information remains stable and accessible over time through two fundamental library functions: archiving and metadata. Archiving of digital information is merely one of the latest manifestations of the eternal dilemma of preservation. Although the digital environment raises new challenges, such as ensuring backwards compatibility and selecting the most important works from the sheer volume of digital information, such technological and selection issues have always been a component of collection management.

'Content rating' should be added subsequent to the act of publication by experts in the field who have determined the work's significance through their own use of it; 'audience level' should indicate the target audience and should be added by the work's creator; and 'use history' should indicate the frequency of use by specific groups and should be generated automatically. The role of collection development in a research library should be given back to academics, it is unlikely that this will happen. Rather, the creation of the content ratings and the audience level ratings in metadata will be done by experts, but these experts will be collection management staff—the subject bibliographers and selectors who already evaluate information on an ongoing basis.

●●

3

Theory of Classification Schedule

When we speak of the consistent use of a term we mean merely that in the bringing together of things to form a class the name by which we call any thing shall represent that thing and that alone in the class. It does not mean that such a word as engine when used in the class Railways shall mean exactly the same thing as it means in the title The Engines of the Human Body where the class is Physiology and the term is used merely pictorially. A certain resemblance is admitted; otherwise the analogy the terms imply would not exist, but they are really quite different terms. We need not pursue at any length the various examples that were given formerly of inconsistency in the use of terms; they were often examples of words used analogically, metaphorically or carelessly, as when it was shown that "spring" may stand for an action, a season, a stream, or a thing; and when we use the word "sharp" of a needle, a street-arab, or a sensation of grief or pain, and so on. Intelligent people are able to detect such ambiguities from the context in which they are found. This emphasis we place upon the choice of class-terms is justified because they are the brief statement of the principles which we have recognized in making the class itself. Some part of the meaning has emerged already, it is hoped, but further explanations may be forgiven. Every classical reader knows that the word "class" in our sense has the same meaning that was given it in Ancient Rome when the effective nobility were arranged in six orders or ranks according to their real or supposed qualities of blood or wealth. These were the classes of the population, as distinct from the lower orders. A classis, then, was made up of a number of persons having a certain quality in common, or as we should say now, using words a little inaccurately but with a meaning we all understand, being of the same class. So in our study a class consists of a number of things which are alike in some particular, have some quality in common by which they may be sorted out from other things and which at the same time makes their own unity. It may safely be assumed from the outset that every thing in the universe is a member of some class; it cannot be affirmed with absolute certainty but clearly if there is a thing which has no likeness to any other thing and therefore has no relationships it is unique and such things, if they exist, must be few. We can test this readily if we consider any of the common things of life-plants, animals, men, houses, streets, stones, stars, clothes and what not.

A class, the definition requires, is made up of like things. This means clearly an assembly of things but as a necessary result it means also their separation from other things. The rule, stated briefly, is "Classification assembles things according to their degrees of likeness and separates them according to their degrees of unlikeness." Likeness has been dealt with in admirable manner by Richardson in the introduction to his Classification. It is not sameness, because no two things have absolutely that likeness which would mean that they were alike in every particular and both occupied the same position in space, which is manifestly impossible. In common speech their distinction is often confused as when two men order drinks and the second after hearing the first says "I'll have the same." He could have something from the same cask or bottle but it would not be the same liquid. A better definition for us of likeness is the quality or qualities in things which enables them to be substituted for each other, as, for example, the cartridges in a particular type of machine gun, the cards used in a catalogue, the letter a in a font of type of a given size, and pennies. Each of these resembles the companions in its class in a high degree. It is clear that there must be many ways in which things are like, as is seen in the simple example of a collection of pennies, as by the sovereigns who reigned at the time of issue, their date, their size in differing periods, their stages of wear; it is possible to arrange them by any of these likenesses, the only qualification being that the arrangement chosen serves its maker's purpose. The example may seem trivial, but as we saw in our description of the many viewpoints from which maps of an area may be drawn, the condition it implies is necessary to all practical classification, for it leads us again to the principle already emphasized that the arrangement must be that most useful to its user.

If, then, a class is a group of things brought together by a chosen likeness, how do we proceed to make this class and to break it up into sub-classes? It is clear that while such a term as Botany is the name of a great-class, the members of which have all the likeness of insentient life, growth and decay, the class is too vast for any detailed study and must be broken up into its parts. The first process is one of assembly. A quality of likeness is chosen as the characteristic, by which we assemble things to make our class. The second process is to sub-divide our class into its parts. In formal phrase a classification proceeds from terms of great extension and small intension to terms of great intension and small extension. Or, more simply, it proceeds by taking class terms which connote great areas of subject-matter and divides them by gradual steps into terms less and less extensive until division is no longer possible. This definition is convenient but obviously depends upon the order adopted, because as Carveth Read shows "Classification may be either deductive or inductive; that is to say, in the formation of classes, as in the proof of propositions, we may, on the whole, proceed from the more to the less, or from the less to the more general; not that these two processes are entirely independent." If a classification were in the developmental, historical or evolutionary order of a subject, it would proceed from such a term as Being; which might connote all existence past, present and possible, to the atom by gradual stages, and there we have an excellent example of the meaning of our rule but, as we have shown, there may be as many arrangements of things as there are kinds of likeness to be found amongst them; It is therefore quite possible to reverse this order and to proceed from the special head to the general one.

In this short paragraph have been used some words which an advanced worker on our subject may assume to be commonly understood, but for reasons already given I repeat a few of the simpler explanations.

Extension and Intension, Denotation and Connotation are words from formal logic representing certain powers and applications of terms. A further series of qualities which may be predicated of terms is that described as the Five Predicables and the application of all these terms is illustrated by the Tree of Porphyry or the Ramean Tree as it is also called. By the extension of a term we mean all the things to which it may be applied. John Stuart Mill and some of his successors use denotation in the same sense. The term "Man" denotes any human being, "Animal" any living creature, and so on. By the intension of a term we mean the qualities implied ""in the thing named. Connotation is used as an alternative to intension. In intension "Man" connotes a mammal of upright gait who possesses reason, and "Animal" an organized living being, vertebrate or invertebrate, with sensation and capable of voluntary motion. The greater the extension of a term the smaller its intension and, conversely, the greater its intension the smaller its extension, as the Tree, below, may be used to demonstrate. The term "Being" already used is one of great extension, seeing that it covers all that is, but the term "pen" or "dog," although it has extension, is of enormously smaller extent and of much greater meaning or intension. The name of an individual, as Edward Edwards, is the example of a term of the smallest extension as it is limited to one man, but of the greatest intension for it implies every quality, racial and individual, that an English librarian of the middle of the Nineteenth Century can be known to have possessed.

The Five Predicables are a group of words which indicate qualities which may be predicated of terms. They were an addition to the Aristotelian Logic taken in the Third Century from Porphyry's Isagoge or Introduction to the Categories. They are Genus, Species, Difference, Property and Accident.

(i) *Genus* is a group of things which may be divided into sub groups, or species.

(ii) *Species*, then, are the group into which the genus may be divided.

The character which determines the division of the genus into the species is the difference, which may be defined as something added to the genus. The species, therefore, is the genus plus some quality or property which is over and above the unifying quality or property of the genus as a whole.

(iii) *A Species*, however, may, and does in frequent cases, itself become a genus; that is to say, if it may be divided into sub-species; so far as these sub-species are concerned, the species is the genus; and, again, the sub-species themselves may each become a genus for possible sub-sub-species.

(iv) *A property* is some quality of a thing or class which is common to that thing or class, but which is not necessary to the definition of that class. The possession of a heart is a property of man, but is not peculiar to him since reason is his distinctive characteristic; and many things possess properties which are not exclusively the possession of the group or class to which they belong; thus, the emotions and certain physiological functions are not exclusively human although possessed by all men; they belong also to other animals.

(v) *An accident* is a quality which is incidental to a class, may or may not belong to it, and has no necessary effect upon its other qualities. The size of a man is a mere accidental quality; so is the cut of a man's clothes; so, too, is the colour of his countenance, if we take man in general.

The Tree of Porphyry

Porphyry was also responsible for the Ladder or Tree which is usually employed to illustrate the division of a term and the uses of extension and intension as well as the predicables. Pierre de la Ramee, the French savant (1515-72), seems to have revived it in the sixteenth century with such effect that some thought him to be its creator and gave it the alternative name of the Ramean Tree.

This is an example of what is called the bi-furcate method of classification, or classification branching in pairs, and in some ways it is a classification of broad character, but its value for us is to illustrate terms and to show the inevitable method of dividing terms. Substance is a term covering everything that exists, it is the most extensive, has the greatest extension, of any terms readily available. Conversely, it is so wide that it is impossible to indicate the multiplicity of things implied. Therefore it is a term of great extension and small intension. Corporeal Substance is still a term of great extension, but it has less extension, connotes fewer things, than Substance; it is therefore a term of greater intension, more qualities in it are definable. Animate Corporeal Substance is again of less extension and greater intension than Corporeal. The addition of the quality of Sensibility continues the process of lessening the extension and increasing the intension while the further addition of Reason completes the process by bringing us to Man who alone possesses it and who is divisible only into individuals such as Plato and you and me.

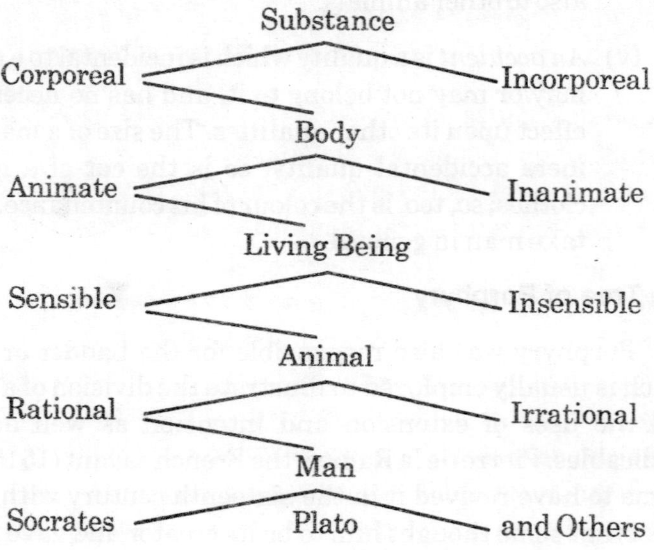

The Tree illustrates the predicables as simply. Substance is a genus which by the addition of the difference Corporeal (or possessing a body) divides the genus into the two species, Corporeal and Incorporeal. Leaving aside Incorporeal Substance, and, following what may be called the biological or living line of sub-division, we add the difference Animation to Corporeal Substance and break it into the two species Animate (the Living Body) and the Inanimate. Thence, adding Sensibility, we make the further species, the Animal, and leave over the living thing that is not Animal (the plant, etc.); and, finally, the difference Reason is added to the Animal to sort out the Rational Being which is Man, and the Irrational Animal is left over. Property and Accident are two predicables which are not illustrated in any obvious way by the Tree, although so far as Property is concerned words could be stretched, in a way unnecessary here, to prove that life is a property of all the left branches of the Tree and lifelessness those on the right.

What Classification Does

As the value of a classification scheme to its user is its cardinal quality it follows that in constructing its schedules the examination of the material to be classified must be of first importance. Librarians think this to be specially so of books, but no arrangement of books which does not follow the principles of logical classification is likely to meet general needs or to endure for long. That there are differences between the book classification and the knowledge classification is obvious to simple perception, but the resemblance between them is even greater. The purpose of knowledge classification is to assemble things in classes in order that their causes and effects may be examined, and where a cause seems invariably to produce an effect the process is regarded as a natural law of the things. Such classification clarifies thought, advances investigation, shows gaps in the sequence of knowledge and promotes discovery; revealing, as it should, the relationships of things, it enables a more or less complete survey of knowledge to be made. The variety of schemes of classifications of knowledge is a necessary condition of knowledge; it cannot stand still, it is infinite.

If that is the condition of the classification of knowledge, to some extent it is reflected in book classification which, primarily, seems to have another purpose. This is to place books in their relations to one another from the point of view of the reader. That reader must to a certain extent at least be a hypothetical person as we see when we encounter the university professor who blandly advises alphabetical author order or when we meet Jevons's statement that the classification of books is a logical absurdity it is, of course, if we pretend that any method of book arrangement will resolve into a precise set of relations the welter of cross-classification which almost every book is. The library classifier makes no such pretence; he says that every book deals with an area or several areas of knowledge or is in a form which gives it its chief interest; in short, has a dominant character and the placing of the book by that character is a convenience and a library economy. The problem is to discover a way of putting books on shelves in an order which will be recognizable, be in harmony with current studies and enable the finding of books together which have likeness in a greater or less degree. So we reach the condition that while an examination of books precedes the final arrangement of the classification, the scheme must first be known to the mind in outline at least. If, then, books are to follow the order of studies, by which we mean broadly what Mr. Hawkes calls the vocational activities of men, the order which the workers in the various branches of knowledge work must be the groundwork of the outline of principal divisions or main classes and their important sub-divisions.

Theory of Knowledge

The assembly of things into classes and the setting of classes in order to bring out their relationships has been the occupation of all creative, system making philosophers from the earliest recorded time until now. To realize this we may revert to our analogy of the map of the world. The position of the traveller or geographer before the making of the maps of Ptolemy must have been very like that of the scientific worker in his early efforts to discover the nature and order of phenomena. In like manner he had to discover and name the continents and by gradual stages of enquiry reach to the whereabouts and character of seas, countries, rivers, mountains and so on. The parallel is a good one, for as the geographer has his divisions of the globe, so has the classifier to divide knowledge into its great classes or continents, its countries or sub-classes and its lesser parts. His task has been the more difficult, because while the geographer surveys a concrete, physical and visible set of phenomena, the scientist has much wider and less defined territories with which to deal. But as geographical maps have grown, changed and improved at every successive stage of discovery, so the classifications of knowledge have progressed. There the parallel may end, because there is a limit to the terrestrial globe; there is no limit to knowledge either in the physical or mental field, there is much more that is unknown, is possibly unprovable, subject to changes. No scheme of classification goes far beyond its own age, if it passes beyond it at all. Therefore we see that successive philosophers have suggested at intervals new characteristics on which to base the outline and the development of their systems. We can mix general and library classifications in our consideration of schedule-making because either form will illustrate the principles, which may be written briefly thus:

A classification is an assembly of classes in their relations.

Classes divide from the general head to the special by gradations of likeness and difference.

The gradation must bring about the subordination and co-ordination of the sub-classes.

The arrangement must be uncritical.

It must be exhaustive.

The process, either of assembly into classes or the sub-dividing of the classes when made, must depend upon some theory of knowledge. Even when we are arranging in the roughest manner a group of books, we do it by some order in our minds that must precede the act of arranging. So the classifiers in turn took some theory that we may say to be their characteristic. Thus Callimachus took the kinds of writer as his basis; Gesner, the order of the studies as they were pursued in the medireval university; Bacon the products of the operation of the mental faculties memory, imagination and reason.

Classifying Process

The process may be illustrated from more limited and simpler things. Instead of the whole of knowledge, we can take clothes or domestic equipment or dwelling houses, indeed anything that is capable of assembly and of division, either in the actual objects or as mental concepts or ideas. In the clothing trade it is possible to arrange garments by their material, their purpose, sizes, prices and many other ways. In domestic equipment, purpose, material and position are some of the possible characteristics. In dwelling houses, style, size, building materials, position and so on may each serve. All such characteristics may in turn be used but only one at each stage of the classifying process. If, then, we are arranging clothes, we may begin by considering their purpose, pursuing this line until all the material is exhausted; for example, under and outer garments would possibly be two great main divisions. Each of these could then be divided by the part of the body the garment is intended to cover, and, having exhausted that, the size of the garments might be taken up and exhausted, and so on with any other characteristic which clothes will exhibit. This homely example exhibits many of the conditions of all classification schemes; thus the whole field of knowledge covered is assembled by the characteristic "that which covers and protects the individual body"; to this we add the difference "for outdoor wear" and immediately produce the two species under and outer garments which, being its parts, are subordinate to clothing generally. They are also co-ordinates as they must range together in the mind and they are correlatives as an outer garment necessarily implies an inner one as brother implies a brother or sister and parent implies child. The two divisions thus made cover all clothes and thus far exhaust its extension or connotation. Further, it may be seen that while it was the difference "outdoor" which divided off or abstracted a sub-class of garments from clothing generally, "outdoor" is also the likeness which brings all the garments together and separates them from all others. Our first characteristic has been exhausted and on the broadest lines the classification is complete. But, for practical purposes, sub-division must proceed and a new characteristic, to be exhausted in turn, must be provided. This can be the parts of the body to be covered by the garments: footwear, legwear, bodywear, neckwear, headwear, and again each of these is subordinate to outer or under clothing as the case may be, each is held by the likeness of the part of the body, and they are coordinate classes.

Characteristics of Classification

Thus we see, if we use another set of illustrations, that when we arrange a series of things, for example, money by value, animals and plants by their physical structure and functions, buildings by the uses to which they are put, the chemical elements by their atomic weights, we have arranged each of them by a principle. The principle employed value, physical structure or use we have called the characteristic and the word, although not employed except by library classifiers in that sense; is a convenient one to indicate a definite notion.

The characteristic, then, is the quality, property or feature by which things are divided. The Library Association examiners have declared several times that "the characteristic is not a subject." The point involved is a fine one but is accurately made, because the subject is the thing divided or classified, and the characteristic is the likeness or quality by which the process is carried out. This now obvious principle is worth stating again since it has caused discussion and some discomfort to those who have not realized the distinction. An example may clear up the matter sufficiently. If we arrange a group of shells by their relative degrees of whiteness, whiteness is the characteristic, shells are the subject. On the other hand, whiteness as an abstract quality is certainly a subject of thought and itself can be arranged, because clearly there are imaginable or conceptual degrees of whiteness and therefore divisions of it; and anything that can be divided is a subject for classification. The fault of which the examiners complain lies in the fact that the candidate committing it had probably confused the subject with the characteristic in the application of the one to the other.

Artificial Classification

One sympathizes with Man in his early effort to reduce chaos to order; he had such a multiplicity of things with which to deal. It is not remarkable, is it, if in his earliest efforts he used his eyes, and reasoned from first perceptions? The appearances of things were there, and if two things "appeared to be like each other," he naturally brought them together. Thus, whales to him were fishes, bats were birds, spiders were insects. He reasoned in general from analogy which, to give a rough and ready definition, means the likeness in things which have a similar function, however different may be the plan upon which they are constructed. Or it may mean, in a sense sufficient for our argument, a likeness in appearance and purpose. Homology, on the other hand, means the likeness in things which resides in the fact that they are constructed upon the same plan, however different may be their functions. These definitions are usually drawn from Biology as we show in the next paragraph. There is also the definition of analogy as any form of likeness or comparison between things which in their essence may sometimes not be alike: as when the engines of the human body and those of a motor-car are said to be analogous; or when two historic events appear to have occurred in similar circumstances; as when two cases in law seem to resemble each other. Every form of likeness, in a sense, provides an analogy, including forms which are also homologic. Homology, however, implies a more total likeness founded upon the essence of the things, which is fundamental to them and which makes them conform in character and purpose. And this may apply, not only to living things, as we are about to show, but it may also apply, indeed does apply, to all things man makes for his purposes. Thus chairs, to use an example, given me by A. J. Hawkes, are a homologic group assembled by the purpose for which they exist-their use-not by their construction.

Let us illustrate a little from the older classifi-cations. We find that in the earliest animals were arranged by the element in which they lived; it was the most obvious thing about them; thus we got:

Animals.

Terrestrial.

Aerial.

Aquatic.

with the result that seals and whales and many molluscs were classed as fishes, while, as I have just said, the bat became one of the birds. This system would also naturally make such flying insects as butterflies into birds. There were variations of this characteristic for centuries, but of course men saw the inadequacy ot it. Even Linareus, who arrived at a more reasonable classifying method, arranged by analogy, choosing as the characteristic of classification the "general appearance and economy of the animal"; and making classes wherein the place of a creature was determined by such factors as the arrangement and number of toes, teeth, claws, beaks and scales. This leads, does it not, if we choose the number of limbs as a characteristic, to the frog and toad getting into the same class as tigers, as they evidently have four legs? Clearly these arrangements depend upon accidents and are artificial classification.

We had almost similar deficiencies in the early attempts to classify in the botanical sphere. The first classifier saw that some plants were larger than others, and he took size as a reasonable basis for his classing with incomplete results. So he obtained: Trees, Shrubs and Herbs as a first outline, the inadequacy of which soon became obvious. Linnaeus, again, offers us the most striking example of classification by a few qualities or properties, which often had no real relation to the nature of plants; and resembled, in some degree, the classification a child makes when he arranges flowers by their colours: everything white being a daisy; everything yellow-celandine, dandelion, buttercup, king-cup, etc. being a "buttercup." It is worth while to consider the various Linarean classifications with some care, as the classical examples of classification according to arbitrary factors, pursued without a due examination of all the characters of the things classified. Briefly, Linareus chose the arrangement and number of the several organs of plants as the basis of his arrangement; the two main classes being

A Flowers present.

B Flowers absent (or stamens and pistils not evident).

[Stamens are male organs, and pistils are female organs.]

These he sub-divided by certain appearances in the plants. Thus in class A we get

A Flowers present.

I Stamens and pistils in every flower.

II Stamens and pistils in different flowers.

III Stamens and pistils in the same or in different flowers.

And again he sub-divided AI into

AI Stamens and pistils in every flower.

Ala Stamens of equal length.

Ala I. Having I stamen.

II. Having 2 stamens.

III. Having 3 stamens.

and so on, until he reached flowers having twenty or more of these organs. Now note the effect of such a system. It depends entirely upon the floral organs, as we have seen; but plants are in flower only at certain seasons, and if, when we went to classify them, they were not in full flower with all their stamens and styles perfect, it would be impossible to determine their class. Moreover, in various stages of growth, as Balfour has pointed out in his Manual of Botany, different flowers on the same plant vary in the number of their stamens; and consequently the classifier would get like plants into quite different divisions.

Nearly always when we classify by number, size, or position in space, we get some such results as those with which we have been dealing. If we classified buildings by the material of which they were built, we might get villas, mansions, churches, townhalls, theatres and what not, all into one group, without any disting-uishing difference between them; and I need not say how inadequate that would be as a classification. Another simple example would be the arrangement of tables by the material of which they were made; or of bottles by their colours which would tell us nothing beyond their hue, and not even that satisfactorily. Everyone has met with the classification of the alphabet which is essential to the study of philology—especially to the study of such languages as Greek, where whole rules of phonology and speech turn upon the classification of the alphabet. In the accepted natural form the alphabet is classified according to the parts of the vocal apparatus which are brought into action in pronouncing them.

Focusing the results of this mode of classification upon books, we shall see how far it would lead us astray. Some libraries, even to this day, arrange books by size. It makes the library look very nice, the shelves being ordered as are properly "sized" ranks of infantry; but it would mean that if we had ten editions (say) of Milton they would be in ten different places. Examples can be multiplied. Again, if we arranged the books by their printing types (typography), the results would be similarly valueless, except for the student of typography for whom, be it remarked, it might be a perfectly "essential" arrangement (but, mark this, too, only if the books are regarded as "museum specimens," and not as having any other meaning). In a rather similar manner, if we arrange books by the language in which they are written, we get a very wide separation of subjects; although, again, if they are arranged for the student of language who is interested only in language, that would be a perfectly justifiable arrangement. All these arrangements, it will have been observed, are dependent upon one or more properties of the things classified; and those properties (or, to use our technical term "characteristics") are accidental ones. All these classifications are artificial ones; and to crystallize all we have here considered into a definition: An artificial classification is one in which some accidental property of the things classified is adopted as the characteristic of arrangement.

The incomplete and partial nature of artificial classifications can be seen, but I have also tried to show that they are not necessarily wrong; their use may in some circumstances be supremely right. What we want our classification to do—the end we have in view—must govern our choice of characteristics. This is merely repeating the rule that they "must be essential in relation to the purpose of the classification."

Natural Classification

A natural classification is one that is made by the inherent properties in things; by those properties without which a thing could not be the thing that it is. If we return to Zoology for our examples, we shall find that one great fact cuts the animal realm into two parts. This is, the possession or absence of the vertebral column or backbone; and, although in the lowest forms of animals held to be backboned the manner in which they differ from those without backbone is not at once obvious, it is quite definite. This then is the primary natural characteristic relating all the higher animals, the vertebrates and, dividing them from the lower forms, the Invertebrates. Thus we get as the basis of all natural zoological classification:

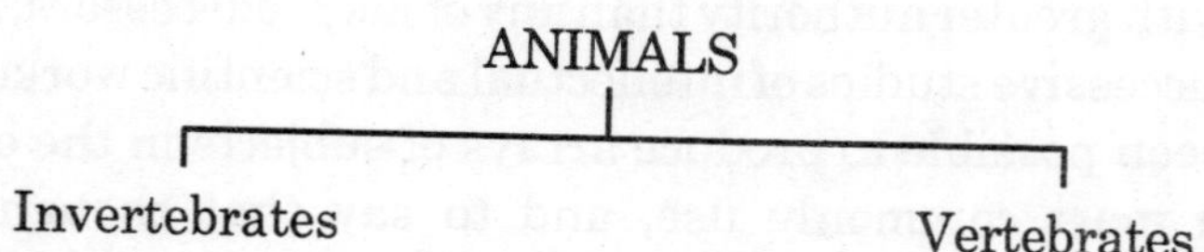

and additional structural differences, in blood, breathing apparatus, method of propagation, etc., continue to increase the intension of this primary characteristic until we reach Mammals in the Vertebrates and Insects in the Invertebrates.

Take, as a further example, three different insects and examine them—a butterfly, a beetle and a blue-bottle. In the first place we shall notice that they have no vertebral column they are not vertebrates; in the second, that their bodies are in three parts or segments, which seem as though they were hinged together; that on the second or middle segment each has three pairs of legs; and that each has two pairs of wings. In the butterfly the wings are apparent, are visibly seen to be a fore and back pair of wings; in the beetle the fore wing has evolved into a hard shining sheath, which when the creature is at rest is an enveloping case for the hind wings; and in the blue-bottle the back wings are rudimentary, are two little button-shaped nobs, but they are still wings from a zoological point of view. Thus, when we chose the characteristic of structure for their arrangement, and reached the name insect, we formed a class in which all the members had this triple-segmented body, these three pairs of legs, and these two pairs of wings. The word insect connotes a whole series of qualities.

Accepted Order

The application of what we have learned of characteristics by the educationist, scientific worker and others is bound in a way to be artificial because, as we have hinted, such schemes are 'based upon limited knowledge; nearly the whole of them have been broken down or destroyed altogether by increasing knowledge. Nevertheless, as Bliss has shown more tellingly and with greater authority than any of his predecessors, from the successive studies of intellectual and scientific workers it has been possible to produce arrays of subjects in the order these most commonly use, and to say that though the foundations of knowledge are all axioms unproveable and liable to disproof, yet there is a certain permanency about the main pillars of knowledge and it is chiefly in the details of knowledge that change is inevitable. To alter our architectural metaphor into a surveying one, a classification scheme-maker, then, takes his field and divides it into its larger areas as we have already shown. This seems to be the converse of the process of assembly of things into classes, but, not to make a mystery of simplicity, both processes, of assembly and division, work together in classification. Knowledge is an assembly of all things; knowledge is a genus to be divided by differences; each difference is a quality in the things divided, which the other things in the genus do not possess, and the possession of this difference is the likeness which assembles them in their own class. Thus, when we divide Science into the Physical and the Biological Sciences for ordinary purposes each excludes the things that the other contains. At the same time all the physical sciences—Mathematics, Astronomy, Physics, Electricity, Heat, etc. are assembled by their likeness, in not possessing life, under the first of these terms and are thus separated from the Biological sciences which form a class in its turn comprising by their likeness—which is life—past and present plant and animal life. These, then, the Physical and the Biological sciences, are the primary great divisions of knowledge, and all things opening from them, because Life (Biology) naturally gives rise to the highest form of life (Anthropology) and this, which is the study of man, proceeds from his natural beginning through his ethnic development to his work in society and in nations and on to the records of his mind, his worship, morals and the products of his mind. The order may, and does, vary in its sequence according to the approach of the thinker proposing it, but the order has a wide general acceptance and, as we shall assert, a definite permanence. This question must recur frequently in our study.

Choice of Characteristic

The essential characteristic will differ for different men, as we have sufficiently stressed. Richardson says that the possible orders on which a classification may be based include:

(1) Logical Order—from the complex to the simplest;

(2) Geometrical—according to the position of things in space;

(3) Chronological—according to position in time;

(4) Genetic—according to likeness in origin or race, the "family" order;

(5) Historical—according to position in space, order in time and genesis and therefore a combination of many of the preceding characteristics;

(6) Evolutionary—the order of likeness from simple to complex, the converse and complement of Logical order;

(7) Dynamic—order of power;

(8) Alphabetical—according to letter-order of terms, the commonest artificial order;

(9) Mathematical—according to numerical symbols; or order by means of a notation.

We may put aside alphabetical classification as not a classification order in our modern sense; it is an index order; and when Richardson defines mathematical order as "the prince of artificial classifications and the servant of all natural classifications" he really means that whatever order we give to things we record it by means of symbols which have a mathematic aspect, fix the order and are its means of reference; in other words, it is classification or arrangement supplied with a notation. Many schemes of classification employ several of Richardson's characteristics: are logical, evolutionary, genetic and geographical in turn, the characteristic changing as the scheme requires.

These enumerations are intended to show that for the student of classification-making the modes available to him are many. That one way is better than another for this or that purpose is true enough. In knowledge classification Bacon, Coleridge, Comte, Karl Pearson, Spencer can be named again as each in turn insisting upon his own as an advance; so in library classification the only reason for the work of Dewey, Cutter, Richardson, Brown and Bliss is that each thought his order was an improvement. The student could express a preference with any assurance after the most careful study of the theory of knowledge used in each. He may find that most of the book classifiers were working, as was Comte—most certainly, towards the position as stated by Bliss when he says of science order: "One study may be applied to, or introductory to, another, as mathematics to physics, physics to chemistry, chemistry to biology, biology to society, sociology to economics, linguistics to literature, and logic to philosophy"; and so a logical order of main classes emerges on a characteristic of progression from one science to another.

Classification is Non-Critical

There is a tendency in all men to view things as they are beneficial or inimical, useful or useless, right or wrong, in relation to themselves. This tendency a must be resisted by the classifier both in his construction of his scheme and, where it may be more likely to be indulged, in his application of it. This can be illustrated by examples more easily than by much assertion. The position of Astrology in Science is settled summarily even to-day by many orthodox scientists; that was so also in 1876 when Dewey in his schedule made a class under Mind and Body in Philosophy for Delusions, Witchcraft and Magic and sub-divided that into Apparitions, Hallucinations, Divination, Witchcraft, Astrology, Palmistry, Humbugs and Spiritualism. One can imagine the reactions of the convinced student of Astrology as well, it may be added, as the members of the Society for Psychical Research! The modern revisions have removed these indignities by renaming the heading Transcendentalism and Occultism in Dewey, and both Dewey and Bliss admit Astrology admirably under Astronomy, although Bliss prefers it to be placed in Folk Lore. Perhaps the cardinal example of criticism comes from Dewey, too, in the 800, Literature, class: he arranges the nine writers he considers to be representative under each period of literature and lumps all the others together as "Minor Writers." That too has been revised in subsequent editions. But the fault of criticism in classification (and in classing, as we shall see) is much more subtle in other ways. An author may represent views that are anathema to the classifier, for example, write a book like Brandes's Jesus Christ a Myth, or on some political question from a violent political bias.

Classification should be Exhaustive

We may complete with one more principle our survey of the mechanics of knowledge classification. It is this: In the construction of our schedules the enumeration of parts must be exhaustive. On the face of it this means that the schedule must name every subject that exists or can exist. It must exhaust every subject. But it will be said at once, and quite rightly, that this is an impossibility. To begin with, no living man knows everything about everything. Bacon took the whole of knowledge for his province, he said: he did not; he took what he thought to be the whole of knowledge. No man can have more than an external acquaintance with the sciences as a whole or can know even one of them, or even a part of one of them say chemistry in all its branches. No man, it has been asserted, can construct an entirely satisfactory general classification; a corps of philosophers and scientists might produce a satisfactory one. Even they, however, can only classify the known things of the universe. They cannot give names to things which have not yet been discovered. All this may be granted, and yet our rule will stand if we read it thus: A classification must enumerate the whole of known things, and permit the insertion of additions to them. It is in the words I have stressed that the vital implication of the rule lies. A classification must be elastic, expansible and hospitable in the highest degree. That is to say, it must be so constructed that any new subject may be inserted into it without dislocating its sequence. If a classification has not this quality it will become obsolete in a very short time. We shall see the all-importance of this principle when we come, as we shall now shortly come, to focus all we have learned so far upon the art of bibliographical classification.

●●

4

Library Computerisation

Early specialists in library computerisation were for the most part recruited from the commercial world. They brought with them these simplistic views and attitudes and a very large burden of ignorance about library operations. They seemed to specialize in yanking fish out of water to teach them how to breathe air. Quite understandably, they were accorded the enthusiasm usually reserved for Martians at a high-church picnic or burnoosed Arabs in Grosvenor Square. From the beginning the computer unit in libraries was viewed as a foreign body, destructive to the larger organism.

In time, events proved this to be the case, and this first wave of computerisers was dashed on the rocks of its own ignorance-ignorance of library operations and the demands on them, ignorance of the complexity of computerizing bibliographic projects, ignorance of the complex variations that existed in seemingly repetitive operations. Discouraged and discredited by repeated notable failures, this first wave left or were replaced in library operations within a few years. During their tenure, there existed nearly total antagonism between them and the library staff, which they managed to keep in turmoil nearly constantly. There was no possibility of integrating them into the library in any managerial sense. The positive result of their failures was an understanding of the high degree of complexity involved in computerizing library operations.

The second wave of library computer specialists as kind of rebound tended to be librarians who had some experience with programming. In most cases, they did not have exposure in depth to an understanding of the computer, generally had not worked in other kinds of computer operations, and very few of them had high skills as programmers. They generally worked together with programmers from industrial, backgrounds. This was the situation when I surveyed computer operations in eleven major university libraries in 1969, when every university of significant size had its in-house computer staff, some of them larger than the whole the short-coming of this generation of computerisers was inadequate programming skill, and, with the reduction of library budgets, in house-computer staffs largely disappeared in the early 1970s, although the last large staff of its kind persisted at the University of Maryland until 1978.

Although this second wave of specialists was far less antagonistic to librarians, they still were held at a considerable distance, partly because they were thrust into library operations by library directors and partly because of the long drawn out agonies inflicted to their colleagues by programming methods that they prevailed. The computer unit was still something 'out there', and if it no longer was engaged in guerilla warfare with the library staff, it nevertheless seemed to work largely at night in mysterious ways, and to slip things into operations that were not completely understood, often not needed, and even worse full of what were called 'bugs', for which there never seemed to be any truly effective exterminator.

There was much raging in the literature during this period of computer fumbling against the inherent rigidity of librarians who hated change and were obviously evil in many other ways, when you come right down to it. Re-reading these articles demonstrates how alienated computer people felt at the time, and rightly so. In thirty-five years of librarianship, which falls short of the introduction of the typewriter but encompasses the advent of microfilm, we have never seen any worthy librarian who did not embrace any new tool or machine that clearly helped do what he was doing. By its very nature, every library pullulates daily with change of every kind; nothing goes on the same from day to day in any operation, and the problems and demands shift constantly. There are few other agencies in the spectrum of human affairs so constantly involved in change.

The fact is that computer efforts in libraries from 1958 to 1970 contributed almost nothing to library computerization except disruption of libraty processes fantastic waste of money, and a heritage of bitterness through arrogance that has disappeared only in recent years. The Ohio State University Library circulation system we believe is the only significant in-house computerized system that has remained more or less intact until the present day, and it came on line late in 1970. By the end of 1970 OCLC was still in a batch card production system, BALLOTS (now ARLIN) still in its programming stage, the University of Chicago system, (offspring of the atomic bomb) was still under cloak-and-bagger cover behind vault doors, and MARC (the dinosaur with tiny brain that may yet devour us all) was still building up to solidity.

The achievements in library computerisation, then, are the product of the last seven years, and it is useful to speculate the changed conditions that made them deviate into sense and begin the Modern Age in library computerization, for which any sane operation would have waited before plunging. First and most important of all was the radical drop in library support that began to hit us in 1970 and has increased to the present day. It shook out the monkeys from the orange crop, and within three or four years stamped out library computerisation as cottage industry (every library it on IBM company). The fact, blatantly obvious in the failures of the sixties, that skilled computer programming is one of the rarest commodities in the world (and rarely, seen in a library setting), began to be recognized, and we looked for help to the few large computer operations outside where it seemed to have focussed.

The second factor, for which we had to look to England for guidance, was realization of the impossi-bility of local collection autonomy, and the promise of the computer as an information transmitter in a country as large and complex as the United States (conditions which influenced developments in Canada and Australia as well). This emphasized and in some ways exaggerated the importance of central production sources of basic library computer needs. Networking was in (and that rhymes with 'E' and that means Computers).

Third was the carly success in producing the bricks with which we all were building-catalogue cards-by OCLC, in an area of service which we all were accustomed to buy from a central source. While MEDLARS had preceded OCLC in distributing a widespread computer service, it was remote because it serviced only doctors. But OCLC reached real people-librarians at a central point of their existence, and we quickly learned to love it, despite its additional costs, and to look to centralized production for a whole range of our computer needs. Enter BALLOTS, WLN and a whole series of new actors to provide that lovely element, competition, so long absent "from our economy, which is now getting intense.

Fourth was the development in the Library of Congress of a totally computerized cataloguing system, which came very slowly and at a cost that no one has ever dared to look at, for fear that it would overthrow our national government, but with national implications. Its totality now threatens to engulf us, as discussed below. With a new set of props under their foundations, libraries could now look sensibly, with much smaller resources, at what they could produce locally, with programming done outside the library, and the present status of the computer unit and its relationship to the management structure of the library emerged. It tends to exit in two conditions. In one condition the computer unit controls decisions on library computerisation, with the advice of concerned departments, and is itself the equivalent of a department. In the other condition, control over computerization is dispersed among the library departments, and the computer specialist provides centralized technology as a staff officer of the library director.

The computer unit or computer specialist in either case represents a new type of power level within the library organization. It is central to the entire operation, a pivotal unit, with no counterpart in previous library history. It can impose' changes by design or inadvertently on departments with which it is not working directly, through the interaction of parts of systems and how they are affected by adjustments in the system. The computer unit, moreover, almost always reports directly to the upper library administration, generally to the director, and while, there are valid reasons for this relationship, it nevertheless places the unit in a privileged organisational relationship.

These two factors cause a change in peer relationships between the computer staff and the rest of the library staff, which are altered further by the mysterious nature of what computer specialists do, procedures which are amenable to simple examination or review by no one. The computer specialist is never as fully integrated into the library structure as other unit heads can be. For these reasons and others, the most successful computer units seem to be those headed by a librarian, with extensive knowledge of library procedures, who has accumulated the requisite systems and programming knowledge, although we know one spectacularly successful exception to this rule. Since he generally does not do the programming, academic knowledge that enables informal interaction with outside computer programmers will suffice.

This kind of a specialist can minimize the impact that changes in computer applications make on library procedures and adapt them to desirable library needs most precisely.

Computerization has changed many relationships between departments in libraries. Its largest effect is the tilt in power balance between technical processes and public services divisions, which had been reasonably evenly distributed previously, in favour of technical processes. The most dramatic instance of this shift in my experience has been that registered in the Library of congress, where the proposal to close their card catalogue precipitated a major battle between the two elements that was finally resolved in favour of technical processes. Evidence of this shift is seen in the emergence in the past five years into high levels of library administration, including the directorship, of librarians whose career had been in technical processes, formerly a rare occurrence.

Within the divisions the independence of the separate units has been considerably loosened. Departments formerly based on rather clearly defined functions have now had those functions changed on the basis of new procedures generated outside of their unit, and to a larger extent than ever before the library organization is beginning to be described in terms of processes that are heavily overlapping in their reach. Boundaries have been blurred, and tensions have arisen over control of various aspects of computerization, such as the nature of processes and the demands they will impose on the department the kind of hardware and software to be used. The nature, location, control, and scheduling of computer terminals are often a matter of bitter dispute. Like elevators, they are far more economical if arranged in banks, but their cost strictly limits the number obtainable.

A typical battle in American libraries occurs in locating the bank of DCLC terminals, which are likely, especially early in the use of the system, to be used by cataloguing, acquisitions, serials, inter-library loan, documents, reference, and even rare book librarians. While the early promise by computer-flappers in the early sixties was that every man could be his own terminal, with access to world information easily achieved by this point in time, there are a limited number that can be obtained by a library because of their cost. The matter of cost is the most frustrating aspect of the entire range of computers in libraries.

We know that it can do wonders for us in the hands of competent computer managers. The computer, in fact, presents the only longterm solution to the two most pressing problems in the entire range of librarianship-short-life paper of books, which is rapidly heading for shorter life with economic trends in paper manufacturing that are irreversible, and even shorter-life bindings (ironically called 'perfect bindings') for books, about ninety percent of which are held together by plastic smeared on the edges of loose pages at the present time.

These crack after seven or eight circulations, and twenty years from now any library committed to preserving books over time will be a mass of loosely-tied sheets. The computer, of course, could store all of our texts, and pump out on demand either microform or hard copy, but the costs of doing so are astronomically beyond our reach. The promise of locating terminals everywhere, which of course is the highest desideratum in any information system, cannot begin to be realized, either now or in the long-term future in the declining state of library budgets. The future will see us with fewer terminals, rather than more, and struggles between departments for control will become even more acute. All departments affected by computerisation (which includes most of them) become dependent on outside technology experts with the introduction of the computer, and this has markedly reduced their autonomy. While this often is not an entirely bad thing to happen, because departments can become rigid, it is futile to assume that basic decisions about what a department is doing and how it does it can be made better outside the department than in it, or better when having to accommodate the needs of other departments than when decided entirely on internal needs.

An automated circulation system, for instance can have an impact of considerable depth on the budget, priorities, and scheduling of acquisitions, cataloguing, and collection management, that is to say, it can rearrange their use of staff and funds, and churn up long standing policies that have emerged from years of negotiation and adjustment between departments within the library and the entire range of academic experts on a campus. The affected departments do not expect the circulation department to have an impact on them, and there is a tendency to resist or reject the new demands that should logically result from circulation information analysis. Nowhere in the costing of computer operations in a library is any account made of the cost of the time required for negotiations and the toll of these tensions on efficiency of departments placed in this new and far less secure matrix of organizational relationships.

Branches pose special problems to the main library in any dispersed system, and they are a special element in the interdepartmental relationship changes that follow computerization. Branches tend to go their own way to a large degree. They have their own support constituency in their academic specialists on a campus whom they can bring to bear on the library ad instruction. They are not constantly viewed, as internal library departments are likely to be, by staff passing through the library.

With computerisation, the branches become far more dependent on the main library. While they may gain access to the records of the entire library system collection, which is highly desirable, this may be in the form of microfiche catalogues which they may not like. They also will lose their card catalogues. However, centralization of the locus of collection records, if on line to branches with provision for defining whether materials are available, can remove a large burden of the curse of branch libraries to students, who are driven made by the dispersal of books among libraries for reasons that seem insane and on a rationale that defies acceptance. The branch libraries under a campus-wide computerized circulation system like that of Ohio State University, become access points for searching the entire system and reserving books for pick-up, greatly broadening the use of materials in all the other branches and in the main library.

The intolerable delay of a minute by telephone to determine current periodical holdings, which led nation-wide to branch library check-in records duplicating the main serials record, yields to sense when the delay is only ten seconds by computer. So critical have fifty seconds become in this century! Computer application tends to standardize methodology in the branches, making transfer of staff easier and cheaper. In public library branches that must respond to rapid change in public demand for the most recent books, easy turnover of book stock is possible with a centralized computer catalogue and computerized checkout of books to the branch, instead of local card catalogues. It is also possible to generate management information about the branches for the library administration that will inform it more sensitively on a timely basis of what goes on in the branches, making them more amenable to central policy control. In general, computer applications tend to make the branches less autonomous, but in the near future we should see the processing of all their materials return to the branches, as it is facilitated by the system.

Although a the present time few libraries have more than a few operations computerized, throughout the land most library departments somewhere or other have tried their little trotters at some from of auto-mation. The following discussion of departments most often involved in automation attempts to describe what tends to happen to procedures and demands on staff and management when their operations are computerized. Early on, some of the wildest computer money was squandered by enthusiastic fools with keypunched brains in converting shelflists to machine readable form with no foresight about what was required for multiple use of these records, and no insight into the requirements for proper bibliographical standards. Enormous sums of money were spent in keypunching, and the resulting carloads of IBM cards lying around in closets throughout the land have scarcely been used and are mostly unusable. The University of Toronto library reports being confronted by "five separate files which had strong family resemblances but were not really compatible," resulting from keypunching that went back to 1965. Before the volume of MARC records at the Library of Congress grew large enough to dominate the scene, most computerized cataloguing records fell far short of standards for reasonable bibliographical access. The data base at OCLC still suffers from the fact that early entries into their computer from some libraries were not subject to quality control. At present computerized cataloguing information is produced almost exclusively by the few large central on-line data bases and bought by local libraries, who enter any local records not already in the data base as well as deriving records from it. When these data bases reached the critical mass that met most of the demands for current cataloguing in smaller libraries, their use increased greatly. This point was reached when two or three of the larger research libraries joined the system and began adding their records to those generated by the computer center. The rapid formation of regional networks with multiple members was accelerated by the need for smaller libraries to have contracting, access lines, and hardware procured by a central agency, and membership in such centers as OCLC has more than doubled in the past four years. The ease of joining these systems has tended to slow the development of local on-line mini and micro-computer systems, which pose many problems identical to those handled to badly during the first decade of library automation.

The impact of automated cataloguing on the staff of cataloguing departments has been beneficial, since one of fits early results was the eradication of inefficient hand-cataloguing operations, of which there were many. The reason why libraries that joined OCLC early could show immediate cuts in staff was that many of them had cataloguing departments with very low productivity. Professional cataloguers who had been performing work easily accomplished by the support staff, practice that had stubbornly outlived the surge of acquisitions of the 1960s, were immediately obsolete and professionals now are restricted to original cataloguing. Except in those libraries expect in replicating inefficiencies, where professional cataloguers are used at computer terminals to summon catalogue cards. There has been retraining of the support staff, and some reduction of total staff in the cataloguing processes. Radical staff cuts in previously efficient cataloguing departments have not occurred.

On the managers of cataloguing departments there have been new demands requiring considerable ability to understand technological processes, radical new demands for training programmes, increased demands for supervision and work-flow adjustment, and infinite patience in coping with the peculiarities, changes, and failures of the on-line centers. These managers, once proudly suspicious of the flawed nature of humankind which generates the chaos in which they flourish, have now become total believers in the new magic that once the button on the terminal is pushed the catalogue cards will inevitably come and that all the cards required in the card-set will inevitably be present in the alphabetical cumulations they receive from remote computer centers. These changes have resulted in cataloguing processes that are more expensive than efficient hand-cataloguing, but which produce much faster processing of the current flow of acquisitions to the shelves. The cataloguing department has become a much more central department than formerly, because it is the closest in need to the data base terminals. Its high priority demands on these terminals make it a host department to other departments using the terminals in most libraries. This department has experienced the largest change through computerization of any large library department.

Processing department, which is often absorbed into the cataloguing department, spent most of its time before computerized cataloguing maintaining files from which were drawn the bibliographical base for production of catalogue cards, an din producing the proper number of catalogue cards, in a variety of ways. This process has been entirely eliminated, and the largest cuts in staff produced by library automation have occurred in this unit. There still remains the task of filing cards in the various library catalogues, and the magnitude of this task is leading to the closing of library card catalogues in the large research libraries throughout the land. No satisfactory substitute for the card catalogue has yet been found short of local production of catalogues in microform or on-line access to local computerised catalogues, a process that is still excessively expensive.

This new condition has reduced the requirement of extremely high typing skills and high bibliographical skills in the staff of this department, making replace-ments easier to select, in a unit that characteristically has a high staff turnover.

Order department has been computerized in both its bookeeping and its order placement functions. One of the earliest applications of the computer to libraries, often generated by self-seekers outside of the library was to bookeeping records of the order department, which are fairly simple records sub-divided into allocations of the book budget by categories. While this is a simple, common place computer operation in business, we have seen more of them in libraries that did not seem to work effectively than one could imagining. By now, most of them have been straightened out, but in libraries that programmed their own systems, departure of the librarian programmer has generally left behind an undocumented system that had to be re-programmed.

These systems often make out the order forms, but the multiplecopy handtyped order form is still in common use. In the 1960s systems were designed to track the exact stage in the order process that each order has reached, but low use of this information has not justified its cost and effort. At present the on-line cataloguing data banks are used by order departments for verification, which has greatly speeded up the search process. New processes have required staff retraining, but there has not been much change in the size of the staff. However, the nature of the searching, which formerly required educated, intelligent, and bibliogra-phically skilled staff has changed, making it possible to recruit at a lower level of skill for these positions although they have not yet been downgraded in most libraries.

The new demands on the manager of this depart-ment require heavy interaction with the computer specialist, negotiation for the use of terminals controlled by others, and heavy dependence on outside sources for programme maintenance, re-programming, failures of the reporting schedule, and incorrectly paid bills. On balance, this manager has less control over this operation than before computerization.

Since computerized circulation records essentially involve manipulation of numerical data, they were among the very earliest to be automated. Like everything caught up in the forefront of the wild enthusiasm of early computerization, the butchery that resulted often made even computers. At one time information generated at this point was made the basis for all other computer applications in the library from cellar to attic, with disastrous. In 1969 I saw one large research library operation that updated its circulation print-out only once every four days because of the cost of paper. In the same year, we assured at one university that computeri-zation had for the first time given them the ability to produce totally accurate circulation records.

Computerised circulation demonstrates nicely some of the basic weakening of control that can come in a library that automates. The library at the present time almost always depends on an outside computer for processing its data. It is not rare for these operations to wipe out completely the entire circulation record. While this can be regenerated to some degree of approximation by using previous computer tape records, there is no possibility of ever recovering completely from such a disaster. One library was about "to shorten its circulation period from three weeks to two weeks, only to discover that the outside agency that handled its data was about to change to a new computer. This required total re-programming of every operation serviced by that computer, and two-and-a-half years later, when the computer operation had been converted and the library circulation system had worked its way into the re-programming schedule, it was possible to change that circulation. period. A prime example of that fact that although the computer initially can be a great accelerator of change, once imposed it becomes a powerful agent against change.

The difficulty of managerial control over pro-grammers was demonstrated in one system that generated a daily Computer Output Microfilm circulation record. When you located a specific call number, it would tell you the date it was charged out and the date it was due, but both in Julian Dates, which completely defy normal human understanding. The record, you see, had been generated for the machine and not for the public although it was intended as a public record.

Although very small high school and public libraries that could in no way justify it either on functional or cost ground computerized their circulation records to get with it, there were nevertheless valid reasons for computerizing this operation in larger libraries. The volume of circulation had so swelled the bank of circulation cards. in larger libraries that adding and retrieving information from them was ponderous. In addition, the process of defining overdue books and issuing recalls would churn up the files for days. The computer eased both of these problems. It also imported new problems—the difficulty of the user finding the circulation record by himself (either in a wad of print-out paper or on microfilm), the lag in updating the filing of newly charged out books (in large libraries three or four thousand on busy days), which can reach two or three days if the timing of the system misfires, and errors in records caused by system lapses in collecting or discharging data.

At present, most computerized circulation systems are remnants of local programming (some still the relicts of wild-and-woolly local library programming), and they yearn toward on-line systems, the simple and obvious condition for the solution of circulation record problems. Few can afford them. In the interim, lightpen collector systems are being used more and more, but instead of using packaged software programmes (with known effects and predictable costs) these often are subjected to local programming, with all its attendant evils. Computerised circulations systems, once past the gargantuan task of keypunching cards for each book in the library, have eliminated the staff formerly used for filing and overdues, and have greatly eased the space-crush at the central circulation desk. They require very little staff training, and have imposed no great demands or the department manager. Except at times of re-programming, when dislocations in the records (until de-bugged) are so frequent and irrational that he must become a psychiatric social worker to avert hysteria on his staff, and an international diplomat to smooth the ruffled senses of library users.

This department has become the center for three kinds of computerized information services-on-line bibliographical data bases, specialized analytical programmes of statistical sources, and local service information in public libraries (occupational or carpool information, volunteer clearing houses, elected officials list and the like). These sources have in some libraries divided reference service into two sub-units for information sources and for in-depth traditional reference service.

There are now about 300 on-line data bases available for purchase. Larger libraries tend to subscribe to two or three of the most comprehensive in their fields of greatest demand with others added, as specialities and finances dictate. They are all extremely expensive, and the main-line bibliographical services are computerized versions of printed indexes with only slight extension of their coverage. Their virtue is the saving of time involved in manual searching of indexes, a factor of importance to advanced research workers. Costs of using them tend to be passed on to the user, which eliminates use by the ordinary library user or by the staff, useful as these services could be in routine reference work. They require extensive training, study, and experience in depth of veteran professional reference librarians, preferably educated in a discipline (science, social science) in the area on which the data base focuses. There is a certain amount of prestige connected with this retrieval that enhances the status of the librarian engaged in it.

The use of COM catalogues, spread around the university, or on-line catalogues with multiple terminals, reduces the use of reference departments for card catalogue assistance, which is provided at the other access points in the system. The extension of reference power that will be possible with the advent of on-line catalogue information accessible in all the ways now possible at the card catalogue, and with expansion of ways of approaching the data base, must wait for the day when libraries can afford such services.

The added computerised services have been assumed by reference departments without additions to staff and at a time when, indeed, public service staffs are being cut all over the country. They have required transfer of skills from the lower level users (typically at the student level) to the research level user at a time when services to students is deteriorating at an alarming rate. They have imposed no perceptible burden to managers of reference departments, and have equipped them with the new magic carpet—a computer terminal, to achieve which soine good librarians give up librarianship. The man in the catbird seat, the runner between the redoubts of staff and higher administration has been affected by computerization more than the rest of the library put together. In the first place he is completely without choice as to whether or not to use it. In the view of one of its exponents, "[technology) does not permit the luxury of not using it." At the present time, it even forbids reasoned judgment in its application. In any sensible social or economic condition, decisions about whether to use technology or what kind to use depend entirely on what you are trying to achieve and what you should buy to attain the largest library service at the level of quality you require. In a condition where magic and w"itchcraft predominate in any of their manifold forms the arcane rituals must be applied, though they kill the body. With the radical decline of personal confidence of librarians who shudder at the thought of being labelled obsolete, not 'with it', defenders of 'the old manual system' and other cock-a-many nonsense, the magic words branded on our bosom are 'change' (for all changes are obviously good) and 'technology' (for machines are undisputed friends of man, ousting the dog from this once honoured status).

But once it is used, the Director is not off all of his hooks. There were more sound and mature directors squeezed out of their positions in the late 1960s in disputes over computerization than you could count. Ironically, they were fired for being on either side. If they did not apply the computer, because they saw the messes in library computerization throughout the land, they were pressured by the local computer boys and the administration; if they did apply the computer, with the level of results usually attained at that time, they were pressured by their agonized staff and users. The budget squeeze of the 1970s made university adminis-trators look at the costs of what they referred to as 'free' computer time, and prudence in approaching the computers was allowed. In addition, as recounted above, programming had moved out of the library and conditions of choice had improved. The pressures on the director became less irrational. After all, any fool can join OCLC, and no one can possibly object to catalogue cards.

However, at the present time the directors of research libraries are heading into a major decision with very long term implications for the entire library, depending on which cataloguing data base they will choose to contract with. On this decision will depend a whole range of computerized processes for their library's operations (managed by an outside source), the scope of bibliographical retrieval possible within their library, and their standing in the research library cqinmunity. In some libraries this of will involve major commitments of budgets.

Outside sources, as of this date, cannot to all of the work in the library, and dealing with local application of what is always an unruly technology presents the director with some of his most difficult problems. In many ways the director is the prisoner of his staff, dependent on them for information to cope with the bewildering range and numbers of complex problems that continually expand before him. However, a director with broad experience in library operations (and we are getting very many now who have very little) can review with some degree of sophistication the information supplied by most library specialists and question them when necessary.

In the case of the computer unit, however, this is virtually impossible, leaving this operation to a large extent on the honour system. The director is far more dependent on the technologist's expertise than on any other unit head. For reasons which range from frivolous to profound, the computer head's decisions are questioned by more peers in the library than are those of any other librarian. The director is left to unsnap these department rivalries. In many cases, the internecine disputes lead to hiring an outside consultant to help make decisions on a level above the emotional entanglements within the staff. The ability to manage with any degree of sensitivity the development of a computer programme in terms of its time-table, its economy of machine time and storage, its documentation (so others can run it), the avoidance of programme-play (a speciality of professional programmers), and cleanness of the programme to minimize misfires is almost never within the scope of the director. Someone else controls it, in the library or elsewhere. Consequently, there is a looseness of control over the computer unit that would be inconceivable in the case of any other department.

And yet, this relationship is crucial in a library, especially in one dedicated to rapid change, since application of the computer can produce more change in less time than any other factor in existence short of total budget withdrawal. If the changes are not good, the resulting difficulties can take five years to repair. For all these reasons, some of the younger library directors who are beginning to emerge here and abroad are those with deep experience in computer applications.

Management information, which the computer can generate by the mile, is not used very much and generally not used effectively at any managerial level in libraries at the present time. The ability of the computer to identify exactly which books have circulated is not often used at a time when radical constriction of books budgets requires precise information about what kinds of materials to buy. At the director's level the computer is used for accounting purposes, but for cost accounting, work-flow scheduling, staff balance, collection manage-ment, resource allocation and budget preparation it is used sporadically and often very badly. A recent visit to a library discovered a monthly statement of management data about three inches high on the director's side table, including more statistics than anyone could digest and correlate in three days. Yet when the director produced for me his per-volume cost for cataloguing a book, an extremely useful statistic to have, we recognised it as being somewhat less than the cost for he catalogue cards produced by OCLC alone, the system he was using.

Many of the director's problems with the computer, including early detection of poor performance, could be relieved by one-line information systems, whose costs still place them a considerable way in the distance. Smaller operations, such as public library branches, with small demands for information storage can move to on-line micro-computers more easily than large and complex libraries with huge information demands, and to some extent this is happening, although movement into computerization by American public libraries has been very slow.

A sizeable portion of the library budget has been transferred to computerization and the staff to run it. Almost without exception, this constitutes additional costs, even after deducting cost savings resulting from the change. Only one major voice, Dr. Gordon Ray, President of the John Simon Guggenheim foundation in New York, has been perceptive enough to state in public that computer operations will have to be funded at the expense of conventional library services (at a time when these are being cut). This balanced view of what is giving way to supply computerized processes is seldom applied, and cost considerations seldom play a major role in decisions on library computerization.

This looseness of careful cost control -in such decisions is best illustrated in the application of the computer to new academic libraries that began in the 1960s and even now are drastically short of collection strength, without regard for what could have been done with the money by forgoing computerization. This use of computerization as a public relations cosmetic to disguise basic inadequacy is illustrated in such cases as the Australian library 1,500 miles from the nearest substantial collection, supporting ten Ph.D. programmes on a collection of 60,000 volumes, which boasted of being computerized up to the ears. Or tiny public libraries in remote areas of the Rocky Mountains who have been forced against their better judgement into on-line systems using expensive terminals which have been foisted on them by the State Library. Or the proud report that 70% of English university and polytechnic libraries, most of them with inadequate collections, are using on-line bibliographic search services which are extremely expensive. These are computer diversions from library inadequacies. The sloppy management, or non-management of the costs of computers in libraries is not as bad today as it was ten years ago, but in the present state of library funding here and abroad, many of us should have been hung long ago for some of the things we have done. The lynchings still may take place. Computer costs are now visible enough in many library budgets to be targets for cuts by university administrations in the budget squeeze besetting the academic world.

Computerisation tends to divert more money into equipment than formerly occurred, and as we become more dependent on on-line access from multiple consoles this will become increasingly the case. As we move into microcomputers, where obsolescence is a daily rather than an annual fact, even more money will have to go into equipment replacement, and nothing short of short-term contracts at a fixed annual price on a lease purchase basis will be practical. A final factor in the library budget is the competition generated against it on academic campuses by the computational computer center that serves faculty information needs. This is the only other large information source on campus, and it has a power base in the science and statistically-oriented social science, and language teaching faculties, and at the same time is critically important in generating research rant proposals. These departments have fairly consistently had better response to their budget requests than libraries in this country.

The critical change in the library-campus depart-ment relations brought by the computer is in our dependence on an outside computer, generally the one that handles administrative data for processing library systems. This dependence on an out house computer has reduced the library's control over its own operations to a noticeable extent. We are dependent on their choice computer on the skills of their programming staff on their schedule on changes in their programme systems, and on breakdowns resulting from volume of which the library is a small part.

The demand by state legislatures for rapid response to requests for what they consider to be accountability data, which they always consider to be statistical and the mounting volume of such requests has been a large factor leading computerization in libraries. Yet the ability to respond has created additional demands for information, and has made public academic libraries even more subject to political control at a time in our history when this has become noxious.

Legislatures have decreed by fiat a 20% blanket cut in all state computerization budgets. They have removed computer budgets from separate departments and centralized them in one local computer unit, with little knowledge of and no regards for the consequences. As computer budgets grow larger and state financing tightens as is likely to be the case in most states in the next few years they will be prime targets for a sweeping cut. All of these factors make for reduced control of the library over its own operations. The very large computer systems with profound implications for libraries are MEDLARS, MARC, CONSER, BLAISE, OCLC, WLN, ARLIN, the University of Toronto system, the Canadian National Library system. Suddenly librarians are confronting big business, which these systems all are. Previously, it this occurred at all, it was on terms such as Blackwell North America's blanket order programmes, that gave a wide range of choice. Instead now a choice must be made among systems, all of which impose very large demands and have large rigidities which must be absorbed, if the benefits are to be obtained.

The networks which are the offspring of computer tie-ups and which are leading rapidly to a national library network again require the surrender of local autonomy with no clear realization of what balance of benefits and obligations they will produce. Already the grounds on which these stand are being shifted after a few brief years. Because of data base networks, the functions of the main bibliographical centers in this country are changing and their importance is decreasing. The centrality of DCLC is being eroded by the networks, and will erode further with the incursion of WLN and ARLIN aggressively into the field the latter two requiring total acceptance of their bibliographical structure and procedures.

Looming above all is the impact of the Library of Congress on the library economy of the entire country. For a long time its handling of library cards on while we have depended since

1902, has become less concerned with its clients and more concerned with its own internal operating problems. With the completion of computeri-zation of its cataloguing processes and the expansion of its comprehensive coverage of books published, it has now become totally free from major influence by the entire library community and has gone is own way. For some time its subject headings have been changed to suit computer reading rather than user needs. Now that shortened budgets have made it totally impossible to break away from the bibliographical data that it generates, LC is imposing a radical discontinuity on practices of the past than within a year will churn up the entire academic enterprise to furies of frustration. While early in its development of computerization the library of Congress presented the glowing picture of their catalogue totally on-line. The financial realities dictate that the catalogue generated up to the present will not be computerized. The early promises of pushing a button to change the subject headings on all pertinent records when new subjsct headings, more in tune with changing times and terminology, were appropriate turn out to be something we cannot afford to do. Instead, we are confronted with a split catalogue that at the same time will consist of author and subject entries that break radically from practices in establishing these formerly.

The loss of control over our operations involved in this development is immeasurable. Academic libraries ill spend the next five years trying to make their faculty believe that we in no way connived in the chaos that descended upon us on January 2, 1980 and trying to make them believe that there is some point in continuing to support our budgetary requests, and that money hitherto spent on libraries should not be diverted to some other more useful corner of the campus. It is the ultimate take-over of libraries by government, but not even that because LC will not have even token responsibility for any of us. After all, we are completely free not to use their cataloguing data directly thlough networks if we so choose, even though financially it is impossible not to do so. While the computer has helped us perform some of our tasks in libraries to a large degree its potential to help us has not been used, largely because of the extreme rarity of high quality programming skills and what was produced by lesser brethren in the past. Computerization has led to some reductions in standards in the error rate in circulation and bookkeeping records, in unchecked catalogue cards and has virtually eliminated prompt and accurate repair of errors when detected. The sum of what of the computer has done for us in the library has increased our total costs over efficient hand operations.

Balanced against these achievements have been major losses in control over own operations caused by dynamics of the computer in our libraries, In its connections to networks, and in national computeri-zation policies largely uncontrolled by libraries. While libraries in the further may be managed from a remote center, local management has been greatly impaired. For a number of reasons among which the computer looms large, libraries will become in the near future less satisfactory for more people than before and their importance in their institutional setting will gradually decrease. In this fast changing world information technology and information management are going to play an important role. Information has already been recognised as one of the basic resources for the socio-economic development of a country. Information has now rather acquired the status of the most sought after resource of the resources. The newly emerging 'high tech' disciplines such as computers, tele-communi-cations, biotechnology, etc. are given importance because they store, generate, manipulate, communicate infor-mation the result of poor results in programming that most of us have experienced in the past.

We are experiencing the impact of the new technology on every facet of information handing. The advent of digital computer has opened up new possibilities in information management, and it is likely to change the information infrastructure by merging itself with other related technologies. The increasing use of computer systems for the control of management of information important implications for our thinking about information. And this information processing, storage, and dissemination with the aid of computer is probably called the Information Technology.

When the first computer, called ENIAC, was developed in 1946 it was a huge as it used electronic tubes with a slow speed and clumsy peripherals. It was the first generation computer. However with the development technology the tubes we re replaced by thee transistors and later the integrated circuits etc. and consequently the size of computer has been considerably reduced, while the processing speed has gone up marvellously. The computer systems we have in the late eighties or rather at the end of the eighties are based on Large scale Integration and very Large scale Integration. And with the availability of the micro-processors, we in India are on the way to developing computer networking.

In India computers have already invaded the library and information field and some of the liberties in the special and research organizations have introduced computer systems to automate some their functions. These functions include book ordering and acquisition, cataloguing serials control, circulation, generation and publication of bibliographies, indexes, and other documentation lists. The application of the computer system can also be extended to storage and retrieval of bibliographic indexes, and other documentation lists. The application of the computer system can also be extended to storage and retrieval of bibliographic information, and SDI services. The first computer in India imported from the UK, was installed at the Indian Statistical Institute, Calcutta in 1955. And in the first decade since as many as 16 computers were installed in different parts of India.

The first indigenous computer was designed in India in 1964 by the ISI, Calcutta in collaboration with the Jadavpur University, Calcutta. This was the introductory phase for computer systems in India, and since then India did not look back in the field of computerisation. During the period 1965-72 the process of computerization speeded up with the installation of 170 more computer systems, although most of them were imported from the Western countries. Then the ECIL, Hyderabad took over the responsibility and installed as many as 94 indigenous computers during the period 1973-78.

Meanwhile, the Government of India gave the responsibility of the computers to the Department Electronics which looked into the question of computer acquisition and evaluation. In 1975 the Government of India set up the national Informatics Centre at New Delhi, and two years later NICNET which now is proposed to be extended to each state capital and district level. Besides, many more computer networks have been established in India during the last decade or so. These include, in addition to the NICNET, the INDONET it is the commercial net work for the country as a whole. We have the RAILNET it is the computer network for the railways; OILNET computer network for oil sector; EDUNET computer network for linking educational institutions; another related one is ERNET computer network for education and research purposes; IANET-computer network for Indian Airlines etc. Besides, there are others which are being. developed as the BANKNET for the banking services: STEELNET for linking steel works across the country to form a communications network etc.

●●

5

Digital Cataloguing Resources

Descriptive cataloguing is concerned with creating catalogue records for items, describing their characteristics as just noted—author, title, and so on. Subject cataloguing is concerned with classifying the subject matter, the intellectual content, of an item. It is the subject cataloguer who assigns an item to a class within a classification scheme which in turn determines a place on the shelf. A distinction is also made between bibliographies and catalogues. Both of these in practice describe items. The difference is that a bibliography describes works and editions of works, but not actual physical items. A catalogue, by contrast, primarily describes particular, physical items in a particular collection. It does this partly by describing aspects of a work (*e.g.* title and author), as does a bibliography, and partly by indicating physical properties, including its location. The development of highly sophisticated, systematically organised catalogues and cataloguing procedures is a product of the modern library era, which dates from the second half of the last century. Book catalogues (lists of entries bound in book form) were the first kind used in the U.S.; these began to be displaced by the familiar card catalogues around the turn of the century.

Digital catalogues (called OP ACs, Online Public Access Catalogues) began to appear in the 1970/s and are now widespread; they are rapidly displacing card catalogues Entries in OPACs are commonly encoded in MARC (Machine Readable Cataloguing) format, a standard which permits them to be shared among institutions. To a great extent, the MARC standard encodes those features previously recorded on cards; it enables a fairly straightforward translation of card contents into digital form. In libraries today, cataloguing is considered part of "technical services"—those services generally concerned with the maintenance of the collection, such as acquisition and binding.

Technical services are distinguished from "public services/ " such as reference services, which involve direct contact with library users. Nearly all libraries have cataloguers, although in very small libraries one person may handle other tasks, *e.g.* reference work and acquisition of new materials, in addition to cataloguing. The cataloguer's job is to produce catalogue records for newly acquired materials. "Original cataloguing" is the process of creating catalogue records from scratch—creating a record primarily using the item itself, *e.g.* by inspection of the book, including, but not limited tot its title page.

Catalogue records that can be used as sources for copy cataloguing are maintained by several institutions, including the Library of Congress, OCLC, and RLG. While it may take only a few minutes to copy catalogue an item, it is not unusual for the original cataloguing of an item to take on the order of an hour.

Cataloguing Rules

Cataloguing rules are the area where there is arguably the least international standardisation. This could be a barrier that remains when format issues etc are resolved. The Anglo-American Cataloguing Rules (AACR) is the most widely used code, but its influence is confined largely to the English-speaking world. However, the growing interest in AACR from other regions, including LIBER members, has prompted a review by the Committee of Principals for AACR, which is looking at internationalisation of the code's development and governance. The virtual library environment means that not only must cataloguing rules cope with digital documents, but they must be also be capable of facilitating access to items from a collection that now expands well beyond the physical confines of one institution.

The Committee of Principals held an international conference in 1997 to discuss how AACR might have to change for the new environment. The recommendations of the conference shaped the development process that has been going on ever since. One of the major conference recommendations was that there needed to be a new logical data model underpinning the standard, to provide a solid foundation upon which to modify and extend the structure. The obvious choice for the data model was the IF LA Functional Requirements for Bibliographic Records (FRBR), and work is going on to fit the Rules to the model.

The aim is to avoid a step change like there was from AACRl to AACR2, which required substantial conversion of existing catalogues. The most significant changes are in the definition and cataloguing of serials. The situation has already been complicated enough in the print world with three codes in use: AACR, the IF LA International Standards Bibliographic description for Serials—ISB (S)—and UNESCO's International Serials Data System (ISDS). Fortunately, there has been a major breakthrough with the recent agreement to harmonise the codes.

In parallel with this harmonisation the defir,ition of what constitutes a serial has been substantially revised, and it is now much broader to reflect the changing patterns of publication, especially in the digital world. Another area of change being considered is whether one continues to catalogue the work in hand (currently prescribed by AACR) or the intellectual work, where the physical manifestation acquired by the library is recorded at a secondary level. This has been characterised as the "content versus carrier" debate. The FRBR favours a tiered approach working from the intellectual work at the highest level, as does ONIX, since it has adopted the FRBR model. So work is well advanced to adapt at least one major cataloguing code to a hybrid print and digital environment. What's more, provided AACR does increase its international appeal by being more welcoming to non-English speaking communities, it may offer a common code in which catalogue data can be more readily exchanged.

However, the difficulty of overcoming cultural differences between national codes should not be underestimated. Cataloguing is often singled out for scrutiny in trying to pare costs. Cataloguing has adapted to these pressures by collaboration, and there are many success stories, *e.g.* OCLC, the Research Libraries Group and the Consortium of European Research Libraries. However, even more collaboration will be needed to contain costs in the digital environment. Indeed, as libraries try to cope with constrained acquisitions and operating budgets, collaboration becomes a major driver in itself. For instance in the UK university and national library sectors much work is being devoted to developing collaborative acquisition, retention and preservation schemes, and cataloguing systems need to be able to cope with the demands this collaboration places upon them. Collaboration is also a major force in the trade sector. Book publishers, music publishers and video companies want to ensure their products are readily available from the on-line retailers. So they, too, are collaborating. For collaboration to work interoperability is paramount. The trade does not want to have to re-key data between applications. Nor do libraries want to convert records between formats as they exchange records.

Issues in Library Community

There are a number of issues for the library community that also have to be taken into account when weighing up the answers to the questions about the future. The first is the systems support for the new formats. We are seeing hybrid systems beginning to emerge from some of the larger vendors. Support for XML will improve as the database management systems that underpin many of the library vendors packages improve their XML support. For example Orade, which underpins several popular packages, supports XML and is introducing more features with each new release, *e.g.* a better nesting capability. The cost of creating metadata is a major issue. Preliminary results of trials by the British Library show that the effort to create a metadata record for a digital publication can take up to three times longer than cataloguing a printed book.

Indeed the ideal time to make preservation decisions is at the time of cataloguing, so that the decisions can be recorded. Then there are the time penalties of having to load digital documents, especially from DVD, CD-ROM etc, in order to discover the technical and descriptive data. All this slows the process. Record transfer and other forms of collaboration have already been mentioned as a way of minimising and sharing those costs. Another parallel strategy is the creation of productivity tools to gather the information automatically. An example of this approach is the range of productivity tools developed and being refined as part of the CORC (Cooperative Online Resource Catalogue) programme initiated and led by OCLC. Another issue for libraries are what records are available, at what cost and whether they are of useful quality.

A traditional problem at the trade/library interface has been the quality of records produced by publishers, whose staff in many cases do not have appropriate training. This is still an issue to a degree, but, whatever one thinks about the descriptive cataloguing data provided by publishers, there is still value in capturing the rich additional data produced by them. And, of course, the increasing role of commercial bibliographic agencies is helping to provide cleaner descriptive data, too. The last major issue, especially if common standards prove an elusive goal between different sectors, is the interoperability of standards, in particular the availability of crosswalks. It is encouraging to note that these are being developed, for instance between MARC and ONIX. The assembly of materials from many different sources and of many different formats is a challenge to techniques of bibliographic control developed in the context of static, print-based collections.

Digital resources can be created with no information about their provenance, change location or disappear without warning, have content which changes rapidly and lack any kind of quality control. Some more familiar media found in digital libraries also pose problems, such as still and moving images, which are especially difficult to describe for effective retrieval. Unfortunately, providing access to information remains a sophisticated task not amenable to automation. There are two levels at which cataloguing of digital libraries might be considered. The "micro" scale of describing individual items has seen extensions to existing cataloguing rules to cope with the vagaries of digital information outlined above. Of fundamental importance in the digital library is the information represented by a link between two resources, such as scholarly papers, and there are several proposals for maintaining these relationships against passing changes in URLs. At the "macro" scale of describing collections or archives and ways to access them, there have been new approaches to integrating catalogues and much reflection on the purpose of those catalogues. Resources likely to be combined in a digital library are sufficiently various in type and distributed in location that it is sensible only to attempt interoperability rather than centralisation. For centuries, they have successfully managed, classified, and filtered information of many types by creating surrogates. This is true of traditional materials as well as new electronic resources. But now as the amount of accessible electronic information increases, the cost of accessing this information will increase and the communities unfamiliar with library science are beginning to grapple with the problem of metadata and the organisation of large collections of data. So there has been a general push to apply and develop techniques to make these resources searchable and more widely accessible.

But all electronic resources can never be humanly catalogued. It's just too expensive and also librarians are so overburdened that they can barely keep up with their traditional workload, let alone begin to catalogue and organise the vast amounts of information available electronically. Clearly, automated tools to apply library science ideas like classification and filtering to electronic resources at high speed and low cost are needed. The whole scenario of information management can be divided into two worlds. These two worlds-the seemingly unorganised Web and the organised world of librarieshave much to offer one another.

The Web can offer automated tools for searching raw information and the library world can offer experience organising and understanding information of all types. By combining their talents and techniques, these two communities can bring powerful resources to bear on the problems of accessing, maintaining, and supplying electronic information. But this is not an easy task. Even though using latest technologies, searching the raw content of every document still seems to be almost impossible since it's not uncommon to retrieve hundreds of documents for a given search.

MARCit. MARCit is an aid to easy cataloguing of web sites, working with a web browser. Cataloguing a site involves viewing the site with the browser, clicking on the MARCit icon, adding other information to the cataloguing screen, saving the cataloguing to a file, and importing the file into a library automation system. A user's manual, which can be downloaded, is very helpful and written so that it can be understood by a nontechnical person. The web browser opens when MARCit is opened. Then, while viewing a web site, one can click on the MARCit icon. The URL and title information appear in the MARCit screen directly from the web site. Several fields are catalogued automatically; other fields can be filled in manually. The software allows the cataloguer to rate the site. Different records can be saved to different files. A saved file can be emptied, renamed, and deleted without leaving MARCit. The method used for importing the file into the library's online catalogue depends on the automation system used.

After cataloguing Internet resources, if the user searches for items on "Monalisa" for example, s/he might find a web site dedicated to Monalisa's art. The user can then access the site and get the information needed. The user doesn't have to wade through the millions of hits a search on Monalisa might yield with a search engine. MARCit makes cataloguing such sites simple. The librarian who catalogues it can also rate each MARC record. Users seeking the best information available can use the ratings as a valuable guide to quality sites.

MARC it adheres to the July 1997 Library of Congress MARC Standards. The comprehensive MARC records it generates comply fully with these standards and include all mandatory fields. Indicators are set automatically. MARC it even sets whether the site is a web site (http) or an FTP site automatically in the 856 fields, in accordance with the MARC Standards. MARC it also automatically handles one main author entry, which can be either personal or corporate, but not both, and several other author entries—both personal and corporate. MARC it also sets the correct MARC fields, subfields and indicators for different types of subjects and subject divisions. It automatically checks ISBNs entered. It makes sure whether title is entered. MARCit does all of this automatically, ensuring that the records are of the highest quality. Computer running Windows XX or NT, 5 MB hard drive space, 16 MB RAM, Netscape Navigator v.3.0 or later OR Microsoft Internet Explorer v.3.0 or later and Internet connection.

The explosive growth of the Internet and the World-Wide Web in recent times has caused great excitement in many quarters. Suddenly an extraordinary wealth of materials on a huge range of subjects is instantaneously available from desktops all over the world. This excitement is tempered somewhat by the awareness that this material is poorly organised, and of variable quality and stability; it is difficult to conceptualise, browse, search, filter, or reference. Increasingly, people are wondering how this situation can be improved. At one extreme are those who believe it is up to current institutions to take on the task of cataloguing, and generally organising, these materials; at the other are those who imagine new sorts of tools and techniques—sophisticated search tools and "agents"—will obviate the need for these traditional methods.

ORDER-MAKING

Order-making is a set of practices which quite literally put a library's collections in order and provide access through a set of systematically organised surrogates, and it is therefore a crucial part of the system by which books and other materials are maintained and made available to readers throughout the world. The work is ever ongoing, not just because new items are constantly being acquired, but because a collection will crumble-like the old barns one sees in the countryside-unless it is continually maintained: books disappear and need to be reordered, they are damaged and need to be repaired, they are misshelved, and so on; catalogues need to be similarly maintained. This might seem like an obvious enough point, but cataloguing shares with many other forms of order-making a certain invisibility. For the ordinary library patron, the machinery by which the collection is maintained is out-of-sight, illunderstood, and the order it produces taken for granted. The typical library patron might be excused .for not knowing how much work is being done behind the scenes to make an item available; indeed the invisibility of this system is largely a measure of its successful functioning. But it is more curious to observe that within the library community itself, in some quarters, at any rate, the work of cataloguing is denigrated.

Cataloguing is not simply a matter of reading off self-evident properties of items, but is a highly skilled interpretative activity by which the properties of items are not simply described, but stabilised and even created. Over the last decade, discussion has ranged over many topics, including: how and whether to catalogue digital documents, the future of cataloguing, the politics. of cataloguing, the relationship between cataloguing and reference services, teaching cataloguing in library schools, and cataloguing humour. But perhaps the central core of discussion is a steady, daily stream of questions, in which cataloguers ask one another for help with items they are cataloguing, for help in interpreting the cataloguing rules, and for advice with materials that the cataloguing rules don't address. What emerges is a much more complex and interesting—picture than Manley's parody, or lay understanding, will admit.

Bibliographic materials, it appears, do not always wear their bibliographic properties on their sleeve, and the rules for determining and "transcribing" these properties are quite complex and require interpretation to be applied. Anyone who has written a dissertation or a paper requiring a formal bibliography has encountered this problem in a small way: an item that is hard to categorise, that lacks an expected property, or one of whose properties is ambiguous. Cataloguing is not just a matter of "reading off" the properties items have but of normalising or regularising the material to conform to standard categories of description and thereby making the properties in the act of describing them.

Digital Order

From a cataloguing perspective, the Net is the wrong unit of analysis, for the Net does not constitute a library in any interesting sense. It may be part of the technological infrastructure which could support a library, but it is not a library-not in the sense of an institution which oversees and provides access to a collection. Moreover, the materials on the Net do not constitute a library collection—not in the sense of a selection of items organised to serve a particular clientele. Instead, we should probably talk about cataloguing digital materials on the Net. Digital collections will need to be organised and maintained if they are to remain stable and usable. To those within the library community this point may seem too obvious to make, since it is one of the central premises on which the modern library movement has been built. Yet it is not widely understood outside this community, to judge for example from the way the Web is often talked about. There seems to be a fairly widespread presumption, tacitly held, that materials can maintain their identity and their currency without continual intervention, without continual work. Moreover, it seems certain that the work of stabilising and maintaining digital collections will require a great deal of systematic human activity.

Certainly, powerful technologies will be involved as well as human labour, as is the case now. Again, this is obvious enough to librarians; technologists, by contrast, tend to see the technical infrastructure but not the "invisible" social infrastructure by which most things, not just library collections, are maintained. There can be no doubt that people will continue to make lists of digital resources which they will want to make available to others. Some of these will have broad scope and utility, while others will be of limited scope. Whether we call these lists "bibliographies" or "catalogues," there will be an ongoing need to maintain them, to keep them current and stable; and whether or not we call this ongoing maintenance work "cataloguing," it will no doubt be supported by a complex, and largely invisible, Socio-technical infrastructure. Of course to say that there will continue to be catalogues still leaves open many important questions.

Some, however, may already be amenable to analysis and may yield at least partial results, but they will require to bring knowledge from multiple work communities. Take the question of a universal catalogue of digital materials. While there is something quite appealing about this vision, research in anthropology suggests that there is an inevitable tension between the desire to generalise, to make universal, and the need to tailor to local conditions.

Miksa and Doty emphasise the collection and intellectual access to it. Levy and Marshall's emphasis is on access and use of the collection by a community, and since their emphasis is on practice, the collection is used in conjunction with other information sources. The apparently dichotomous nature of the digital library architecture has broad consequences for its maintenance. However, most technical architectures will be some combination; it will be argued below that this is likely for institutional reasons. In this section, we show that some technical architectures muddy the question of broad versus narrow. It is entirely possible to have both types of libraries simultaneously. The library community has been very successful in maintaining traditional libraries and has developed many practices and ideals to do so. Among them are the ideas of unified collections and access methods. In fact, one could argue that many core library activities, such as circulation, technical services, and even shelving, were created by the library to maintain access to its collection over time. It is essential to note that this set of practices and ideals maintain the traditional library as institution and as community of practice together over time. This equilibrium is in the process of being disturbed or destroyed with the intrusion of new technical possibilities. Only some of the practices of the traditional library will carry into the digital world, perhaps only for a narrow conception of the digital library.

Furthermore, the hypertext and computer science communities have no such traditions and practices for the broadly-construed library. In the management of most resources, managerial control can play many roles. In the digital library, different control mechanisms over the collection are possible, and these control mechanisms will influence the possibilities and necessities for maintenance. These control mechanisms are influenced by collection types, as an examination of different collection types demonstrates.

Collection Types. Libraries have always managed their collections, selecting and removing items from their shelves. This has been viewed as a critical function of library management. According to the collection management literature, the practices of collection management are dependent on the type of library collection. For example, Drew and Dewe distinguish ephemera in special collections from other items, and Kovacs distinguishes among types of libraries. In a traditional, or paper-based, library, there is considerable control over the collection. Versions of publications are stable. More importantly, because the collection is physically contained, there is conside J;able control over the collection.

Library staff can decide what is and what is not in the collection. Maintenance of the collection is within the purview of the institutional members. At one opposite is the World Wide Web. The Web nodes often change, in content, location, and even existence. On the other hand, the content in a location does not shift rapidly; it tends to remain relatively stable. There is no control by any given individual over the entire Web. An individual has control only over his nodes and the selection of pointers to others' nodes (URLs) that provide the capability for extended collections. At another opposite is Usenet or similar computer-mediated communication (CMC) systems.

The control over the collection for this type is also very low for any given individual. In the middle of both dimensions is the organisational information repository. Since the information resides within an organisation and since the organisation generally provides a sanctioned organisational member to manage the system, there is considerable control over its collection. Nonetheless, organisational memories tend to be more dynamic than traditional library collections; for example, they may include informal information, time-sensitive information, or bulletin board mechanisms.

Collection Maintenance. The variation in collection control determines the type of institutional and technical maintenance possible. Collections that are closer to those in traditional libraries can use more traditional control and maintenance mechanisms. Digital libraries that incorporate more individualistic, dynamic, and informal information may need to find new maintenance mechanisms. Digital libraries, if self-contained in a manner similar to traditional libraries will be able to draw upon traditional methods and practices. Traditional libraries, as noted above, have developed methods for maintaining their core set of institutional ideals, thear community of practice, and their collections of materials. Although many maintenance practices will need to be adapted—such as preservation and circulation control as extreme examples—the existing practices can serve as the bases for new norms and practices. We have argued above that such norms and practices are required for the long-term viability of the digital library as institution. Therefore, if the adaptation of current practices is successful, then the narrowly-construed digital library will stand a much greater chance of success in the long run. These traditional practices, however, have had their limitations.

A traditional library could never cope with much ephemera; it would require too many resources. To adequately index, catalogue, and otherwise conform to the institutional ideals for the broad range of ephemera would be overwhelming. In the past, there were strong institutional reasons to constrict the bibliographic universe. Going digital, however, changes the cost structure, and collection and maintenance costs need to be revisited. It is not necessary, for example, in a digital universe to hand-index all materials; there are other methods of access. There is considerable evidence that this change in the cost structure is affecting organisational memories.

However, the dynamism and volatility of organisational memories tend to be close to that of traditional libraries. That is, organisational members can reliably return to the same location in the organisation's information repositories to find the same materials. However, the widespread interest in Lotus Notes, which combines electronic messaging and document storage, argues that combining formal organisational materials with informal is valuable. Nonetheless, because institutional adaptation is much more manageable and amicable than extreme change, we expect that there will be pressure to have digital libraries as discrete and contained collections. The broadly-construed digital library lacks practices that will maintain itself over the long run. The same incentive that promotes use of the Web or of Usenet—namely that there is no intervening institution between the author and his potential audience—also brings its own disincentives to systematic use. The location of Web nodes can change without notice. Usenet groups do not change locations, but the message traffic changes constantly. The individualistic orientation of both the Web and Usenet argues against easy control over the collection. Without institutional control, each individual using the collection must deal with the maintenance issues himself. If the informal materials are dynamic or volatile, then there is a constant maintenance problem.

Users must determine whether materials will continue to be available, accessible, and even understandable. Collection maintenance, then, will be a critical limitation of the broadly-construed digital library. If the broadly-construed library, with its access to multiple sources, is to be viable, users cannot have a high maintenance cost over the long run. It will be necessary to reduce the cost of long-term use, and without mediating institutions, this reduction will need technical solutions.

Collection maintenance tools will be necessary for the digital library. As examples of these tools, we briefly consider here several potential mechanisms for reducing the user's maintenance cost in his continued use of the World Wide Web. These examples are limited. Although many of the same issues exist for other informal materials, the mechanisms for dealing with them I may not. For example, trying to capture traffic on Usenet groups might require methods of summarising series of messages. Still, the Web is a valuable test-bed for dealing with maintenance issues.

The Web may be traversed by owner, site, or document tree, and it is possible to mark areas for the spider to avoid. However, for efficiency reasons, MOMspider performs the traversal from the perspective of a site administrator. Furthermore, MOMspider cannot analyse changed materials to see if the changes are significant to the user. This centralised focus makes it harder for individuals to use MOMspider for personal collections and limits their ability to customise the maintenance process to their needs.

Web:Lookout is a semi-autonomous agent that can periodically examine a compiled list of interesting Web nodes or areas. Web:Lookout can determine when links or nodes have been added, removed, or changed. Like MOMspider, the purpose of Web:Lookout is to avoid manual maintenance. Its major use is to automate the examination of "hot lists" or "favourites pages". It is fairly common on the Web for individuals to have nodes with links to other individuals' interesting nodes. These interesting nodes may be associated with a given topic, making them extremely valuable to researchers.

Additionally, individuals may have pages with pointers to work in progress, pre-press or published papers, informal descriptions of projects, data, and the like. Again, these pointers can be extremely valuable to researchers. Unfortunately, without examination, there is no way to know when an author has added in a new link. Similarly, one cannot know when an author has added nodes to his Web area, perhaps providing new descriptions or progress on a project. Instead of having to manually traverse these lists to look for new items, Web:Lookout allows users to automate this process. Unlike MOMspider or other robots that periodically examine specific locations for any change, Web:Lookout notifies the user only upon interesting changes. Its heuristic examines nodes for the specifics of content and link changes.

●●

6

Cataloguing by Multimedia

A precedent is set by various agencies which issue single-medium lists and catalogues. Some of these agencies are firms and other organisations which deal with specific medium and so of course these examples cannot be said to advocate separation in retrieval systems in libraries. A well known example is the British national film catalogue, recording the stock of one organisation. However, we should mention that the Library of Congress, which receives all materials under copyright deposit, issues separate catalogues for such forms as films and filmstrips; and phonorecords; and in the past it issued one for maps and atlases. We should also mention that BNB issues a separate publication of scores and works about music in the British catalogue of music, even repeating the entries for works about music as compared with BNB itself, although classified according to the BCM's own scheme. Notwithstanding, we recommend the principle of integrating, as far as possible, entries for all forms. The chief reason for this is that information enquiries do not necessarily cite a particular form, and even if they do they may not cite yet other relevant physical forms. This may happen because of ignorance on the part of the enquirer, who may be, say, book-oriented, and may not know of other forms. Current awareness services might include, under certain subject headings, not only bookform materials but any form of presentation of a subject. Such a facility would, we suggest, be of direct value mainly in teaching institutions, at all levels.

A further factor in favour of integrated catalogues is the increasing use of various forms in conjunction with each other. This situation is no novelty. The fact of accompanying material' has been long known and catered for in codes. A very common example is that of a recording, which will perhaps be on disc, with accompanying letterpress material, such as one of Chaucer's Canterbury tales together with a copy of the printed text. In the past, the accompanying material has usually be regarded as subsidiary, even though in fact it may have been necessary for the full exploitation of a document, *e.g.*, a film strip intended for instructional purposes with accompanying teacher's lecture notes, or records. Contrary to current emphasis on the audio-visual 'kit' as a new phenomenon, we suggest, then, that this form has been with us for it is difficult to decide which is the predominant medium, *e.g.*, as to whether a sound recording 'accompanies' a text, or the text' accompanies' a sound recording. For this reason, as well as to ensure that all materials are exploited as fully as possible, we suggest that a so-called multi-media catalogue is needed. However, since accompanying materials is often in textual form, it seems reasonable to reach the logical 'the media' and conventional textual material in the same catalogue.

Nevertheless, there will still exist the need for a physical form approach, mainly, we feel, for the librarian's benefit for stock record and housekeeping purposes, but also in some cases for the immediate use of the library's clientele. The latter may happen, when, say, a teacher is making up a film or record programme for general use, or when a new piece of equipment has been acquired and the teacher particularly wishes to experiment with it. The librarian's need may arise from the need for a stock record for such purposes as stockchecking, statistics, accounting, and calling up of items not received. Strictly speaking, these last are not catalogue uses, the basic object of a catalogue being the exploitation of stock by users, whether directly or indirectly. However, as we know, much of the data for housekeeping purposes is the same as that used for exploitation. Inevitably, with the use of a basic set of data for various purposes, there arises the concept of an integrated systems approach, with the use of a computer for selecting from a comprehensive store, and manipulating the data to specific ends. From the user's or librarian's housekeeping point of view, entries for documents in a particular form could be selected, manipulated and printed out in whatever order was required for the purpose. An essential need is to be able to list all materials in a particular form, *e.g.*, filmstrip. In turn, this means that each physical form must not only be represented, as in standard, eg AACR, cataloguing practice, but also it must be a field on its own, and with a tag to facilitate its use as an access term.

Phonodisc could reasonably be made a field, with its own tag. Similar provisions apply for other physical forms starting with the stem 'phono...', such as phonotape and phonowire. It should be possible to enable a search to be made on the stem 'phono' to facilitate retrieval of all sound recordings, whatever their physical form. "Incidentally, in the example given above, the full stop (period) has been omitted at the end of the author heading, and following 'Phonodisc', despite its being, inconsistently, included in the code. However, by accident, the code may have provided a means whereby nonbook, as differentiated from book, forms of material might be retrieved by computer, the full stop acting as a searching and retrieval device for most 'special' materials as opposed to conventional materials. According to AACR, other special forms are not so conveniently indicated by a potential field attached to a uniform title.

A problem exists for music scores, which are not designated as such in headings or uniform titles, although in some instances the word 'score' occurs in the collation. Yet another problem occurs even when a potential field is suggested in

AACR; this is when there is a possible difference of opinion over a term to be used. This would not pose much of a problem for locally generated data, but it could cause some degree of difficulty at least it locally generated entries using the 'British English' term had to be merged with, say, LC generated entries, which naturally would use 'American English'.

Similar types of problem are manifested by the many other forms of document, when it comes to computerised manipulation and retrieval of selected forms, as well as of subjects. And, as we feel we can assume, computerisation is the only feasible hope of achieving a multiple-access approach to both information as such and special forms of presentation. We wish to sum up, at this point, that not only a multi-media catalogue may be needed, but also that a generously multi-approach catalogue is needed. There should be approaches along the lines of a principle which we feel Cutter would have approved. Potentially, in one sequence, one could approach or trace information according to, not only author-type and title headings, but also subject headings and physical form headings; subject headings could consistently be subdivided according to form of presentation.

Some libraries are already computerising, or planning to computerise, their bibliographic data on special materials. In some cases, systems are being, or have been, introduced for certain individual forms, depending on local need, eg the Library of the Western Australian Institute of Technology has a multiple-approach computer-printed catalogue for slides. At the time of writing other media have not been planned for in this particular instance. Despite some academics' pipe dreams of an integrated systems approach, there is a lot to be said for experiment with a single medium. Problems relating to programming, computer storage, and access can be identified and solved comparatively inexpensively. However, we suggest that such achieve-ments should be regarded as research and development projects rather than as ends in themselves. A most important aspect of such an experimental project is actual use of the resultant catalogue or index. In a comparatively 'closed' situation, as in the library of an educational institution, potential users of such a system can be canvassed and their comments recorded and analysed.

When libraries reach the point of finally appreciating that so-called 'special' materials are not so special that they may be rejected as 'normal' stock, or if actually acquired hidden away and largely avoided, it should be possible for multi-library catalogue use studies to be made. From these could emerge an idea of what library clienteles really need in relation to special materials. Judging by one experiment, in Pearl River Public Library, New York, when a multi-media catalogue and even stock-integration-policy is implemented, the users readily respond to such facilities: 'Users do like to find related materials on a given subject on one place'.

Just as normal monographic materials are being recorded on centrally produced computer tapes, as it happens MARC tapes, so there is more and more talk of doing the same for special materials. Also, as is commonly known, there are central computer stores, regional, national, occasionally international, of bibliographic data relating to articles, reports, etc. in certain subject fields. These can be searched on demand for specific subject requests. At the moment, MARC tapes for monographic materials are sold to interested libraries to use as they think best or apparently, at present, to be merely accumulated with a view to future use. Also, as one useful by-product, MARC tapes are used centrally as a basis for the computer output microfilm production of the 'micro-microform' Books in English by BNB. There is not as yet a convenient facility for libraries to draw upon a national, let alone an international, central computer store for only the data which they require, either for documents which they have in stock or for searches on demand from users. However, there is a proposal, and presumably a hope, for setting up such a central, national, store, in Britain, to be tapped on demand for certain special materials.

The Gilbert Report is confined in scope to audio-visual materials used in education. However, education and modern teaching techniques are probably the main stimulant to the increase in use and acceptance of at least the large audio-visual sector of special materials likely or even unlikely to be encountered by most librarians. Further, the report interprets 'education' in a broad sense, and some documents which might formally be dubbed 'recreational' are likely to be embraced by its proposals. This interpretation does not affect the variety of physical forms, but it could affect the size of any central store established, and this in turn could mean that any local library's stock of nonbook materials may stand a reasonable chance of being as well comprehended by the central store as, say, a general library's book stock might be covered by MARC tapes.

The physical forms contemplated are listed as follows:

SOUND OR AUDIO RECORDING

Gramophone record: a recording of sound on disc.

Sound or audio tape: a recording of sound on magnetic tape carried on an open reel.

Audio cassette or cartridge: a sound tape contained in a cassette or cartridge.

Visual images: still

Slide: a small unit of transparent material containing an image, mounted in rigid format, usually 2" x 2", and designed for use in a slide viewer or projector.

Filmstrip: a roll of film containing a succession of images designed to be viewed one at a time.

Transparency: a sheet, or combined set of sheets, of transparent material, carrying information, designed for use with an overhead projector.

Flash card: a card having words, numerals,. or pictures, designed for rapid identification, with or without an integrated sound track.

Print: a picture with accompanying text which makes the print significant for study purposes.

Wallchart: a large sheet of information arranged in tabular or diagrammatic order, designed for public display.

Flipchart: an integrated graphic presentation on separate sheets hinged together in easel format.

Art Print: a printed reproduction of a work of art-eg painting, drawing, sculpture, etc.

Visual images: moving

Film: film, bearing a sequence of images which create the illusion of motion when projected, and carried on an open reel.

Picture or Drawing: a two dimensional drawing, painting, portrait, photograph, or a print of any of these, produced on opaque backing.

Film loop: an endless loop of motion picture film usually contained in a cassette.

Videotape: magnetic or other tape, carrying a series of TV images recorded magnetically, electronically or holographically. (Any of these may bear an integral sound track.)

Film cartridge: a length of motion picture film contained in a cartridge.

Visual Images with Sound

A recording of moving visual images may carry an integral sound track (*e.g.* Sound Film).

A set of slides, or a filmstrip, may be accompanied by an associated sound recording on a gramophone record or, more usually; tape (commonly referred to as Tape-Slide).

Programmed Materials

Carried on transparent, opaque or magnetic substrates and designed for viewing directly or by projection, or for use with a computer; may have the physical form of a book.

Artefacts and Realia

Map: a flat representation of part or all of either the earth or the heavens.

Relief model: a three-dimensional geographical map other than a globe.

Model: a three-dimensional representation of an object, either exact or to scale.

Globe: a sphere with a representation or a map of the earth or of the heavens.

Chart: a sheet of geographic or other information arranged in tabular or diagrammatic order.

Diorama: a scene reproduced in three dimension by placing objects, figures, etc. in front of a re-presentational background.

Realia: actual objects or specimens.

Microforms

(Microreproduction: a miniature reproduction of printed or other graphic matter which cannot be utilised without magnification.)

Microfiche: a microreproduction on a flat sheet of film.

Micro-opaque: a microreproduction on opaque material.

Microfilm: a microreproduction on a roll of film.

Aperture card: a card with an opening or openings within which micro-reproduction on film is mounted.

Combinations

Kit: a combination of items in two or more media designed to be used as a unit.

Game: a boxed set of materials designed for educational play.

It is envisaged that any records of documents would include commercial;, 'semi-commercial' (from, say, professional bodies), and even some locally produced items. Incorporated in fact the core of such a data base-would be entries from large national collections in Britain such as the National Film Archive and the British Institute of Recorded Sound.

We might note at this point that in 1972 a proposal was made from another source that there should be a 'British national discography' along the lines of the British catalogue of music and of course BNB itself; if such a work were realised its contribution to the type of database contemplated could be substantial. Also here we might recall that the Library of Congress has a potential which has progressed beyond this stage: its catalogue coverage already embraced audiovisual materials thanks to US legal deposit, which appears to be automatically comprehensive of all physical forms of documents.

To return to the Gilbert Report, with its attempts at cumulating such data as is at present available in Britain, we have to appreciate that, at the moment, a large variety and types of records would have to be drawn upon to realise the hope of a comprehensive collection of bibliographic data on nonbook materials. It is anticipated that such information could be reconciled, and incorporated consistently into a central store, without the central cataloguers having to sight the actual documents. This situation may, at first sight, seem to be analogous to that of compiling union catalogues of, say, books, or serials. However, in such cases, it is usually expected, or at least hoped, that entries have been compiled by professional cataloguers and, at least to some extent, according to a standard recognised code. We feel that Gilbert possibly minimises the technical difficulties in such a process. However, we feel that such a process. However, we feel that such a project is possible, and that bibliographic niceties so dear to some dare we say, conservative—cataloguers must give way to the immediate need of producing data of use to many libraries. To digress, but with a purpose, we might recall that some BM cataloguers seem to have wanted to delay indefinitely the photo-printed BM catalogue while they indulged their penchant for bibliographic perfection on the bibliographic information needed all over the world. We had the privilege of meeting Sir Frank Francis, then BM's director, in the early 1960's and he commented that, in effect, he had to get his cataloguers to eschew academic bibliographic niceties and to get on with producing a catalogue for real live use. Librarians must have in mind not colleague-cataloguers' academic criticism, but the ultimate use of their product in document and information retrieval. In short, if any minor errors emerge hard luck. The main concern should be use of the data to enable documents to be identified and exploited by users of libraries all over the country or even the world. In sum, then, we support the layman's proposition of integrating data from whatever source so that it can be drawn upon in real live situations. It is better to have some however inconsistent sort of information about nonbook materials, and soon, than wait for the millennium when all material is catalogued perfectly down to the last punctuation mark. We do not apologise for this apparent tirade: there are still far too many cataloguers who derive more satisfaction from the use of a square bracket than from the knowledge that they are serving users' needs for information today, not in three months' time when they finally have finished their games and pass on their toys to a vague depersonalised public whom through unfortunate library management-they never meet.

So, then, we keenly recommend the concept of the centrally accumulated data base hoped for in GILBERT, and we further hope that people can be found to do the accumulating, assimilating, and production for use of such information.

However, to realise such a hope, two needs must be borne in mind: *(a)* an overall organisation; and *(b)* a detailed organisation for the manipulation and output of bibliographic data according to the needs of requesting centres, assumed to be libraries which receive and formulate enquiries.

An overall organisation is worked towards by a system as reproduced from GILBERT. This includes four components: *(a)* the actual producers of documents; *(b)* central cataloguing agencies; *(c)* a computer store; and *(d)* printers for producing usable hard copy as required. It is technologically possible for *(c)* and *(d)* to be parts of the same apparatus: a lot depends on the physical type of product expected in reply to an enquiry, and the type of physical presentation acceptable by users. A single enquiry might be satisfied with a 'one off' computer printout, but a resource centre's own complete catalogue may demand a more sophisticated physical presentation.

An overall organisation is further enhanced by the system reproduced from GILBERT. The essential advances of this system on the previous diagram is that it introduces the real users of nonbook materials, and it shows how they are integrated into an information retrieval system ranging from producers, via a central store and enquiry coordinating service, through catalogue agencies, and back to enquirers. A major component of this system is the Central Bibliographic Service, linking libraries and similar information service centres with a computer store and with cataloguing agencies, and, ultimately, with users of nonbook materials the final objective of the exercise.

So far, we could envisage the service as providing computer-printed lists for individual enquiries. However, this concept would, in effect, put the cart before the horse. Before individual searches are initiated, it is reasonable to expect general lists to be searched, in much the same way that Index medicus may be searched manually before a MEDLARS search is initiated by computer. The report, then, envisages a printed bibliographic service, which corresponds to the records of normal books covered by BNB or—in the film world—works covered by the British national film catalogue. A noteworthy quotation from GILBERT is that 'no significant problems were encountered, and that there is every reason to suppose that the MARC system can be used for the cataloguing of NBM. The inference is that all nonbook materials could conveniently be catered for in the MARC format, and presumably entries for all forms could be integrated into once catalogue.

The sample catalogue entries would be part of a so called HELP IS system: Higher Education learning Programmes Information Service, as an adjunct to LERMISTOR: Learning Materials Information Store. But, confirming what we said earlier, the range of types of materials and of actual documents prepared for the system make it seem likely that the actual store of bibliographic data, and the spadework which would go into programming in the broadest sense, would encompass a lot of the work of all sorts needed to make the hole system operative. It may be useful at this point to try to consolidate the main components of creating the type of integrated system envisaged in the report as a whole, and as demonstrated micro-economically by its sample Catalogue of materials available for exchange produced in March 1971 and including a variety of audiovisual materials.

First the documents have to be made, and, as with printed monographic media, they come from a great variety of organisations, and may range from commercial materials for national or even international distribution, to perhaps items locally produced for use in just on equcational institution. An example of the latter-local products which comes to mind, though in fact Australian, is a series of video-taped lectures made in the Princess Margaret Hospital, Perth, for the education of nurses. A decision must be made somehow and somewhere as to which documents are to be recorded in the central system.

We then come to the need for all such worthy documents to be catalogued, adequately and according to a generally accepted method. An obvious need is that documents on one subject but in varying physical forms and from a diversity of origins must finish up with a uniform subject heading, whether verbal or codified. This operation would call for the recognition of a uniform subject approach if it were to cater ultimately for a wholly consistent integrated record at the projected central store.

Then comes the need for items' entries to be selected and to be notified to the central store. Approaches and description need to be either consistently expressed or given fully enough in whatever form for consistent records to be brought together accurately at the catalogue compilation centre. The problem of integrating dissimilar entries for similar documents is as old as the compilation of union catalogues, and goes back to at least medieval England when a union catalogue of the manuscripts in monastery libraries was compiled. The problem is vastly intensified nowadays because of the fantastic increase in the quantity of documents, and in the present context it is inevitably exacerbated by the variety of physical forms. A J Wells has stated 'The largest single problem in system terms arises at this point since there is no unique identifier for each item which would provide a ready means of eliminating duplicate standard descriptor fields from the file. This is a major problem since the same item may be input into the data bank from any or all of the agencies. Inevitably here we must bring up the fact of standard book numbers, and further, international standard book numbers. There is an obvious need for some form of unique identifying tag for nonbook materials, just as there has developed a system for normal books in several countries, eg Britain and the USA. To plan and execute such a system would involve a lot of planning, and in fact we find it hard to envisage it being carried through. Presumably a prefix for each form would be required, as well as a unique number for each document. A unique identifying system does already exist for sound recordings in disc form, even though the notation used, assigned by manufacturers (ie publishers), is often complex.

The next stage is the assembling and editing of bibliographic data at the relevant centre and its feeding into the store, say in computer disc form of facilitate the random access envisaged. This stage necessitates the allocation of tags and fields in a uniform way: this is why we have inferred that initial compilation of data should be made if at all 'possible, according to an accepted code for author/title and description and according to a standard system for the subject approach. UDC is the most widely accepted system-whatever faults it may have at present. An advantage of UDC is that it has built in symbols for various types of physical form, which can be represented either through the use of the colon for linking 'main' notations, or through the addition of symbols, to represent physical forms. We suggest that in a central store the use of 'main' notations would represent the type of flexibility required for access according to physical form, as well as the obvious requirement for access according to the subject of a document. Further, experiments have demonstrated that UDC-despite its occasionally awkward facet indicators can be computerised. The inputting of bibliographic data might, we feel, be the most difficult part of the operation possibly even more difficult than locating information in the first place. However, experiments with MARC-based formats seem to indicate that the project is viable. Input would embrace the functions of both bibliographic-oriented and retrieval-oriented catalogues, as we call them. This means that bibliographic detail in description and approaches would have to be as detailed, minute, and varied as might be needed by any user of such, a system. If, for example, the system were to be completely acceptable and useful, it would have to embrace' depth indexing' as well as the more conventionally expected approaches and detail.

We now come to the ultimate objective of the system: use. It is envisaged that the data base would be drawn upon in four main ways:

(a) Machine-readable data, in the form of magnetic tape, could be obtained as required by user-libraries and resource centres, preferably using 'Standard Nonbook Numbers' for access, but the system should cater for other approaches such as conventional author/title headings as commonly cited and as arrived at by the application of, say, AACR. We reiterate here that work is in progress on a new compre-hensive nonbook code in Britain, but at the time of writing this had not been produced.

(b) A more sophisticated application approaches the limit of accessibility to data stores usually envisaged, in that a local centre could possibly be on line to the central store. We know that mainly, according to our observation, on-line systems seem to be operated by industrial and commercial organisations. So, it is technologi-cally feasible that a similar system could be used for objective information retrieval via a local community-oriented service.

(c) The central store could be used for printouts resulting from searches initiated by local libraries, etc. in response to requests for comprehensive information according to any approach: subject, physical form, author, collaborator and so on. Such a function would be similar to that performed by various data banks in selected subject fields at the moment. *(i)* and *(ii)* could overlap in that a local centre may acquire magnetic tapes to use in local specific subject and/or form searches.

(d) Finally, comes the vital factor of location of required documents. In this respect, the central store would serve as a union catalogue.

Despite the lists produced in the US by NICEM (National Information Center for Educational Media), there is not in progress any system attempting to do all that needs to be done. We feel keenly that the time will come when either such a system has to be realised or we shall lose contact with nonbook-based information and its sources.

●●

7

On-line Cataloguing

The development of online catalogues, on the other hand, has not reached a comparable stage of maturity. There is no common agreement even about the major features or basic approach that should be provided, much less about how the major functions should be performed in relation to one another or how much and what types of information should be provided to the system user. Some OPACs stress simplicity of operation above all else, even if the resulting product is little more than an electronic card catalog. Others are highly sophisticated retrieval systems that allow the user and greater flexibility than is available through other from of the library catalog. This level of sophistication, however, is often achieved at expense of simplicity of operation. The sophisticated system may require catalogue users to master techniques to which they have had little or no previous exposure, either in the library or elsewhere. Most OPACs attempt to draw a balance between extremes, striving for simplicity of operation and, at the same time, attempting to provide benefits that are lacking in other forms of the library catalog. This compromise may be the prevailing philosophy in the design of OPACs, but there is a great deal of room for interpretation as to what constitutes the limits of "simplicity" of operation or "sophisticated" retrieval capabilities. Compounding this problem are very basis differences of opinion as to what library users need in a catalogue, and how sophisticated a system most people can handle effectively or even want to use.

Online catalogues can be looked at from several perspectives. Many issues pertain to their design and use in libraries, ranging from the number of terminals required to service a given number of users, to the ergonomics of terminal placement, to the types and amount of information to be included in a catalog, as well as its arrangement on a screen display. But in examining any from of library catalog, online or other, the distinction between its implications for the internal operations of the library and its implications for library users must be kept in mind. Even though these two perspectives do act on one another in the creation and use of the final product, the distinction is important.

The introduction of off-line, computer-pr0duced book and Computer Output Microform (COM) catalogues was a significant step in the evolution of the library catalog, but aimost exclusively in terms of production and maintenance. Computer-produced, off-line catalogues addressed many of the problems inherent in card catalogue production and maintenance, and many labour-intensive tasks that were fundamental to card catalogues were eliminated with the use of computers and machine-readable records. With offline computerised catalogues, only one unit entry record had to be created for each item; the computer expanded this record into as many individual catalogue entries as necessary and performed all alphabetisation and filing tasks to maintain the catalog. It was also much easier, at least in theory, to change a major catalogue heading; the change could be made once and applied to all effected entries by the computer-quite a difference from manually typing a new heading onto each which a change applied. However, as far ass the library user was concerned, the benefits of computer-generated off-line catalogues were far less pronounced. The actual format of the catalogue certainly changed in some instances, but the basis content, and the basis avenues through which records in the catalogue could be found, rally did not. The principles used for access to entries in computer-generated book and COM catalogues mirrored those of the card catalog, an the information was often identical and sometimes even less III amount. From the users standpoint, computer-produced book catalogues were little more than card catalogues in bound volumes, and COM catalogues little more than card catalogues m a box. Given such frustrations as dealing with multiple parts of a catalogue issues in editions and supplements, and equipment breakdowns with COM catalogues, more advantages of computer-produced offline catalogues were not noticeable to the user and, at any rate, could often be overshadowed by the logistical difficulties in using them.

In contrast, many OPACs, represent a radical departure both from card catalogues and from off-line computerised catalogues in their implications for the user. Access to records can be enormously broadened in an online catalogue over what had typically been provided in other forms, but these benefits are accompanied by a new set of requirements and demands on the catalogue user. The relationship between user and online catalogue is fundamentally different from that in use of other catalogue forms. The online catalogue is interactive, not passive, and requires the user to engage in a dialogue quite uncharacteristic of card, book and COM catalogues.

A search must be physically, not just mentally, initiated by typing onto a keyboard issuing a command through some other means. The system will respond according to the very specific action initiated by the user. In many instances, the user will then have to initiate further action based on the system's response, and so on back and forth until the user arrives at the desired end of the search or otherwise terminates the dialogue. This interaction and the nature of system responses represent a significant departure :or the user from simply thumbing through catalogue cards or pressing a button, turning a knob, or sliding a handle on a microfilm or microfiche reader. The fact that a OPAC is intended for users of library materials in perhaps the fundamental dis tinction between this application of automation and those which serve strictly internal processing functions. Such matters as simplicity of operation or sophistication of retrieval capabilities should be important considerations in the design and selection of any automated system regardless of application, but self-evidence in operation may be less important in a technical processing system in which the library is able to exercise a certain degree of control over the selection, training, and monitoring of system users.

The design of an online catalogue must take into account a quite different set of circumstances. Considerable diversity exists among users in their level of knowledge about library catalogues and in the extent to which they are familiar with the use of computerised systems. The library will usually have little or opportunity to balance its diversity though a planned programme of controlled instruction and monitoring. Most peoply will not use the OPAC as part of everyday routine, and hence their knowledge and skills will not be constantly reinforced.

An example of the well-placed emphasis in discussions of OPACs on users and their interaction with the catalogue is the series of studies sponsored by the Council on Library Resources (CLR) during the early 1980s, aimed at gaining a better understanding of what users want and need in online catalogues, their likes and dislikes, and the dynamics of their interaction with catalogues. Despite the vast array of differences among existing OPACs and lack of specific guidelines for development, at the base of these differences is a common goal: to design online catalogues that will allow the user maximum flexibility and yet will be easy to use. Investigations like those sponsored by CLR should help to establish a stronger foundation for realising such a goal. Phrases such as "user friendly" have become almost meaningless because of their sometimes indiscriminate use to describe systems or features that commonsense observation show are 'anything but.' Yet the overuse, and ever misuse, of well-worn phrases does not negate the relevance of the concepts they represent.

Technical processing systems can be evaluated largely in terms of functional capabilities, or what a system can do. But the circumstances in which OPACs are still used are too different for such a simple evaluation. Equally and perhaps more important is the question of how easily system functions can be learned, understood and applied to the fullest extent by a diverse group of users. For any given characteristics in their operation, OPACs are still simply too new, and their use still too little understood, to be able to state categorically that one approach is somehow "better" than the other. Fundamental to all of the features described is the most basic improvement that OPACs have made on other forms of the library catalog: the expansion of avenues of access to catalogue records.

Bibliographic Records

The usefulness of different forms of library catalogues can be compared in a variety of ways. One of the most important criteria is simply the extent to which a catalogue fulfils its basic purposes. Although the purposes of the library catalogue are not case in stone and depend on one's perspective, one set of standards by which library catalogue functions have been measured throughout the twentieth century is the principles of Charles Ammi Cutter as noted in his Rules for a Dictionary Catalogue.

- Cutter enumerated three major "objects" of a library catalogue.
- A catalogue should fulfill a gathering function, showing what a library owns by a given author, on a given subject or in a given type of literature.

- A catalogue should allow someone to find book if its author, title, or topic is known.
- A catalogue should provide assistance in the change of a book, either as to its edition or its literary or topical character.

A fourth commonly recognised catalogue function, although not explicitly noted by Cutter, is collection, having to do with the arrangement and relationship of headings within the catalog.

Underlying most of these functions is the fundamental matter of access top bibliographic records in the catalog: the points of entry through which a record for an item may be found. Cutter's first object—the finding function—is the essential basis for access, nut the gathering and collocation functions also have to do with accessibility to records. The function least directly related to access is assistance in the choice of material, which has more to do with content of a bibliographic record than access to it. Whether Cutter's objects still provide the most viable criteria for defining the purposes of a library catalogue in an online era is debatable, and some have questioned the degree of completeness to which these objects have ever actually been realised in libraries. Cutter's principles stem from a time quite different from the 1980s. New factors-including but not limited to those of a technological nature-should not be disregarded in defining the purposes of a library catalog. Nevertheless, Cutter's principles serve as a point of departure in many decisions of online catalogues, and concerning access to bibliographic records they still provide a convenient framework for comparing online catalogues with one another and with other forms of the library catalog.

Access to bibliographic records in library catalogues has traditionally been marked by a high degree of rigidity, requiring considerable knowledge and exactitude on the part of the user. Generally, access is gained through four types of bibliographic elements: author, title, series, and subject. Multiple author and subject headings are assigned to an item as rules or judgment dictates, but the number is usually kept to a minimum. The terminology selected for headings is also tightly controlled, with the library usually trying to establish a one-to-one correspondence between headings and the persons, corporate bodies, or concepts they represent.

These practices may be understandable from a practical point of view, but they do impose certain limits on accessibility to records. The user can indeed locate an item in the collection for which the author, title, or subject is known, but only under some rather inflexible conditions. To find a record under the title, the user must know the full and exact wording of the title-not some or most of the words, but all of the words, and in their correct order.

For access by author, because of the pre-AACR practice of establishing full and singularly valid forms of names, it has not always been enough to know the from of an author's name as it appears on publications or by which the person is popularly known. It has been necessary for the user somehow to know the exact from of a person's or corporation's name as it has been established by the library, often on the basis of considerable research. Where there are discrepancies in name form, it has been up to the user to figure out the form selected by the library. Access by subject is even more problematic. Singularly valid forms of headings are selected from among all possible equivalents, but because of the greater conceptual complexity involved, there is even greater likelihood in subject searching that discrepancies will arise between the terminology selected by the library and the vocabulary chosen by the user. The problem is further compounded by the general conservatism in libraries toward changing the vocabulary used in headings and by complicated subject heading formation and filling sequences.

Such practices, which result in a lack of flexibility, are all but dictated by necessity in card catalogues; however, they were also carried over generally intact to off-line versions of computerised catalogues as well. Given the capabilities of computers and the elimination of the need for manual filing, there is no strictly technological reason for some of these practices to have been retained so uniformly. Additional access points, such as by keywords appearing anywhere in titles or assigned subject headings, could have been provided with little or no appreciable increase in human labor.

Some OPACs adhere quite closely to other forms of the catalogue in the ways in which access to records may be gained, requiring just as much exactitude and exhibiting just as little flexibility. These are essentially electronic card catalogues. Other OPACs significantly broaden, and even fundamentally change, the traditional concept of access. An over few of several techniques by which this is accomplished is presented in the following pages. One technique that many OPACs use to allow greater flexibility of access to records in the catalogue is keyword, or term, searching. This feature enables a user to retrieve records on the basis of single terms or combinations of terms appearing anywhere within specified fields of a bibliographic record, such as author, title or subject heading. In finding an i1em by title, for example, a User can retrieve a record simply by entering one or more words in the title, regardless of sequence or position.

A user can find a record for The Peoples of the Soviet Far East, for instance, by entering the title-search terms "Soviet," "East," and "Peoples." The record can also be retrieved simply by entering the term "People," or any other single term or combination of terms in the title. A number of OPACs also allow keyword searching on author fields and on fields containing assigned subject headings, and some permit retrieval on the basis of terms appearing within a variety of other bibliographic fields. Keyword searching has certain advantages over the exact order full-phrase searching required in other forms of the library catalogue. In corporate author searches, the keyword capability means that the user does not have to know the exact hierarchy and order in which a corporate author name appears in the records. For title searcres, the user does not have to know the full and exact wording of the title to be able to find it in the catalogue. A key work search capability expands, and actually alters, the traditional concept of locating an item for which, in Cutter's terms, "the author or title is known."

Keyword capabilities are particularly useful in subject searching. When a catalogue permits retrieval of terms appearing anywhere within assigned subject headings, the user does not have to know the full and precise working and filing sequences of assigned subject headings and subdivisions as they appear in the records themselves. Many OPACs allow a broadened view of the subject elements in a bibliographic record; for instance, by allowing keyword searching on title fields. Given the usually high level of correlation between the subject content of works and the terms appearing in their titles, a keyword title search composed of one or two terms can be a viable from of subject searching in online catalogues.

Some OPACs, in fact, automatically retrieve from title fields when subject searches are initiated. When the user carries out a subject search, records are retrieved for items in which the search terms appear either in assigned subject headings or in the title field of a record. Whether or not this combination is provided automatically by the system, the ability to search assigned subject headings by keyword, supplemented with term searching on other fields of the bibliographic record, makes subject access generally far more expensive in and OPAC than in other forms of the library catalogue. Some OPACs allow a use to truncate, or abbreviate, search terms. For example, many online catalogues allow retrieval of records with an author's surname and first initial.

Even though the full forename may be stored on the bibliographic records, the use of an initial is sufficient for retrieval.

In a search on assigned subject headings. truncation on most OPACs requires an explicit expression by the user. A special character must be keyed to indicated that a term or phrase is being entered in truncated rather than in complete form. In title searches, some OPACs require the user to supply a special truncation designator; others provide an implicit form of truncation whereby the system automatically truncates a search term or phrase for retrieval according to an internally prescribed number of characters or words, regardless of how many the user has entered. By either means, the net effect of truncation is to broaden the set of records retrieved over what a possible in a search requiring complete and exact terms or phrases.

Use of Boolean Operators

Most OPACs allow the user to combine two or more search terms through the use of Boolean operators, such as "and," "or," and "not." In most OPACs, a Boolean "and" is assumed when two or more terms are entered in a search statement, especially if the search is conducted of a single field or type of information such as author, title, or subject. Only records containing all specified search terms will be returned. In the earlier example of entering the terms "Soviet," "East," and "Peoples" in a title search, one records for works containing all three works in the title would be retrieved. Some OPACs allow the combination of terms from different fields or serving different functions, such as an author's surname and a title word, in which case the user is generally required to enter a economic code preceding each term indicating the field or function to which it applies and then linking the terms with an explicitly stated "and." OPACs with fuller Boolean capabilities allow the user to construct search statements with other operators as well as the most common being "or" and "not." Depending on which operator is used, the result of Boolean search capabilities is to allow a user to other broaden or narrow the set of records retrieved.

Capabilities such as keyword searching expand access to records through traditional avenues like author, title, and subject. Some OPACs index other fields of bibliographic description as well. In a few OPACs, virtually every tern in every field of a bibliographic record are replaced by an all-encompassing concept of access by "bibliographic description" the more specific elements of author, title, and subject headings become simply qualifiers for refining the scope of a search. OPACs generally have not taken quite this broad an approach, although some have indexed certain additional elements, such as names of publishers, for retrieval on tern searches that act upon several different fields simultaneously.

A number of OPACs offer a more restricted idea of nontraditional access points in the from of bibliographic qualifiers that the user can employ to limit the results of a search. The two most common are language and data of publication. By including a language code or publication data or range of dates in a specified manner as part of a search statement, a user can block the retrieval of records for items that would otherwise qualify but are considered too old or too new to be useful or are in languages that the user does not read. Other bibliographic elements could be incorporated into OPACs for purposes of qualifying search statements. The possibilities depend largely on the types of information discretely identified and consistently entered into records in the bibliographic database. For libraries with records in the MARC format, one likely source of qualifiers is from the elements constituting the fixed fields. Based on these elements, an OPAC could provide the ability to limit retrieval according to government publication, conference publication, fiction, juvenile literature, and a host of other categories. Few existing

OPACs, however, currently offer a range of qualifiers beyond the elements of language ad data of publication.

In a somewhat different but not unrelated category, OPACs have attempted to address traditional limitations of access in library catalogues in the treatment of alternative forms of name headings and subject terminology. The most frequent method used by card and off-line catalogues has been to provide cross-references guiding the user from variants in the form of a name or subject term to the authorised, library-established, heading under which full bibliographic entries are listed.

Online catalogues generally fall into two categories in attempting to deal with likely alternatives in the terminology through which users might seek access. One technique essentially mirrors the approach commonly used in card catalogues, namely, by cross-references guiding the user to the authorised terminology. When an online cross-reference is displayed in response to a search, the user must then key in or otherwise instruct the system to search under the authorised term or phrase. Although this approach is similar to that used in most other forms of the library catalog, the presentation is usually more distinctive because the cross-reference message will be displayed prominently on a single screen instead of being buried among other information. Other OPACs have taken a different approach with respect to cross-references by essentially dispensing with them from the user's point of view, using instead a recognition of equivalent terms as valid for retrieval. If the library has assigned "Women" and "Females" as equivalent subject terms in an online authority file, for example, the user will retrieve the same full listing of records in a search on assigned subject headings regardless of which of these two terms is entered in the search statement. This approach still requires the creation and use of an authority file, but the linking of terms is strictly internal and visible to the user.

Other features, such as the use of word proximity in term searching, have been incorporated into some OPACs father expand the accessibility to records in the catalog, but those described here are the most common, and they significantly broaden the ways in which library users can approach catalog. Now of these features is new to online information retrieval systems used in the library environment in general; they have been standard in such systems as DIALOG and BRS for many years. What is new is their incorporation into the public catalogue librarians have long assumed that systems such as DIALOG and BRS require special expertise and training for effective use.

What is most challenging about OPACs is that at least some of these same sophisticated features are intended for people without formal training and with only limited need to use them. Taking these factors into account is perhaps the most crucial element in the successful design of online public-access catalogues and their implementation in the library environment. Because they are interactive and can offer far broader approaches to access, OPACs are a fundamentally different from of catalogue than their predecessors. The overall difference can result in greater value for the library user, but not without costs in human terms. Interaction with computerised systems and the use of such techniques as keyword searching, truncation, Boolean combinations, and so on, involve skills that many users do not have, especially within the context of application in a library catalog. For many, lack of familiarity with computers and retrieval techniques extends well beyond use in an Online library catalog. There are still many library users for whom interaction with a compute for any purpose remains an alien experience. This situation is changing rapidly as more and more of the population become educated in computer use, but for some time to come, unfamiliarity is a condition that must be taken into account in the design of online catalogues.

Catalog Interaction

Using an OPAC requires the interaction of three primary participants: a library user, a computerised system, and a library catalog. With an OPAC as both a system and a catalog, the rules governing behaviour can be fairly mechanically and consistently structured, even if at times they are complex. As an online computerised system. an OPAC incorporates certain rules that dictate how a user must enter commands and how the system will react to them. In the library catalogue function, certain aspects of interaction will be governed primarily by rules and conventions adopted by the library regarding descriptive cataloguing, summation of subject content, and so on. Rather than distinguishing between on OPAC as a library catalogue and as the mechanical means of conveyance, some discussions blend the two functions together. However, it is important to recognise such a distinction on at least a conceptual level, for each purpose has characteristics that can independently contribute to success or failure in using an OPAC. Some patrons may be well versed in the use of computerised systems and their retrieval techniques, but may be almost totally unfamiliar with the library's cataloguing and other bibliographic practices that do, in fact, influence the degree of success in using the system. Other patrons may have a fairly comprehensive understanding of the structure and organisation of library catalogues, even in online form, but may be unskilled in the mechanics of using computerised systems and unfamiliar with retrieval techniques. Any advantages gained by introducing clarity, case of use, and greater flexibility at one of these levels can be offset by undue complexity or lack of clarity at the other. By taking advantage of the power of the computer, an OPAC can be more flexible than conventional catalogue forms, but it must be so in a way that allows these new methods to be easily learned and understood.

Although the rules that govern the behaviour of an OPAC as a system and as a catalogue can be fairly mechanical and consistent, the rules that govern the behaviour of the library user are not. First and always, "the library user" is an elusive entity. Human factors that influence online catalogue use, such as levels of knowledge, skill, and motivation, vary widely from one user to another, and even within the same user at different times. Complicating matters is the user's perception of how an OPAC works. It is one thing to say that an online system performs a certain way or that certain rules govern the structure and organisation of a library catalog, but the more important consideration is the user's own perception about how the system works or how the catalogue is structured and organised. The design features of an OPAC can either facilitate or inhibit interaction between user and system. As noted earlier libraries are not always able to provide the desired level of guidance and assistance when making as significant a change as introducing a sophisticated online public-access catalog. Therefore, an OPAC must be designed to minimize the need for off-line guidance, taking on some of the instructional responsibilities and burden of assistance itself.

An OPAC must be easy to use and its features easy to learn, and it must be a free as possible from retype language, confusing conventions, and complex rules that are meaningful only to the system. The term "user friendly" may be ambiguous and trite, but the concepts it represents are perhaps the most crucial criteria for evaluating systems designed to handle the interaction between a computer, a library catalogue, and a diverse group of library users. There are certain similarities from one online catalogue to another in terms of the sequence of stages in which dialogue occurs. For most OPACs that are not entirely menu-driven, dialugue between a user and the online catalogue generally conforms to the following:

- USER: Enters a command to begin session
- OPCA: Acknowledges user's command.
- USER: Enters a search statement.
- OPAC: Provides "first-level retrieval" of records conforming to the user's search statement.
- USER: Manipulates and refines results of first-level retrieval in order eventually display record(s) desired.
- OPCA: Responds accordingly to manipulation and refinement until the user terminates the session or enters a new search statement.
- USER: Enters command to terminate session.
- OPAC: Acknowledged user's command.

OPACs vary in the extent to which each stage in this general sequence is explicitly necessary, especially in the earliest and latest steps-the begin-session, file-selection, and terminate-session procedures. Many OPACs do not require the user to instruct the system that a new search session is about to begin or to explicitly select the catalogue file. Instead, the OPAC is constantly set for a bibliographic search, enabling the user to begin searching immediately on arrival at the terminal. Similarly, many OPACs do not require the user to explicitly information system when a session is completed. The user terminates the session simply by walking away from the terminal, and the display remains on the screen until a new search statement is entered. Even when specific begin-session or end-session procedure are required or available, their execution is normally simple and straight forward. The real substance of interaction occurs between the time a user enters as search statement and the time at which he or she feels the search is completed. The end of a search may be the display of a single bibliographic record for an item, a list of abbreviated bibliographic records containing one or more of the desired items, or a response or display that leads the user to conclude that the item or items are not in the catalog.

The dialogue from entry of a search statement through final resolution may require any number of user-initiated actions and system responses. But in terms of the general nature of the user interface, it is important here to moment on two of the stages in particular. The first involves entry of a valid search statement and the initial system retrieval of appropriate records. In other, there are two or more interactive steps involved. For example, the use may first be required to indicate the type of search being conducted—author, title, subject, whatever-to which the system responds by acknowledging the type and issuing instructions to enter search terms. The user then keys in the appropriate term or terms, and the system responds by providing first-level retrieval of all records in the database matching the two-step search statement. Some OPACs, depending on the complexity of the search statement, require even more that two interactive steps before the statement is complete and records are retrieved.

The second major stage of interaction involves the manipulation and refinement of the search results provided by the system at the first level of retrieval. If the search is satisfied at the first level, this will be unnecessary. In many cases, however, the search is not satisfied at first stage, and final resolution may require several steps in manipulating and refining the initial results. For example, a user may seek full bibliographic detail about a specific work, but can remember only one or two words in the' title. If the words are very general, for example, "History" or "Education," a keyword title search will retrieve a large number of records at the first level. To identify the specific work and arrive at a full bibliographic display, the user may have to wade through a rather lengthy discourse worth the system.

These two crucial stages of interaction—entry of a search statement and manipulation and refinement of first-level results—are in fact, part of a continuum in interaction worth an online catalog. The distinction between them is made partly on the basis of convenience for purpose of discussion, but also partly on the basis of the crucial role that first-level retrieval plays in establishing the content for subsequent interaction. There are few areas in OPAC design that exhibit as much diversity as does presentation of the initial system response to a search statement. First-level retrieval in some OPACs involves simply an indication of the number of records retrieved, even if there is only. The user must then enter another command to actually see any bibliographic information at all. Another approach indicates the number of records retrieved, but immediately displays bibliographic information only one record is retrieved. Other OPACs display at least some bibliographic detail at the first level, even if a number of records are retrieved.

The way in which this is done, however, can very considerably.

For searches where very large numbers of records are retrieved, some OPACs group individual records at a general level if necessary so that everything can be summarised on a single screen display. In others, the first level consists of brief bibliographic information about each item, regardless of the number retrieved or the number of screens required for brief display, so long as a system limit is not exceeded. In some OPACs, the system automatically scrolls through the entire list of enters until the user initiates some action to freeze the display. In other, a single "page" of entries is fixed and the user must then enter a command in order to see subsequent pages of information, one at a time. A variable in this approach is the criterion used for arranging individual entitles in the list.

The basis for arrangement of records in such a listing can vary from one OPAC to another. Entries are displayed in so online catalogues alphabetically according to author, title, or subject heading. The primary basis in other is reverse chronological order by data of publication. In others, the basis is by some principle strictly internal to the system or something that may not be immediately apparent to the user, such as sequentially by system-supplied bibliographic record control number.

These examples underscore the diversity among OPACs at this crucial stage of interaction. Whatever method is employed, the first level of retrieval is the starting point from which interaction between user and online catalogue will progress.

For any of the stage of dialogue outlined previously, there are specific issues that have a direct bearing on the degree to which an OPAC can clarify and assist interaction between a user and the catalog. But underlying the specific issues are more general concerns that are pertinent to the user/system/catalog interactive process regardless of the stage at which interaction is occurring. Among the more important of these general concerns are the explicit features designed to assist the user in conducting dialogue with the system, the language and related conventions employed in OPACs, the nature of the progression of dialogue, and the extent to which a system accommodates different levels of users.

COMMERCIAL CATALOGUING SYSTEMS

Commercial firms have also become interested in the possibilities of on-line systems. The System Development Corporation began development of a project called LISTS (for Library Information System Time-Sharing), which would allow libraries connected to the system to perform a variety of technical processing tasks, including not only production of catalogue cards but also printing of orders and acquisition reports, maintaining outstanding order and in-process files, and even circulation control. The system began in 1968 with seven libraries (two public and four academic, plus the SDC library) connected by ASR33 teletype terminals to a 360 Model 67 located at SDC headquarters in Santa Monica, California, but it has never been seriously marketed.

The Information Dynamics Corporation announced a service called BIBNET, which uses Data-point 2200 or Hazeltine 2000 terminal connected via regular telephone lines (though Tymshare's TymNet service) to a computer owned by System Development Corporation. The Data-point terminals have not only a keyboard and a cathode-ray tube but also a small computer memory and provision for insertion of two magnetic tape cassettes containing programmes or data; in effect, therefore, they are minicomputers themselves. When a desired record or information is located by searching. It can be stored on one of the cassettes and them called up on the screen at a later time and edited without tying up expensive telephone lines. GE Terminet printer terminals are also available, with rated speeds of either 30 or 120 characters per second.

Searching may be done by the LC card number the International Standard Book Number, by author, by title, or by Use of a "Ruecking algorithm" (a code made up of several characters from the author and title, as in the OCLC system). In early 1975, company was still in the process of leading MARC record into the system, but brief "index" entries for many records were already available, providing the full author, titles and imprint, as well as LC card number and ISBN. If the full bibliographic record is desired, a key on the terminal can be depressed to ask personnel at IDC headquarters to search manually for the full record, convert it to machine-readable form, and send it back, several days later.

The New Mexico State Library has used the systems and a Hazeltine terminal to add holding codes for eighteen libraries in the state, and then search for locations on request from interlibrary loan librarians around the state. SDC's ORBIT programme is used for the searching operation. The costs, in addition to the cost of the terminal and its installation, are $45 per hour, plus 20 cents per location added and 90 cents per location retrieved. All of the systems described above use on-line input and searching techniques in connection with the production of catalogue cards; one other large on-line system, however, has book catalogues as its final product instead. This is the New York Public Library system, perhaps the best and certainly the biggest book catalogue system, in existence at this time. NYPL is really two libraries in one-a large research library, and public library with eighty six branches-so two book catalogues are produce, each containing records added since February 1927.

The catalogues are produced on a schedule of so-called "continuous re-accumulation". This means that in order to locate a particular tiles the user must consult only the cumulation for that portion of the alphabet, plus the cumulative supplement, plus the old card catalogue for entries prior to February 1972. 36 To reduce printing costs, all added entries are condensed, omitting "title page extension", publisher and bibliographic notes, "the assumption being that the user who is interested in such data will take the trouble to refer to the main entry."

Input to the system is off-line but three 2740 terminals are used for inquiry. An IBM 370 Model) 45 computer is used for processing, and production of the book catalogue pages in done by an RCA Videocomp photocomposer. In 1972, the cost of production was about $100, 000 per year for 550 to 600 copies of the branch libraries catalog, and about $90,000 per year for 200 copies of the Research Libraries, catalog, of which about forty are sold. The costs of development for the system have been estimated at anywhere from $2 million to $4 million, and the annual computer bill is around $360,000; of this latter amount however approximately $200,000 is paid of by renting out time to private industry. The project traces its origins to the work of a Columbia University doctoral candidate who found that at NYPL approximately 20 percent of its nine million cards showed substantial deterioration. This study led to a fuller report, which recommended that the library cease adding to the card catalogue cards for new titles using automated techniques. By 1968, plan had been developed for new card catalogues which would grow for five years and then be converted to book form; by 1969 however, the idea of using catalogue cards had been dropped, and a decision was reached to use book catalogues exclusively.

The largest programme in the system and its strong feature is its authority file control; a single machine-readable file includes all subjects, series titles, and names used in the system, and every new record is checked against this file before being entered in the system. This provides valuable assistance to the catalogers and avoids the problem of variant forms of entry, a problem that has plagued other similar systems, notably OCLC. This feature also makes it possible to change outdated terminology for new, readily and efficiently, both in catalogue headings and in the cross-reference structure.

Other products of the system include processing information lists, cataloguing work sheets and two shelflist cards for each book which are sent to the branches or divisions. Several other book catalogues, including one of the Dance Collection of the Research Library of the Performing Arts, have also been published. At least two systems have been ·designed to produce both catalogue cards and book catalogues fro on-line input. The Western Kentucky University library in Bowling Green originally began its project as a means of reclassifying from Dewey to the Library of Congress classification. Ten IBM ATS (2741) terminals were installed in 1971 on-line to an IBM 360 Model 40 computer and temporary workers were used to enter data. The computer printed out proof-sheets of the data daily, and these were then proofread and edited by catalogers, reinforced as needed by librarians from other parts of the library. Labels, pockets and book cards were produced of reprocessing of some 250,000 items, and both catalogue cards for a divided card catalogue and book catalogues were then printed.

The UCLA Biomedical Library's cataloguing application differs from most other in that it makes no attempt to use MARC records, and is designed to accommodate only "original" cataloguing. The majority of the records acquired by the Biomedical Library are not available on MARC in any case, since the Library of Congress by policy avoids adding works in clinical medicine or other areas covered by its sister institution the National Library of Medicine. The cataloguer for the Biomedical Library types information on a "cataloguing coding sheet" which a clerk then rekeys on a terminal, the redundant keyboarding action apparently necessitated by the objection of the cataloger to using the terminal. The terminal itself is a Delta Data Systems device with a cassette section added; the information is recorded on the cassette, and periodically the computer reads the information from the cassette into disk storage. A prooflisting is printed periodically, and is used by the cataloger to make editing changes. Corrections are then input by the typist. Catalogue cards are produced once a week on a 360 Model 20, prearranged in filing sequence, and a list of new accessions is produced once a month. The same programmes that arrange the cards are also used for the book catalogue, which is produced primarily or regional interlibrary loan purpose.

A few libraries have taken what some regard as the ultimate step and devised systems that use on-line terminals not only for input and searching but also for regular conciliations of the catalogue file, thereby eliminating the use of catalogue cards and book catalogues altogether. Perhaps the first such system was the Experimental Library Management System (ELMS) at the IBM Advanced System development Division Library in Los Gatos, California, parts of which have been in operation since 1965. Catalogue information is input via IBM 2741 terminals and is consulted by both library staff and patrons using IBM 2260 display terminals. There are four of these-two in the processing area, one at the reference desk, and one in a carrel.

Public use appears to be successful but since this is a small, specialised library it is difficult to estimate the problems that might result if the same techniques were used in a large research library. Before the on-line reference function was implemented, the system produced nine separate book catalogues or listings, and apparently this capability is still used. Spine labels and book pocket labels are produced. On-line reference to machine-readable catalogue files was also the subject of much intensive study during Project Intrex at the Massachusetts Institute of Technology. Intrex was a multimillion dollar research project, which began in 1965 and was finally terminated in 1973. On idea that received much experimental study during the lie of the project was the concept an "augmented catalog", which would be consulted on-line and would contain not only the usual bibliographical information, but such additional data as the "author's purpose", the "level of approach", excerpts from the text, all except the author being what the project staff referred to as "content-indicating" fields. Main entry and publisher were deemed helpful only 9 percent of the time, and such fields as edition, place of publication, and physical dimension were ignored completely by the users. A variety of terminals was used, some of them designed by the project and some commercially available. Not surprisingly, those terminals with full screen displays were preferred to those that had only a typewriter for communication from the computer to the user.

The other major effort of Project Intrex that is pertinent here was the attempt to store and retrieve, via on-line terminals, the full text of documents. Storage of the text was in microform, scanned and transmitted electrically, on demand, to the same terminals used for searching and other purposes. Permanent copies could also be obtained, either in microform or in full-size hardcopy. A summary of use during the project indicated that:

- Over 80 percent of the experimental sessions involved use of the text-access subsystem. Most user said they found rapid access to full text a crucial element in a fully satisfactory system and that the text-access system, as implemented, was more than fast enough for them.

- Although most user seem satisfied by the quality of the image when text access is used for the purpose for which it was originally intended (the preliminary ex-amination of the document), Most user prefer higher resolution and express the desire to eventually obtains hard copy.

- The system operated reliably; over 90 percent of the commands initiated by the user result in the specified output.

- Users in this experiment employed the text-access system primarily to judge the relevance of documents after preliminaly judgments have been made on the basis of the catalogue data. Users employed text access only to a small extent to read document text for information contained...

- Relevance judgments with the full-text system are made primarily on the basis of document text, as

> such, rather than associated parts such as illustrations, or the abstract. If we assume that academic level (by year of study) is a reasonable measure of a student's depth of knowledge about the subject of his search, the this depth of knowledge is negatively correlated with the utility of full text for the relevance judging function. The more a user knows about a subject, the more he is willing to rely solely on catalogue information.

The average user spends somewhat more time looking at catalogue data than he does looking at text, but since he looks at catalogue data on more document.

Although the Intent Project has been formally discontinued, it seems likely that the results of its extensive experimentation, especially with the augmented catalogue and full-text access, will be important to designers of similar systems in future years.

●●

8

Challenges to Traditional Cataloguing

A user of the Web who has sampled any of the numerous search engines (*e.g.*, Coogle, AltaVista, Excite) might argue that digital content, networks, and full-text indexing have made human-mediated organisation through cataloguing obsolete. Web search engines demonstrate the great utility of such searching and the benefits of over 30 years of research in information retrieval and, to a lesser degree, natural language processing. However, there are numerous inherent limitations to the technology underlying them:

- **Scalability.** Most Web search engines accumulate indexes by scanning the Web and downloading full content from sites. As the volume of Web content grows., it has become increasingly difficult to keep these indexes current or complete. One study indicates that even the best search engines index only about 12 to 15 percent of Web content. Even more problematic are the limitations of the information retrieval (IR) technology used in most popular Web search engines. The nature of the Web as a corpus presents some difficult scalability challenges for IR and often leads to poor results. The sheer size of the corpus is a notable problem; a typical Web query will retrieve a very large set of potentially relevant documents.

In addition, the Web corpus is usually presented as a single, unorganised collection of documents, which makes synonym clashes inevitable. Synonym clashes are well understood and can be addressed with a variety of techniques (*e.g.*, thesauri, user feedback, local context analysis, phrase structure), but these techniques are generally not exploited by Web search engines.

- **Access Limitations and Databases.** While a great deal of useful content is freely available on the Internet, there is a growing and equally valuable portion of Internet content that is proprietary and held in protected systems. Much "valuable" content (from the point of view of the rights holder) is held in databases on special servers that require a password or other means of authorisation for access. These databases also provide enhanced functions beyond what can be done with simple, static Web pages. However, they do not in general support access via crawling, the method used to build most Internet search services.
- **Format.** Existing Web search engines are limited to textual content. 'They index words in documents and process textual queries-for example, "digital imaging"-returning lists of documents ranked according to the appearance of the query words in their content. Extending this approach to images will require tools to analyse image content and respond to queries such as "find images with cars in them" or, at an even more advanced level, to queries that ask for images with features similar to those of another digitised image. The tools to retrieve images, video segments, voice, and music are being actively researched but are currently beyond the capabilities of Internet search engines.

- **Context.** At a more abstract level, the usefulness of indexing based solely on the text content of a resource is compromised by lack of context. The best tools to help a person locate a resource are those that are tailored to the context in which the resource occurs and to the knowledge context of the searcher. For example, content-based searches of MEDLINE (the medical index at the US National Library of Medicine) might be appropriate for a professional familiar with medical terminology and with the body of medical literature indexed by MEDLINE. However, a high-school student might not be able to select documents that are appropriate to his or her background and might not be familiar with medical terms, so he or she might find content-based searching to be difficult.
- **Markup.** HTML, the main markup language of the Web, provides only a very simplified set of tags for labelling the parts of a document. These are primarily oriented to supporting the appropriate display of the document and in general tell little about the meaning of the various sections of the document. Many search engines utilise smart markup to provide more powerful retrieval facilities, allowing users to limit which parts of a document are used to satisfy the search argument. The simplicity of HTML markup severely constrains Internet search engines' use of such facilities, which are very useful for limiting and refining search results.

The creation of structured descriptive records for resources (*e.g.*, traditional cataloguing records or, more generally, surrogates) can help to address some of these limitations. Scalability can improve if surrogates are used instead of the full content for indexing. Content providers may be more willing to distribute freely descriptive surrogates for indexing, in lieu of the full content. Surrogates can be created, and standards are being developed for describing all manner of digital objects. Finally, surrogate records may include descriptive information that is not part of the document itself (usually the result of human analysis).

For example, surrogates to facilitate searching MEDLINE by high-school students might associate more common medical subject terms with the resources, thus making searching easier for this community. On the other hand, there is broad agreement among the committee members and in the general information community that the nature of resource description needs a thorough examination in the context of digital resources. Traditional cataloguing is one kind of resource description, which, in turn, is one kind of "metadata" (information that describes the structure or content of a document but is not part of the document). The nature and use of meta-data are evolving to accommodate the great variety of digital objects. Traditional library cataloguing has scaled up to serve institutions of great size—prominent among them the Library of Congress. However, over the past year the number of resources on the Web has grown to the point that they exceed the number of books in even the largest of libraries and even the number of book pages in the average library. The growth rate of these networked resources substantially exceeds the growth rate of traditional physical resources. Sheer size presents considerable challenges to the economics of traditional library cataloguing, in which meta data records are characterised by great precision, detail, and professional intervention.

The high price of traditional library cataloguing makes it impractical in the context of such growth, and less expensive alternatives are needed for many, if not all, of these resources. There has always been a trade-off between the cost of creating metadata and its value in facilitating access to document collections. Large print collections generally cannot be accessed without some sort of metadata, so the value of the metadata is high. The appearance of digital objects in commercially in teresting collections during the 1970s changed the economic model. Then, access could be provided with relatively little investment in metadata, although higher quality metadata could still be justified for high-value materials. Now, the steady increase in the volume of electronic materials has increased pressure to reduce the cost of metadata, although manually produced metadata are still common.

The lifespan of networked resources differs dramatically from that of physical resources. The well-known problem of "dangling URLs" bedevils any librarian who is trying to incorporate Web pages into a collection. The impermanence of networked resources is rooted in the economics of networked dissemination. The cost of distributing networked content is low compared with the cost of printing and distributing hard-copy content, so there is little benefit to the publisher of maintaining older versions of a document. With no incentive to retain older versions, the management of objects is haphazard and object permanence is problematic. Such an environment has a strong impact on the economics and incentives for producing metadata and also points out the critical need for preservation-oriented metadata and mechanisms to manage the preservation of digital objects.

The breakdown of traditional publishing roles has disrupted some of the traditional mechanisms for establishing the credibility of an information source. In the traditional print model, the pedigree of a document derived in part from the credibility of the publisher (*e.g.*, publisher X publishes good computer books) and the credibility of the information intermediary—library or bookstore—that made the material available. Because the information intermediaries are being circumvented, it has become increasingly difficult to assess the integrity of information resources. A further problem is that information can be viewed in ways that were never intended by an author or publisher.

Since metadata is itself an information resource, the credibility issue applies to the quality of metadata created by external sources (outside the traditional library cataloguing community). The creation of bad metadata can be non-malicious: for example, an author who lacks training or who doesn't care may assign a bad subject classification to a descriptive metadata record. It can also be malicious: so-called "index spamming," whereby content creators seed metadata fields with misleading or incorrect information to affect the ranking of their pages by search engines, is a real problem on the Web. An important challenge for networked information is developing the mechanisms and policies to verify the origin of any information, including metadata.

The libraries, deals with a considerable variety of resources, including books, serials, maps, software, movies, images, and, now, digital resources. The Library's efforts to create metadata for this spectrum of resources can be divided into two categories.

First, much attention has been paid to enhancing the traditional cataloguing mechanisms—AACR2 and MARC, for example—to accommodate these new genres. These efforts are motivated by the central role that the traditional cataloguing formats play in the Integrated Library System and in the cooperative cataloguing efforts described above.

Second, the Library has employed a number of other vehicles for resource description—metadata schemata tailored for individual resource characteristics. Some schemata have been coordinated with external communities; others have been developed internally. The use of other meta-data vocabularies raises the issue of ~ow the.se vocabularies interact to provide integrated InformatIon spaces for users of digital libraries. After all, one of the major strengths of the standardisation on AACR2 and its expression in MARC records has been the uniform search interface provided by library catalogues to large and heterogeneous collections.

METADATA

The field of metadata has exploded into a major area of investigation and development over the past several years. As information becomes more of a commodity Item-and, as many would argue, is the largest product of the "new economic paradigm" -its management is of Interest to a broad spectrum of organisations. This stands in rather strong contrast to the situation in the pre-internet, era, when the standardised management of Information was more or less restricted to libraries with the Library of Congress playing a key leadership role. This broadening of the metadata environment will include many new players and applications and require the Library to think in new ways if it is to reassert its leadership in this area.

Descriptive cataloguing, exemplified by the traditional library cataloguing record, is but one of many classes of metadata. Real-world applications need to make use of a much broader range of metadata than descriptive cataloguing. Some other metadata types are listed below to provide a sense of this range, The list is not in any way comprehensive, nor are all of these types of data appropriately within the scope of the Library of Congress.

- *Terms and conditions*—metadata that describe the rules for use of an object. Terms and conditions might include an access list of who may view the object, a conditions-of-use statement that might be displayed before access to the object is allowed, a schedule (tariff) of prices and fees for use of the object, or a definition of the permitted uses of an object (viewing, printing, copying, etc.).
- *Content rating*—a description of attributes, of an object within a multidimensional, scaled rating scheme assigned by some rating authority; an example might be the suitability of the content for

various audiences, similar to the well-known movie rating system used by the Motion Picture Association of America. Note that content ratings have applications far beyond simple filtering on sex and violence levels., Content ratings are likely to play important roles In future collaborative filtering systems, for example.

- *Administrative data*—metadata that relate to the management of an object in a particular server or repository. Some examples of information stored in administrative data are the date of last modification, the date of creation, and the administrator's identity.

- *Provenance*—data defining the source or origin of some content object, for example, of some physical artifact from which the content was scanned. The data might also include a summary of all algorithmic transformations that have been applied to the object (filtering, reductions in image density, etc.,) since its creation. Arguably, provenance information might also include evidence of authenticity and integrity through the use of digital signature schemes; or, authenticity and integrity information might be considered a separate class of metadata.

- *Structural data*—data defining the logical components of complex or compound objects and how to access those components. A simple example is a table of contents for a textual document. More complex examples include the definition of the different source files, subroutines, data definitions in a software suite, SGML or XML tagged books, or other complex works.

- *Linkage or relationship data*—data indicating the often complex relationships between content objects and other objects. Some examples are the relationship of a set of journal articles to the containing journal, the relationship of a translation to the work in its original language, the relationship of a subsequent edition to the original work, or the relationships among the components of a multimedia work (information on synchronisation between images and a soundtrack, for example).

The need for additional metadata types and for traditional metadata for a larger volume of materials challenges traditional means of metadata creation—manual techniques cannot be scaled up to meet demand. But automated techniques are available that can help in the production of metadata (natural language processing, automatic classification, document clustering). These techniques have yet to be integrated with more traditional manual techniques; such integration will be a huge task for the library community.

Dublin Core Metadata Initiative

The Dublin Core Metadata Initiative (DCMI), begun in 1994, hoped to create a simplified metadata convention that would provide more effective resource discovery on the Web. Over the past 5 years, it has developed and refined a set of 15 elements—the Dublin Core Element Set (DCES)—for resource description to facilitate discovery. The DCMI has broad international participation from librarians, digital library specialists, the museum community, and other information specialists. Its advocates claim that the DCES has distinct advantages over traditional cataloguing methods in terms of simplicity, interoperability, and extensibility.

DCMI, which is hosted by OCLC, represents a concerted effort by OCLC to extend the leadership role it has played with physical resources into the world of digital resources. The DCES plays an important role in one of OCLC's latest projects, the Cooperative Online Resource Cataloguing (CORC) project, which is examining the use of new Web-based tools and techniques for cataloguing electronic resources. One important aspect of CORC is that it examines the mechanics and economics of different levels of representation, whereby resources can be described simply using the DCES and, when appropriate and economically feasible, described more completely using traditional cataloguing techniques (MARC). The Library of Congress does participate in the DCMI: a member of its Cataloguing Directorate has long played a. role. Not only did the Library host the sixth Dublin Core meeting in November 1998, but its Network Development and MARC Standards Office has also developed "crosswalks" (translations) between the DCES and MARC.

Geospatial Metadata Standards

The geospatial community's interest in metadata stems from the difficulty of managing and locating the burgeoning amount of data being produced by geographic information systems (GISs), remote sensing initiatives (*e.g.*, satellites), and the defense and intelligence community. The U.S. Federal Geographic Data Committee has been working for several years to create a complete and complex meta data format for describing geospatial entities—Content Standards for Digital Geospatial Metadata. The Open GIS Consortium, which comprises technology companies, universities, and government agencies, manages consensus processes with the goal of achieving interoperability among diverse geoprocessing systems.

E-commerce and Rights Management

The burgeoning of content available over the Internet has stimulated interest in the business community in mechanisms for managing, controlling, and receiving remuneration for providing access to digital intellectual property. So-called "rights management" is among the most active topics in digital library research and Internet business development. One initiative-<indecs> (Inter operability of

Data in E-commerce Systems)—is an international initiative of rights owners formulating metadata standards to govern the exchange of digital intellectual content.

Content Rating Metadata

The motivation for content-rating metadata grows out of the proliferation of adult material on the Internet and the desire for filtering mechanisms to keep certain individuals (*e.g.*, children) from accessing certain content (*e.g.*, pornography). Faced with this challenge, the World Wide Web Consortium (W3C) developed a description standard, Platform for Internet Content Selection (PICS). The PICS standard enables content providers to label (voluntarily) the content they create and distribute and "enables multiple, independent labelling services to associate additional labels with content created and distributed by others."

Resource Description Framework

The proliferation of standards for meta data has motivated W3C to examine a general infrastructure for associating multiple metadata records with Web resources and packaging those records' for exchange (as MARC does for AACR2 descriptions). The result is the resource description framework (RDF), a major initiative by W3C to facilitate descriptions of Web resources. The intellectual underpinnings of RDF lie in a variety of knowledge representation efforts.

The RDF is based on two key assumptions: *(1)* the diverse meta data needs of networked obje·ts argue for a modular, not a monolithic, metadata solution and *(2)* the different meta-data modules should be created and managed by individual communities of experts (*e.g.*, let the librarians construct the bibliographic descriptions). RDF is an area of intense development within the Web community, and the associated tools and standards promise to enhance significantly the functionality of the Web over the next several years.

Interoperability of Metadata Standards

Cataloguing has evolved from primarily a library practice into an activity engaged in across the Internet economy. As described above, the library itself, faced with a proliferation of resource types and management needs, has undertaken and participated in a variety of metadata initiatives outside traditional. cataloguing. This proliferation of metadata types and standards raises a pressing need for intensive work, both technical and organisational, on issues of metadata interoperability. The problem of interoperability is not new. Specialised metadata standards have been developed in many domains (*e.g.*, law, medicine, chemistry) to help normalise the description of knowledge in each. Interoperability problems are exacerbated by the nature of the "Internet Commons," where multiple communities intermix and interact in nontraditional ways. By eliminating physical barriers, the Internet encourages interactions among formerly separate communities. In such interactions, one community may have good reason to use the work of another. For example, an art museum may put a digitised map, which is the product of the geospatial community, on its Web page to provide directions for visitors. These spontaneous interactions underlie the need for common meta-data standards to support finding, evaluating, and managing content across traditional boundaries.

Metadata interoperability has three dimensions:

- **Structural Interoperability**. Each metadata record expresses a set of values for the categories described above. Humans are often quite capable of translating between unstructured values; many recognise that "Bill Gates" and "Gates, William H." are the same person. On the other hand, us. and British citizens are likely to interpret the date 10-1-99 differently. Computers are even worse at interpreting unstructured values and so require strict definitions of structure. Authority files, described above, have been the primary mechanism in the library community for enforcing structural interoperability.

- **Semantic Interoperability.** Every metadata scheme defines its own set of data elements or categories for data. Semantic interoperability is the extent to which different metadata schemes express the same semantics in their categorisation. Successful interoperation requires clarity about how the categories of metadata across schemes relate to each other: When do elements have the same meaning? When are elements derivatives, subsets, or variations of each other? When are elements completely unrelated?
- **Syntactic Interoperability.** Creators of metadata want to store, exchange, and use metadata records from different sources. Such exchange requires common mechanisms for expressing metadata semantics and structure. These common mechanisms include hypertext markup language (HTML), the resource description framework (RDF), and extensible markup language (XML). The MARC record format, described above, has been the primary mechanism in the library community for addressing syntactic interoperability.

The last two areas of metadata interoperability, structural and syntactic, have been and are being addressed in forums such as the W3C and in the various standards agencies, such as the International Organisation for Standardisation (ISO), the American National Standards Institute (ANSI), and the (U.S.) National Institute of Standards and Technology (NIST).

The first area, semantic interoperability, is the subject of current research activity and the area in which the knowledge organisation and classification expertise of the Library, and the library community in general, has the most to offer. Briefly, the problem can be characterised as follows. Various metadata vocabularies are by nature frequently not semantically distinct but overlap and relate to each other in numerous ways. Achieving interoperability between these packages by means of one-to-one "crosswalks" is useful, but this approach does not scale to the many metadata vocabularies that will inevitably develop.

A more scalable solution is to exploit the fact that many entities and relationships—for example, people, places, creations, organisations, events, certain relationships, and the like—are so frequently encountered that they do not fall clearly into the domain of any particular metadata vocabulary but apply across all of them. Mechanisms for semantic interoperability could exploit this fact by expressing the relationships between the vocabularies of individual metadata sets and the core concepts (*e.g.*, places and events) using notions such as subtypes, supertypes, or siblings.

Although a number of these concepts in semantic interoperability are still in the early development or even the research stage, they address a critical problem that the library needs to recognise: metadata vocabularies will proliferate, and methods for interoperability among them must be developed. The Library needs to take an active role in such research areas if it is going to successfully deal with digital materials and information on the Internet.

Cataloguing Models

Establishing and expressing the relationships among information resources is one of the most difficult aspects of cataloguing. These relationships are multidimensional, bidirectional, and many-to-many. Examples of such relationships are translations, versions, editions, transcriptions, and structures (*e.g.*, the issue of hierarchy and the relationship of articles to serials). In many ways the relationships between information resources are of primary importance in the management, discovery, and accessibility of these resources. Yet, the basic model of the MARC record, whereby cataloguing metadata is packaged into discrete records associated with individual information artifacts (that is, MARC records are resourcecentric), makes it unwieldy to express the richness and complexity of these relationships.

The importance of relationships among entities has been recognised for a long time in the database and knowledge representation communities. Entity-relationship modelling and E-R diagrams are tools to model information that expresses entity types (*e.g.*, books, serials, agents, events), the permissible relationships between these entity types (*e.g.*, authoring, creating, publishing) and the constraints on these relationships (*e.g.*, an article must be "in" a journal). Recent work in the international cataloguing community recognises the importance of relationships for formulating accurate descriptions of the resources commonly dealt with by libraries.

The Functional Requirements for Bibliographic Records (FRBR), defined by an International Federation of Library Associations task force and contributed to by the Library of Congress, provides a provocative starting point for discussions on how bibliographic description might more accurately reflect resource relationships. The FRBR presents a model that distinguishes among intellectual Ideas ("works"), the forms in which they are realised ("manifestation," for example, a novel), and their availability as physical objects (*e.g.*, as an individual book or an individual performance of a play). These stages in the evolution of intellectual content are connected by distinguishing relationships that affect the description or meta data for the objects.

The FRBR is just a start for rethinking the theory behind bibliographic description, but it provides an interesting foundation for the treatment of digital objects whose plasticity will require that considerably more attention be given to issues of relationships than has been required for physical artifacts. (This plasticity poses a serious challenge to AACR2—which is based on describing a specific manifestation of a work—because manifestations can be fleeting in the digital world.)

The importance of relationships in resource description of digital objects is also reflected in the metadata activities on the World Wide Web. The Web has demonstrated, even in its current primitive form, that the linkages (hyperlinks) between information objects are an integral part of their content. RDF incorporates a data model in which relationships, or "properties," playa key role in the description of digital resources.

The committee understands that it will be a tremendous challenge to change the base model for metadata (*e.g.*, from resource-centric to relationship centric) in a world of widespread data exchanges (the MARC records that are the basis of cooperative cataloguing) and reliance on turnkey software (commercial integrated library systems that are based on MARC). However, it is certain that library-type metadata practices will at some point need to be reexamined in the light of a changed world. It is certainly valid to ask when the time will come that there is sufficient understanding of this changed world to undertake such a process.

●●

9

Digital Library Topical Area

The Digital Library (DL) topical area currently lacks clear boundaries with related areas and internal taxonomy, at least in the sense of large group consensus about these factors. We cannot discuss system requirements without tackling these topics, and without straying into the other subgroup focal topics, particularly that of the fourth subgroup. We therefore abandon any attempt to do so, and focus on what we mean by digital libraries, on a system taxonomy for distributed data services, and on system requirements in that order, trying for clarity rather than any form of completeness or precision. Hopefully what is presented is a useful start for iterative refinement.

One may take either an expansive or a narrow attitude about the boundaries of the topic at hand. Retrospection suggests an unspoken and unresolved difference of attitude among DL workshop participants about this. We give scant attention to borderline topics below; for instance, we treat electronic publishing as an outside topic even though a future library enterprise may well include publishing material derived from its own unique contents, as the U.S. Library of Congress is already considering doing. Some workshop participants tended to include topics at the periphery as part of the DL topic; others preferred to exclude peripheral topics whenever possible, especially topics already being tended by other interest groups. Such tension is natural because the technology potentially blurs organisational, human role, and task distinctions that evolved in a world of books and book-like materials. Our report deals only with aspects that distinguish DL services from other topics. This approach is not intended to imply a consensus among the authors, but rather is a practical way to control the report length and to focus attention on topics less thoroughly addressed elsewhere.

Commercial and Academic Activity

To understand what DL technology is already available and what needs attention, it is helpful to remember that in this area commercial activity began more or less at the same time as academic activity. The commercial presence is signalled by promotional material I which claims:

> "[X] offers the most advanced information management system available today. [It] is ... for large integrated collections of textual and image information and... even an inexperienced researcher can use it effectively the first time.
>
> "[X] meets the growing need for document storage and retrieval through integration of optical storage, scanning and optical character recognition, powerful but inexpensive desktop computers efficiently networked, [etc.]. [X] technology is currently being used by:

- Kiosk systems for public information
- Law firms for litigation support and ... knowledge systems
- Public utilities to manage regulatory correspondence
- Newspapers for electronic archives
- Engineers for their technical documentation

- Law enforcement agencies
- Pharmaceutical firms to support approval testing
- Publishers of scholarly journals for CD-ROM distribution
- Universities for full-text books, multi-media manuscripts, periodicals, and catalogs

"[X] features include:

- Intelligent search and relevance-ranked retrieval
- Heuristic, expert search assistance
- Hypertext and access to external collections
- Text, data, image, and video-clip support
- Access via fill-in-the-blank forms and [other common paradigms]
- Call interfaces for embedded reuse in other applications
- Printing, sorting, access control, session logging, and [other utility functions]
- Portability across many operating systems

Inspection of any extant DL, especially with a particular application and user class in mind, readily exposes functional shortfalls. As tempting as it might be to focus on a specific instance, *e.g.*, publication of physics manuscripts, this would not be enough. Since our intention is to be comprehensive and global we must, encompass the requirements extant systems address and also enough of their architectures and data representations to avoid islands of automation.

For this reason, and because of practical constraints and limited current knowledge, our report proposes broad taxonomy while avoiding detailed architecture and identifies essential qualities of requirements analyses by example and citation. In support of this objective, we mention a few specific academic and archive library efforts which illustrate the range of applications that must be considered, without implying that the particular works cited span the range or are a comprehensive source for requirements analysis.

Digital Library

There are many buzz-words for related activities, including, but not limited to: multimedia database, information mining, information warehouse, information retrieval, on-line information repositories, electronic library, operational image applications, imaging, world wide web (WWW), and wide area information services (W AIS). Clearly there are too many topics in the list, with too much overlap of related activities, and entirely too much rediscovery of what is already known.

The NSF/ARPA/NASA Digital Library Initiative, FY 1994 states:

> "Information sources accessed via the Internet are ingredients of a digital library. Today, the network connects some information sources that are a mixture of publicly available (with or without charge) information and private information shared by collaborators. They include reference volumes, books, journals, newspapers, national phone directories, sound and voice recordings, images, video clips, scientific data (raw data streams from instruments and processed information), and private information services such as stock market reports and private newsletters. These information sources, when connected electronically through a network, represent important components of an emerging, universally accessible, digital library."

In a prior DL workshop report, we find:

> "A digital library is a distributed technology environment which dramatically reduces barriers to the creation, dissemination, manipulation, storage, integration, and reuse of information by individuals and groups."

The former quotation, asserting inclusion of all network-accessible information combined with things not yet mentioned, defines DL expansively enough to stymie prioritised choices of action. The latter quotation attempts a narrower definition, but does not proceed far enough to distinguish DLs from other data collections, *i.e.*, does not teach how to recognise a DL when it is presented. The relationship of DLs to libraries of the conventional or traditional sort is clearly of some interest. In particular, we should inquire whether there are essential differences between these two services. If, as some people have suggested, there are few commonalities, we might ask why the word "libraries" was tacked onto "digital" at all. If, on the other hand, there are some differences but also significant commonalities, we should try to understand how such differences affect the transfer of experience gained in the context of conventional libraries to that of digital libraries. If we find that there are no essential differences between the two, then we need to think about why we need the term "digital" at all, and what it implies for changes in the way that things have been done in conventional libraries.

The function of conventional libraries has been described as four-fold: collection; organisation and representation; access and retrieval; and analysis, synthesis, and dissemination of infonnation. Collection includes techniques for understanding what information resources are of use to a client population and for cost-effective storage and preservation of such resources. Organisation and representation have to do with classifying and indexing information resources in ways relevant to their potential users. Access considerations include deign of physical space and organisation of materials within such space to respond effectively to user needs and expectations. Information retrieval has been addressed, of course, in the design of systems specific to that task. Analysis, synthesis and dissemination functions include responding to reference questions, producing evaluative reviews, and devising community outreach programs.

It is hard to imagine that a DL would add many, if any, qualitatively new roles to these, nor does it seem likely that anything that people would call a DL would omit any of these roles. Although DL implementation may well depend on the local context and technologies chosen, there are commonly accepted constraints which must be maintained to please users. For instance, any of us can enter a conventional library in New York, in Stuttgart, or in Hong Kong and confidently expect to find what we want almost as quickly in the foreign library as we do in a familiar one.

DL research has focused on automating activities carried out by librarians, such as automatic indexing and classifying and expert systems for reference desks. Conventional cataloguing presumes people are involved and can only assign a few keywords; digital catalogs can support long keyword and key phrase sets with weights, long user queries, ranked retrieval, etc. Information search via hypertext illustrates that indices can be implicit rather than explicit, giving users a seamless blend of primary and secondary works.

Further, some current library activities may become irrelevant; for instance, circulation problems originating in a fixed number of copies of each work simply disappear. We might redefine and redesign library services to achieve the basic aims more effectively than is possible now. Thus DL involves not only automation of each traditional library activity and service, but also calls for redefinition of services, new groupings' of services or replacements of groups of services with other solutions.

Whether one judges the differences between digital and conventional libraries to be intrinsically qualitative or merely quantitative, the quantitative factors are so immensely different that it will often be better to treat them as qualitative. For example, although photocopying led to problems for conventional libraries similar to problems anticipated for digital libraries, the ease and speed of digital copying and redistribution suggest qualitatively different treatment.

On the positive side, the potential ease of integration of information in different modes from mutually remote repositories creates new social possibilities; for instance, that the California death certificates are now being collected into a digital library enables a test of the conjecture that shipbuilding in 1940-5 led to premature deaths from asbestosis. So there are clearly new problems and new possibilities for which we should seek new answers, develop new techniques, and create new institutions or significantly modify old ones.

To some readers, these comments might appear to be labour the obvious. They were, however, not uniformly agreed among the workshop participants, and are probably still not fully accepted. In view of the foregoing discussion and because the area is sufficiently new that consensus has not yet been reached about its content or the answer to "What is a digital library?", we are in fact free to assert how the term digital library should be construed. To prevail, such an assertion must be sufficiently close to what people expect, and must be repeated often and loudly.

A digital library is a machine readable representation of materials which might be found in a university library together with organising information intended to help users find specific information. A digital library service is an assemblage of digital computing, storage, and communications machinery together with the software needed to reproduce, emulate, and extend the services provided by conventional libraries based on paper and other material means of collecting, storing, cataloguing, finding, and disseminating information. A full service digital library must accomplish all essential services of traditional libraries and also exploit digital storage, searching, and communication. Public, private, professional, school, commercial, and other kinds of library emphasize different services, different kinds of information, and different service styles. While any digital library instance may thus offer only partial services, the technology suite from which library instances are assembled must permit assembly of a full service library. In addition, this suite must shield the user who wishes to draw on multiple libraries from inter-library differences which are irrelevant to him.

What distinguishes a conventional library from a heap of things to read is organisation provided by someone other than the authors of the collected materials. For a small, private collection this could be shelf organisation; for a large collection it is typically a descriptive catalog which is distinct from the collection, with at least one catalog record associated with each item held. Not every database is a library, but every library is a database. What distinguishes a library from an arbitrary database are certain data integrity and security rules that constitute an implicit contract between custodians and users. A few circumstances and characteristics for which we expect DLs to emulate conventional libraries holding books, pictures, and other material objects communicate the flavour intended:

- users are usually elsewhere than the information they want, and often want to correlate items from several sources;
- different patrons are permitted different actions and to see different parts of each collection;

- whoever wants to use a library must show permission to do so;
- the catalog and the collected items are used differently and hot necessarily housed in the same place;
- the catalog may describe items in other libraries;
- to find specific information, each user must understand the catalog structure;
- documents contain cross references to other documents;
- document identifiers are different from document names; a document may have several names, one for each context, *e.g.*, "Tales of Hoffinann" in English, "Les contes d'Hoffinann" in French, and "Hoffinanns Erzahlungen" in German;
- documents are cataloged with text descriptors and also with conventional properties, such as author names;
- each stored item is valuable, often with part of its residual value owned by its authors or authors¢ assignees;
- translations of a document may express essentially the same information, *e.g.*, versions of classic literature in different languages;
- part of the value provided by a library is the provenance information it holds for each item;
- items are put into libraries because, while each is thought valuable for future reference, the specific individuals who will read it and the times when this will occur are not known.

The advantages of a digital library over a paper library are similar to those of any digital database over its paper counterpart: faster addition to the data collection, improved browse and search functionality, faster distribution from the points of creation and storage to the point of usage, better history tracking, finer granularity of control, and enhanced plasticity of its content.

The benefits of improved control and plasticity are not only improved data quality, but also more freedom and reduced bureaucracy for individual users. Only a librarian may add to the collection of a conventional library, because of the discipline essential to create a quality catalog. In a digital library, cataloging discipline and search restrictions to authorised data can be automatically enforced.

Taxonomy

A "complete" library service will contain many components from which each installation selects a subset and each user draws on an even smaller set. We need a distributed computing infrastructure and a framework for such components. Part of such a framework is provided by the concepts resource manager and application enabler, which are well known to architects of distributed computing services. Since they seem to be outside the experience of at least part of the digital library community we summarise them below. The concept of a resource manager will be seen to embrace notions from object-oriented computing and from client-server computing. A very similar notion has been implemented in such advanced information retrieval systems as CODER. Given suitable operating system and communication services, all distributed computing services can be built as a set of application programs, application enablers, and resource managers, with only the resource managers directly invoking operating system and communication services.

Resource Managers

A protected resource is the combination of a persistent data collection and a set of programs which define its semantics.

To define the data semantics with absolute integrity, this program set must constitute the only access path to the data; it is called a resource manager. Services such as authentication, file subsystems, network directory services, database management systems, and digital library components can all be constructed as resource managers. We have in mind a network of mutually supportive resource managers, each providing a relatively specialised service. Each resource manager distributes itself for remote applications and accesses any needed sibling acting as a user, *i.e.*, using the sibling's client interface. Whether sibling service is local or remote is transparent; exploiting propinquity is regarded as a network optimisation issue. A resource manager is a service which combines state and processes and is accessible to multiple, concurrent clients. To qualify and be used as a resource manager, the program set and the data it manages should satisfy the following criteria:

- The resource manager programs provide the only access path to the protected data, and therefore define and implement its semantics.

- The resource manager provides distributed access, doing so by having client and server portions connected by a private protocol. That the protocol is private distinguishes the resource manager approach from one based on open protocols, which must be standardised to be effective.

- Typically, the protected data are highly structured, possibly consisting of well-defined objects. Typically each protected resource consists of many such entities, called items below.

- A resource manager often serves as an access control enforcement function (AEF) between a request initiator and a target, in the sense called for in international standards.

- To the extent consistent with achieving good performance and with practical aspects of software production and distribution, each resource manager avoids reproducing services that it can efficiently get from other resource managers. For instance, a library catalog manager could exploit a database manager, invoking it just as any other database manager client would.
- As well as access control, a quality resource manager provides various data integrity protections, such as these called the ACID (Atomicity, Consistency, Integrity, Durability) properties.

Thus each service instance encapsulates its own data within a cocoon—a form of object-oriented programming which is not necessarily bound to any particular programming language. There typically will be many instances of each kind of protected resource, with its associated resource manager defining the resource class, *e.g.*, Network File Systems (NFS), DB2 databases, X.SOO directories, X-windows services.

Library content is a protected resource in the sense intended, and the library procedures defining access to the content constitute a resource manager. Resource managers are generic services. Not all generic services need to provide network distribution or to hold data if they can do so indirectly by invoking resource managers. Services such as editors, filters, formatters, and other generic software constitute a class called application enablers. The purpose of such enablers is to make application programming easy and quick, or, optimally, avoidable entirely. Just as resource managers can be modularised by having each exploit other resource managers, application enablers can be cascaded.

Document Storage

Document storage and access software can be realised in two layers above a base of file systems and database managers.

The lower one is a storage subsystem which stores and retrieves items to and from each library collection, updates and searches library catalog records, and limits who can manipulate which data—giving only services which are identical for all types of documents. Instances of the higher layer, which we call document managers, help applications or end users with their special kinds of documents and varied forms of presentation and manipulation.

The distinction between the document storage subsystem layer, which would be implemented as a set of resource managers, and document managers, which would be implemented as application enablers, deserves more careful articulation. Part of its reason is that we expect the storage subsystem layer to be difficult for most users to change or substitute, and document managers being made relatively accessible and malleable.

The storage subsystem limits its services to aspects which do not depend on the meaning or representation of items. With at most limited exceptions, items it delivers to requesting applications are faithful copies of items other applications stored. The storage subsystem manages data placement and replication, implements custodial responsibilities for data security, and hides irrelevant network and other environmental dependencies to the extent possible. It is convenient to think of its application programming interface in three parts: a query interface, intended primarily for identifying items of interest to a browser, should allow whatever inquiries do not violate item owners' confidentiality desires; a retrieval interface should deliver items with whatever timing and buffering is consistent with the data kind at hand and with the user's responsiveness and cost objectives; and update interfaces for the library catalog and collection should enforce articulated policies for library data integrity and quality.

Since searches for information may well depend on databases that are not part of what the librarian has chosen to include in the formal library catalog, the storage subsystem should also support queries which combine internal and external databases. In summary, the document storage subsystem provides retention and catalog services and manages inter-machine communications, hiding them to the extent possible. Its implementation follows a client-server approach. To provide enough flexibility for all possible applications, the document storage subsystem interface is likely to have many primitive operators, making it somewhat difficult to program for ad hoc applications. This can be overcome with document managers which implement broadly interesting information access methods. The storage subsystem attempts comprehensive coverage of functional requirements in its domain; good document managers would offer less flexibility and fewer options, but would be much easier to explain and understand. More generally, document managers give those services which vary among access occasions because different document types need different presentation and manipulation and because users have different objectives and preferences. Document editing, transformation, combination, and presentation, and other complex manipulations are conveniently implemented as document managers.

Thus, in a practical system, each of many document managers embodies a document model-the set of concepts that create the digital analog of some collection of papers or other physical objects, or some information network invented for a particular application, such as hypertext, or some flow of documents through a series of routine steps. In contrast, the document storage subsystem layer avoids modelling. Typical document managers interpret scanned data to create catalog entries automatically, manage interrelationships among documents, facilitate the most common search methods, and help move information among workers. For instance:

- A folder manager might include a scanning service for memoranda, letters, contracts, and financial records; such a manager would extract names, addresses and dates to cross-index information received and associate each document with a folder.
- A second document manager might manage moving pictures; it would communicate with its users in terms of movies, reels, and frames and depend on a storage subsystem with video delivery channels.
- A third document manager might feature CAD and be applied to maintenance records of university buildings; it would generate and display building plans with a graphic editor and maintenance contracts with a customised text editor.
- A fourth document manager might model what is found in a university library—books and pamphlets with individually viewable pages, loose collections of papers in folders, manuscripts, video tapes, and so on.

Generic document managers for applications like geographic information systems, and enterprise-specific ones administering conventions and document quality standards, may evolve over time. While a good document manager would support most library services in its domain, the storage subsystem interface is exposed to allow other applications to bypass document managers.

Modular DL Toolkits

Even within a group of similar library applications, no two libraries have a sufficiently similar set of needs that a monolithic library software offering will satisfy many people. Individual users and individual custodians will have evolving views of what they want.

The software that creates DLs will include at least the following module classes. Here we say "module classes" because each tabulated item in the list may be represented by several implementations to create different look and feel, or to provide different data transformations, or for different hardware and operating system platforms. A document storage subsystem is a resource manager that creates a library abstraction implementing all the essential data storage, retrieval, protection, communication, and search functions as primitive operations which do not depend on the interpretation of the data handled. It is middleware that integrates more basic resource managers, such as database managers, video servers, cache managers, and file managers.

Network directory and security servers are intimately related resource managers which help users locate protected resources, limiting each user to what each resource and item owner permits. A name or directory service maps names ·to locations and other descriptors. Authentication and authorisation services combine to control access to what is permitted. A billing subsystem is a component or set of components which collects and validates subject and account information, rate information and resource consumptions, and submits these to a charge-back subsystem.

A source selector and fuser is an application enabler which partitions a query among as many libraries as the query implies, calls on query managers to execute the queries, and assembles the results to hide those inter-library differences that the user considers irrelevant. A search engine is a resource manager which accepts a query and returns item descriptors, but not usually copies of the items themselves. There may be primitive search engines that operate only on certain kinds of database and also more complex search engines which partition queries among simpler query engines and combine results using joins and selections which are beyond the simpler engines.

Part of a search engine might be an external query optimiser intended to overcome the performance problems inherent in multiple, separated library catalogs. A filter service is a separately programmed bit-stream to bit-stream transformation that can be linked into a resource manager or an application enabler for functions like encryption, compression, and partial object access. A link engine is an application enabler which interprets a hypermedia link and calls on resource managers to manipulate a copy of the item indicated, possibly by launching an separately-provided application program, and possibly invoking library services to provide integrity holds on the primary copy of the item.

A preview/thumbnailer is an application enabler which collects from one or more libraries a set of small data objects ("thumbnails"), or creates each such thumbnail from a library item, to present these to a user for selection. Each thumbnail remains bound to the associated item so that selecting it can be used to drive item retrieval or some other action. A presenter or renderer is an application enabler which prepares an object for manipulation in a client machine, possibly assembling item parts from one or more libraries.

There is no clear boundary with a filter or a format converter which edits a set of files to create another set of files representing a subset of the same information, typically executing close to the data source or sink. Data analysis tools, browsers, navigators, and authoring and editing services are application enablers. Source/sink servers are resource managers such as scan servers, print servers, and fax servers. Indexing tools, document analysers, and other tools to recognise patterns and structure are application enablers for creating search indices automatically. An actor or active agent is a persistent process which monitors database state and sends to principals filtered information about changes.

Notice that actors are neither resource managers nor application enablers. Resource managers and application enablers are essentially passive and cannot distinguish active agents from human users. Triggers, a database feature in which an incoming message causes not only database changes and/or responses to its source, but also messages to a third party, share some of the characteristics of actors. Both triggers and actors are dependent on store-and-forward network services because the message target may not be active when the message is ready for delivery.

Requirements Analysis

Any social unit might create and manage its own library, and most individuals will want access to many libraries. All libraries should do certain things similarly-adhere to certain standards-so that people do not need to learn new methods for each library and so that information can be exchanged. At the vague and general level found in requests for proposals, in the trade literature, and in business publications, there is broad consensus on what services the DL should have in 5-10 years. Sensible 2-year objectives are not equally obvious.

For a few generic components, such as storage subsystems and document markup languages and interpreters, detailed needs analyses exist; each of these is characterised by hundreds of well-justified requirement statements. For most generic components suggested above, however, similarly comprehensive requirements analyses are not available in the generally accessible literature.

To prioritise the needs for academic, museum, and archive DL services we must consider a range of objectives which will differ among different institutions and for different kinds of collection. For some libraries, the premier objective will be improved accessibility to rare and valuable materials for scholars. For other libraries, it will be out-reach into troubled elementary school districts. We must start by characterising each community we are trying to serve, what it wants and can handle, and the nature of the collection. A few existing projects suggest the range:

- In the TULIP project mounted by Elsevier in partnership with material science groups at several universities, the objective is rapid communication of recent research activity.
- The Carnegie Mellon University Mercury project extends this by hoping to make information available "in specific disciplines ... as part of a national electronic library".
- In an IBM/Case Western Reserve University Project, the library is intended to be a component of an "electronic learning environment", as part of a campus-wide information system.
- In the Brown University Intermedia project, an objective was a more narrowly conceived repository for interactive instructional materials.
- The Library of Congress American Memory project intends broad public access to unique material.
- The Sequoia project intends to create a quite' specific tool the data management component of a massive scientific investigation.
- A Cornell University project under the auspices of the Commission on Preservation and Access intends rescuing the content of fragile materials.
- A joint project of the Vatican Library, the Pontifical Catholic University of Rio de Janeiro, and IBM intends world-wide access to images of rare, historically significant materials such as a beautifully illustrated copy of Dante's Divine Comedy and the four oldest surviving manuscripts of Virgil's poems.

– Project Envision at VPI&SU focuses on information retrieval and interface capabilities with structured and reusable objects, as well as on technologies for learning about computer science with materials from ACM, IEEE-CS, and others.

Such examples make it clear that part of what we need to do is compile requirements statements from a sufficiently large and diverse application set, in order to distinguish common from unique elements. Accomplishing this is a large enough task to warrant an orderly engineering approach, as illustrated for DL middleware; a helter-skelter approach, in which many individual, marginally correlated projects decide requirements independently, is not enough. Orderly tabulations will reduce wasteful duplicated effort and will help us distinguish what is already available, what is merely a matter of technical development and/or deployment, and what deserves attention and research funding because it is both difficult and needed. Comprehensive requirements statements will provide a substratum which helps each project decide what it can reasonably expect to achieve for its clientele and what its contributions to DL technology should be.

Public and Commercial Policy

The issues of ownership of information, the benefits of rights to information, and whether, when, and how money should flow from information users towards information originators can neither be ignored nor be properly handled in this report. Browning provides a commentary on some key issues:

> "... the Library of Congress is just beginning its own budgetary debate. It is now forbidden by law... to charge more than the cost of reproducing documents, plus 10 percent.... But building l CDROM] publications combining several media—marrying, say, Civil War photographs with letters... from the... vast collection

requires heavy research, the costs of which the Library cannot alone recover. So the Library has asked for legislation overturning the IO-percent restriction, but the proposal has run into controversy.

"The Information Industries Association, representing publishers, fears that the legislation will unfairly set up government-subsidised competition. The American Library Association, meanwhile, fears that the legislation will set libraries on a slippery slope that will lead to the elimination of free services....

"If libraries do not charge for electronic books, not only can they not reap rewards commensurate with their own increasing importance, but [they] can also put publishers out of business.... If libraries do charge, that will disenfranchise people from information - a horrible thing.... It is not really satisfactory either to cripple the technology so that ... texts cannot be stored, or to divvy information into two categories: the free (paid for by the taxpayer) and the commercial (paid for by the consumer)."

It is clear that these issues are very difficult, that they will be hotly debated for some years to come, and that librarians and technologists have no persuasive claim to a special voice in determining the outcome. It is equally clear that the resolution will be different in different political jurisdictions and for different classes of information, *e.g.*, depending on whether copyrights are expired, whether the information is raw data or organised, summarised, and analysed, and so on.

What may not be obvious is that it is feasible to implement DL services to support all possible policies, including situations in which different items in a collection are governed by different policies. So, for the moment, we content ourselves by asserting such feasibility and identifying as a requirement the ability to handle access to each stored item according to rules appropriate to it.

A nucleus for intellectual property rights management must be built into storage subsystem software in such a way that each data custodian can choose options to implement his institution's policies. The tracking software needs to be able to determine reliably who to bill and that bills will be paid. For efficiency such software must be intimately related to authenticators, user registries, access control mechanisms, and electronic funds transfer mechanisms. The solution should have least the following characteristics:

- As much or as little interaction as wanted with each user to advise about charges;
- As much or as little administrator interaction as institutional objectives demand;
- Imperceptible data server responsiveness degradation; and
- Sufficient efficiency to collect 10¢ page charges.

The technical work to achieve this is much less than what will be needed to achieve industry conventions and deployment.

Document Storage Services

An analysis of the DL storage subsystem done by IBM Research identified several hundred specific needs-too many to tabulate here. However, several broadly applicable elements emerged, and are summarised below because they typify what needs to be worked out for each library component class identified above.

- **Distribution.** People are often distant from needed information, frequently in locations for which high speed links are not affordable. Such recipients of large items often want delayed delivery at times of day when communication tolls are low.

- **Accessibility from all Workstation Platforms.** Different people will have different kinds of personal computer because of history, function needed, or personal preference. Increasingly, individuals may use more than one machine type. Library service must be accessible from whatever workstation is chosen for other reasons.

- **Performance.** Updating a stored document is likely to be a rare event and not subject to stringent responsiveness objectives. In contrast, retrieval should be rapid, and search to identify which items are worth retrieving should be even more rapid. Large and small items: Item sizes range from about 10^3 bytes for ASCII notes to 10^7 bytes for high resolution pictures. Digital video and audio items are even bigger and must be delivered with controlled pacing.

- **Catalog Service from all Kinds of Operating System Platform.** A large enterprise may have different kinds of database server in different locations, and should be able to provide compatible library catalog services from these database servers.

- **Low Entry Point, with Growth to Giant Collections.** Library service offers want to start cheaply and to grow without disruption or breakage to large numbers of users and very large databases. There should be no system-imposed limit to collection sizes.

- **Support for all Kinds of Item Storage.** Custodians should be able to house items as economically as possible within their operational and policy constraints. They should be able to add capacity using the currently most effective storage medium hierarchy and attach this wherever needed to minimise communication costs and maximise responsiveness.

- **Low Administration Overhead.** Installation and custodial responsibilities for a library should require only a small addition in time and training for data administrators. Installation and use of the workstation portion of library services should be easy given only "shrink wrap" materials, without help from specialists.

- **Standard Interfaces and Protocols.** The previous requirements imply a long term commitment to an application programming interface for library services, and to how the storage system exploits underlying communication services.

- **Joining Libraries to Other Databases.** People want easy use of library data in unanticipated ways, joining library catalogs to enterprise databases and combining data across agencies and sometimes across administrative jurisdictions. People want to do particular correlations on short notice and with low cost.

- **Open Subsystem.** Emerging work station application packages-text, graphic, image, and audio editors, spreadsheets, CAD packages, and industry support packages such as those for hospitals and for doctors¢ offices-are potential sources and sinks for large numbers of electronic documents. Document storage subsystems must provide application programming interfaces and exit points for enterprise tailoring.

- **Application Independence.** The utility of stored data is hampered by anything that tailors it to one application or one usage paradigm in preference to alternatives. Cataloging documents is economical primarily under the presumption of future pertinence to multiple, unanticipated applications. An application-neutral interface to library services is required.

Application of Digital Library

DL research attention has been more focused on recently generated materials than on managing the cultural heritage. We need to think about the possibilities and limitations for antique material. This includes recognising the special virtues of paper as an archival medium, and also its limitations.

Requirements for Catalogs

The radically new possibility for the DL is the storage and dissemination of collected items. In contrast, digital catalogs have been in practical use for some time, and there is a considerable body of experience and some standards in this area. Instruction and standards are necessary since library cataloging has long been known to be difficult:

> "The preparation of a catalog may seem a light task, to the inexperienced, and to those who are unacquainted with the requirements of the learned world, respecting such works. In truth, however, there is no species of literary labour so arduous and perplexing. The peculiarities of titles are, like the idiosyncrasies of authors, innumerable."

Digitally managed catalogs present many of the same problems as card catalogs and some new problems, and the possibility that automatic processes may improve some aspects. Catalog quality is limited not only by linguistic and technical factors, but also by difficult cost constraints exacerbated by ever larger acquisition rates. Catalog quality receives a great deal of attention from librarians, both in their graduate education and as a research issue. Librarians complain that computer scientists are not adequately involving them in DL deliberations; the criticism is merited.

In the workshop, we did not consider catalog structure, but recommend renewed attention to it, either by resurrecting prior needs analyses and re-examining them for current pertinence, or by constructing afresh something similar to what is available for the storage subsystem.

Document Markup and Interchange Conventions

This topic is critical for documents produced specifically for the digital environment. As this has been realised for some years, markup, linking, and interchange have already received intensive attention, including standards activities and proposed industry conventions. We refer the reader to treatments of the Dexter model for hypertext, of SGML and HyTime for standard document markup language, and to the trade literature for arguments about the merits of Microsoft OLE (Object Linking and Embedding) and Apple Open.

There is considerable overlap among these tools, which are mostly promulgated for personal computers and office applications, between them and World Wide Web markup being popularised in the Internet, and probably between all these and further document markup languages that we have overlooked. In addition, the two standards for document interchange, ANSI and ISO, are mutually incompatible, and have unresolved relationships with the linking conventions. The DL community should avoid further redundant activities. In the workshop, we did not consider the extent to which DL progress depends on the emergence of a limited number of document markup conventions or how the DL community should participate, if at all.

Information Capture

By information capture we mean everything necessary to import each external information item into a DL, including media conversion, creation of primary catalog records, document analysis to extract secondary indices, correlation with prior library contents, and conversion to a format suitable for navigation by following links and conforming to interchange standards, and whatever else is needed to make the DL convenient for the human client. Here, "convenient for the human client" is ill-defined; while we might aspire to some automatic generation of hypertext links, preparation of hypertext for instruction should probably be considered outside the DL topic.

Giant libraries can be achieved only with automatic means of capturing information. The NSFIARPAINASA initiative calls for "an economically feasible capability to digitise massive corpora of extant and new information from heterogeneous and distributed sources". Information capture arguably presents the most difficult technical challenges of the DL enterprise and the largest costs of the deployed DL complex. A National Library of Medicine project suggested that digital replacement of existing books is not economical, at least not yet; its objective was to make its resources available to practising physicians, but it encountered an early obstacle in the cost of turning the pages of each book. So that dream is not yet realised. Information capture from existing sources is itself a thriving field of inquiry, summarised by the ICDAR Conference Chair:

> "The large number of existing paper-based documents and the production of a multitude of new ones every year have raised the important issues of efficient handling, retrieval and storage of the information these documents contain. This has led to the emergence of new research domains dealing with the recognition

by computers of the constituent elements of documents including characters, symbols, text, lines, graphics, images, handwriting, signatures, etc. In addition, these new domains also deal with automatic analyses of the overall physical and logical structures of documents, with the ultimate objective of a high-level understanding of their semantic content... Automatic, intelligent process of documents is at the intersection of many fields of research,... This second conference... is part of a series of biennial conferences.

Information Retrieval (IR)

Information retrieval, being one of the earliest foci of computer science research, needs few words in this report. There are commercial products which create secondary indices from text bodies. Fuzzy indexing and search seem especially promising.

Morris has reviewed research on expert systems for information retrieval and concludes:

> "Current practice cousels expert system development only in narrow, well-defined, homogeneous domains; none of these attributes applies to on-line searching....
>
> " ... Although they have developed beyond infancy, it seems that information retrieval systems will not reach adulthood before the next century. There is much to be done with regard to standardising platforms and formats, in developing and integrating information retrieval and AI techniques,... before consulting an information retrieval system is no more daunting and at least as rewarding as asking one's personal researcher for 'Details about..."

Effective techniques for evaluating IR services and experiments are not yet available. Another topic that has not received sufficient attention, as far as we know, is combining queries over attribute databases with queries over text bodies; we are addressing it. Chaumier surveys recent introductions to the marketplace.

Large Libraries

Problems of scale were not considered in the workshop, beyond recognition of their existence. Our treatment is limited in that it considers the topic Digital Library rather than the topic Digital Libraries, *i.e.*, almost ignores the problem of the user who needs to choose which libraries to search. More recently, Sheldon considers the possibility of content labels to help control the size of query answer sets. Aggrawal introduces database mining, which is discovery of what questions a database might help answer.

Scaling of the storage component is not a research problem. Storage management for very large collections is understood in principle; a document storage subsystem can knit together commercial database management and hierarchical file systems sufficient for the largest DLs practical for the time being. We know how to handle 10^8 objects in a library, with a mixture of sizes from 10^3 to 10^7 bytes per object; what is practical will be determined by information capture capabilities and by costs.

A fully compatible document storage subsystem has also been demonstrated within a single workstation. Such technology has not yet been applied to academic libraries, and performance challenges such as those which might arise in a multi-campus diversity with 10^5 students have not been identified, much less solved.

Every module class defined above needs to be considered along the lines we have started. For some, such as protection services and means for letting users proceed without knowing actual locations of information resources, requirements analysis is well developed. Others are not so well addressed.

●●

10

Textual Material and Digital Library

Methods for storing textual materials must represent two different aspects of a document: its structure and its appearance. The structure describes the division of a text into elements such as characters, words, paragraphs and headings. It identifies parts of the documents that are emphasized, material placed in tables or footnotes, and everything that relates one part to another. The structure of text stored in computers is often represented by a markup specification. In recent years, SGML (Standard Generalized Markup Language) has become widely accepted as a generalized system for structural mark-up. The appearance is how the document looks when displayed on a screen or printed on paper. The appearance is closely related to the choice of format: the size of font, margins and line spacing, how headings are represented, the location of figures, and the display of mathematics or other specialized notation. In a printed book, decisions about the appearance extend to the choice of paper and the type of binding. Page-description languages are used to store and render documents in a way that precisely describe their appearance.

Structure and appearance are related by the design of the document. In conventional publishing, the designer creates a design specification, which describes how each structural element is to appear, with comprehensive rules for every situation that can arise. The specification is known as a style sheet. It enables a compositor to take a manuscript, which has been marked-up by a copy editor, and create a well-formatted document.

An outline of the procedure that several journal publishers use to produce electronic journals. Articles received from authors are marked up with SGML tags, which describe the structure and content of the article. A style sheet specifies how each structural element should appear. The SGML mark-up and the style sheet are input to rendering software which creates the formatted document. In the early days of digital libraries, a common question was whether digital libraries would replace printed books. The initial discussion concentrated on questions of readability. Under what circumstances would people read from a screen rather than printed paper? With experience, people have realized that computers and books are not directly equivalent. Each has strengths that the other can not approach. Computing has the advantage that powerful searching is possible, which no manual system can provide, while the human factors of a printed book are superb. It is portable, can be annotated, can be read anywhere, can be spread out on a desk top or carried in the hand.

Since digital texts and printed materials serve different roles, publishers create printed and online versions of the same materials. A mark-up language can be used to manage texts that will be both printed and displayed on computer screens. By using separate style sheets, a single document, represented by structural mark-up, can be rendered in different ways for different purpose. Thus, journal articles can be displayed on screen or printed. The layout and graphic design might be different, but they are both derived from the same source and present the same content.

Strict control over the appearance of documents via SGML mark-up and style sheets proves to be very difficult.

The says that textual materials are organized, displayed, and interpreted have many subtleties. Mark-up languages can represent almost all structures, but the variety of structural elements that can be part of a document is huge, and the details of appearance that authors and designers could choose are equally varied.

For example, many articles in journals published by the ACM con tam mathematical notation. Authors often supply their articles in TeX format, which provides precise control over the layout of mathematics. During the production process it is converted to SGML mark-up. When rendered using a style sheet the output may appear slightly different from the author's original, which can cause problems.

The Oxford English Dictionary

The new Oxford English Dictionary is a fine example of the use of a mark-up language to describe both structure and content, so that the same material can be used as the basis for a variety of products. The first edition of the dictionary was created by James Murray and his colleagues over four decades. Nineteenth century photographs of Murray at work in his grandly named "Scriptorium" in Oxford show a primitive shack filled with slips of paper. The dictionary was a landmark in lexicography, but it existed only as static printed pages. Keeping it up to date by hand proved impossible.

The typography of the original dictionary is loaded with semantic information. Capital letters, bold and italic fonts, parentheses, smaller type sizes, and other formatting conventions convey semantics that are recorded nowhere else. A highly sophisticated computer program was written that extracted this buried semantic information and marked the textual elements with SGML tags. The new dictionary is maintained as a computer database, in which the SGML mark-up is as important as the words of the text. Lexicographers update it continually. A wide variety of publications can be created with minimal effort, including printed books, CD-ROMs and other digital versions. This new Oxford English Dictionary required cooperation between the world's largest team of lexicographers, in Oxford, a team of computational linguists at Waterloo University in Ontario, and corporate support from IBM. Converting text

Today, most documents are created digitally, beginning life on a word processor, but libraries are full of valuable documents that exist only on paper. Consequently, there is demand to convert printed documents to computer formats. For important documents, conversion projects capture the appearance and also identify the structure of the original.

The basic conversion technique is scanning. A document is scanned by sampling its image on a grid of points. Each point is represented by a brightness code. In the simplest form, only black and white are distinguished. With a resolution of 300 dots per inch, horizontally and vertically, a good image can be made of most printed pages. If the resolution is increased to 600 dots per inch, or by coding for 8 levels of gray, the clarity becomes excellent, and halftone illustrations can be represented. High-quality artwork requires at least 24 bits per dot to represent colour combinations. This creates very large files.

A scanned page reproduces the appearance of the printed page, but represents text simply as an image. In many applications, this is a poor substitute for marked-up text or even simple ASCII characters. In particular, it is not possible to search a page image for specific words. The serious scholar sometimes needs to work from the original and frequently needs to know its appearance. On other occasions, an electronic version that identifies the structure is superior; a marked-up electronic text is more convenient than an image of the original for creating a concordance or for textual analysis, since the text can be tagged to indicate its linguistic structure or its historical antecedents. Therefore the next stage of conversion is to provide an electronic text from the page image.

Optical character recognition is the technique of converting scanned images of characters to their equivalent characters. The basic technique is for a computer program to separate out the individual characters, and then to compare each character to mathematical templates. Despite decades of research, optical character recognition remains an inexact process. The error rate varies with the legibility of the original. If the original document is clear and legible, the error rate is less than one percent. With poor quality materials the error rate can be much higher. For many purposes, an error rate of even a fraction of one percent is too high.

Various processes have been devised to get around these errors. One technique is to use several different character recognition programs on the same materials. Hopefully, characters that cause one program difficulty may be resolved by the others. Another approach is to use a dictionary to check the results. However, all high-quality conversion requires human proof reading. In some systems, a computer program displays the converted text on a screen, and highlights doubtful words with suggestions which an editor can accept or correct. One organization that has developed efficient processes of this type is UMI, which converts huge numbers of theses every year. Since most theses received by UMI are new, clean copy, UMI achieves low error rates from optical character recognition combined with manual resolution of doubtful words.

When the individual words have been recognized, the next stage of conversion is to identify the structure of a document and to tag key structural elements, such as headings. This is another aspect where, despite steady progress by researchers, high-quality conversion requires human proof reading and editing.

There is an alternative method of conversion that is widely used in practice: to retype the document from scratch and add mark-Up tags manually. This approach is often cheaper than a combination of automatic and human processing. Since the work is labour intensive, it is usually carried out in countries where labour costs are low. One of the largest conversion projects is the Library of Congress's American Memory program. The documents to be converted are selected from the library's historic collections and are often less clear than a recently printed document. The conversion is carried out by contractors who guarantee a specified level of accuracy, but are at liberty to carry out the conversion by any convenient method.

Encoding Characters

ASCII

When representing text in a computer, the most basic elements are characters. It is important to distinguish between the concept of a character as a structural element and the various representations of that character, stored within a computer or displayed for reading. A character, such as the capital letter "A", is an abstract concept, which is independent of the encoding used for storage in a computer or the format used to display it.

Computers store a character, such as "A" or "5", as a sequence of bits, in which each distinct character is encoded as a different sequence. Early computers had codes for the twenty six letters of English (upper and lower case), the ten digits, and a small number of punctuation marks and special symbols. The internal storage representation within most computers is still derived from this limited character set. Most modern computers represent characters using the ASCJI code. (ASCII stands for American Standard Code for Information Interchange, but the full form of the name is seldom used.)

Originally, ASCII represented each character by seven bits. This 7-bit encoding is known as standard ASCII. For example, the character "A" is encoded as the 7-bit sequence 1000001. Considered as "a binary number, this sequence is the number 65. Hence, it is conventional to state that, in the standard ASCII code, the number 65 represents the character "A". There are 128 different pattern that can be made with seven bits. Standard ASCII associates a specific character with each number between 0 and 127. Of these, the characters 0 to 31 represent control characters, *e.g.*, "carriage return". The printable ASCII character set is truly a standard. The same codes are used in a very wide range of computers and applications. Therefore, the ninety six printable ASCII characters are used in applications where inter operability has high priority. They are the only characters allowed in HTML and in many electronic mail systems. Almost every computer keyboard, display, and software program interprets these codes in the same way. There is also an extended version of ASCII that uses eight bits. It provides additional character encodings for the numbers 128 to 255, but it is not as universally accepted as 7 -bit ASCII.

Textual materials use a much wider range of characters than the printable ASCII set, with its basis in the English language. Other languages have scripts that require different character sets. Some European languages have additional letters or use diacritics. Even Old English requires extra characters. Other languages, such as Greek or Russian, have different alphabets. The Chinese, Japanese, and Korean writing does not use an alphabet. These languages use the Han characters, which represent complete words or syllables with a single character. Even for texts written in current English, the printable ASCII characters are inadequate. Disciplines such as mathematics, music, or chemistry use highly refined notation that require large numbers of characters. In each of these fields, comprehension often depends critically on the use of accepted conventions of notation. The computer industry sells its products world-wide and recognizes the need to support the characters used by their customers around the world. This is an area in which the much-maligned Microsoft Corporation has been a leader. Since it is impossible to represent all languages using the 256 possibilities represented by an eight-bit byte, there have been several attempts to represent a greater range of character sets using a larger number of bits. Recently, one of these approaches has emerged as the standard that most computer manufacturers and software houses are supporting.

In strict Unicode, each character is represented by sixteen bits, allowing for a up to 65,536 distinct characters. Through the painstaking efforts of a number of dedicated specialists, the scripts used in a wide range of languages can now be represented in Unicode.

Scripts Represented in Unicode

Version 2.0 of the Unicode standard contains 16-bit codes for 38,885 distinct characters. The encoding is organized by scripts rather than languages. Where several languages use a closely related set of characters, the set of symbols that covers the group of languages is identified as a single script. The Latin script contains all the characters used by English, French, Spanish, German, and related languages. Unicode 2.0 supports the following scripts: Arabic Armenian Bengali Bopomofo Cyrillic Devanagari Georgian Greek Gujarati Gurmkhi HanHangul Hebrew Hiragana Kannada Katakana Latin Lao Marayalam Oriya Phonetic Tamil Telugu Thai Tibetan. In addition to the above primary scripts, a number of other collections of symbols are also encoded by Unicode. They include the following:

Numbers General Diacritics General Punctuation General Symbols Mathematical Symbols Technical Symbols Dingbats Arrows, Blocks, Box Drawing Forms, & Geometric

Shapes Miscellaneous Symbols Presentation Forms Unicode does not cover everything. Several modern languages, such as Ethiopic and Sinhala, will eventually be included. There are also numerous archaic scripts, such as Aramaic, Etruscan, and runes, which will probably be included at some date. One important aspect of Unicode is support for the Han characters used by Chinese, Japanese, and Korean. Unicode supports the Unihan database, which is the result of an earlier project to reconcile the encoding systems previously used for these languages. The acceptance of Unicode is not simply through the efforts of linguistic scholars in supporting a wide range of languages. The developers have thought carefully about the relationship between Unicode and existing software. If every computer program had to be changed, Unicode would never be adopted. Therefore, there is a special representation of the Unicode characters, known as UTF-8, that allows gradual transformation of ASCII-based applications to the full range of Unicode scripts.

UTF-8 is an encoding that uses from one to six bytes to represent each Unicode character. The most commonly used characters are represented by a single byte, the next most common by two bytes, the least common by six bytes. The crucial part of the design is that each printable ASCII character is represented by a single byte, which is identical to the corresponding ASCII character. Thus the same sequence of bytes can be interpreted as either Unicode characters (in UTF-8 representation) or as printable ASCII.

Transliteration

Unicode is not the only method used to represent a wide range of characters in computers. One approach is transliteration. This is a systematic way to convert characters in one alphabet into another set of characters. For example, the German 0 is sometimes transliterated oe. A phonetic system of transliteration known as pinyin is frequently used to represent Chinese, especially Mandarin, in the English alphabet. Transliteration may have been acceptable in the days when typewriters were manual devices with a physically constrained character set.

Libraries have a more immediate problem. They were using a wide range of alphabets long before the computing industry paid attention to the problem. In fact, libraries were well-advanced in this area in the days when most computers supported only upper case letters. As a result, MARC catalogues and other library systems contain huge volumes of material that are encoded in systems other than Unicode, including pinyin, and face a daunting task of conversion or coexistence.

SGML

Mark-up languages have been used since the early days of computing to describe the structure of the text and the format with which the text is to be displayed. Today, the most commonly used are the SGML family of languages.

SGML is not a single mark-up language. It is a system to define mark-up specifications. An individual specification defined within the SGML framework is called a document type definition (DTD). Many publishers and other agencies have developed their own private DTDs. Examples of DTDs that are of particular importance to scholarly libraries are the Text Encoding Initiative and the Encoded Archival Description.

Document Type Definitions (DTDs) for Scholarship

Text Encoding Initiative the Text Encoding Initiative (TEI) was an early and very thorough effort to represent existing texts in digital form, with an emphasis on use by humanities scholars. Documents from the past include almost every approach that has ever been used to represent text on paper, velum, papyrus, or even stone. They include print, handwriting, typewriting, and more. The documents include annotation, deletions, and damaged portions that can not be read. Every character set the world has ever known may be present. SGML has proved effective in describing these materials, but designing the DTD provided a challenge. It would have been easy to have created a DTD that was so complex as to be completed unwieldy.

The solution has been to create a family of DTDs, built up from components. A core tag set defines elements likely to be needed by all documents and therefore is part of all DTDs. Each DTD is required to add a base set of tags, selected from a choice of tags for prose, verse, drama, dictionaries, or data files. Usually, only one base tag set is appropriate for a given document. Finally, a variety of additional tag sets are available for specialized purposes.

The Encoded Archival Description (EAD)

The term finding aid covers a wide range of lists, inventories, indexes, and other textual documents created by archives, libraries, and museums to describe their holdings. Some finding aids provide fuller information than is normally contained within cataloguing records; others are less specific and do not necessarily have detailed records for every item in a collection. Some are short; others run to hundreds of pages. The Encoded Archival Description (EAD) is a DTD used to encode electronic versions of archival aids. The first version of the DTD was developed by a team from the University of California at Berkeley. The effort drew on experience from the Text Encoding Initiative.

Much of the information is derived from hierarchical relationships and there are many other interrelationships that must be explicitly recognized when encoding a finding aid for use in a digital library. The EAD has been widely embraced by archivists, who have worked collaboratively to refine the DTD, test it against existing finding aids, and provide extensive documentation. The EAD has become a highly specialized tool, tailored for the needs of a specialized community. For use by that community, it is an important tool that allows them to exchange and share information. A DTD is built up from the general concepts of entities and elements. A DTD defines what entities and elements are allowable in a particular class of documents and declares the base character set encoding used for the document. Entities are specified by identifiers that begin with the letter "&" and end with ";". Here are some examples: α &logo;

In a typical DID, the allowable entities include most of the ASCII character set and other characters, known as character entities, but any symbol or group of symbols can be defined as a entity. The name of the entity is simply a name. In standard character sets, "α", is the entity used to encode the first letter of the Greek alphabet, but a DID could use this code for some totally different purpose. The DTDs used by scientific publishers define as many as 4,000 separate entities to represent all the special symbols and the variants used in different scientific disciplines.

Entities provide a stream of symbols that can be grouped together into elements. A DTD can define any string as the name of an element. The element is bracketed by two tags in angle brackets, with" I" used to denote the end tag. Thus the Text Encoding Initiative uses the tags <del> and </ del> to bracket text that has been crossedout in a manuscript. To mark the words "men and women" as crossed-out, they would be tagged as: <del>men and women</ del>

Examples of elements include the various types of headings, footnotes, expressions, references, and so on. Elements can be nested in hierarchical relationships. Each DTD has a grammar that specifies the allowable relationships as a set of rules that can be processed by a computer program.

Simplified versions of SGML

SGML is firmly established as a flexible apr roach for recording and storing high-quality texts. Its flexibility permits creators of textual materials to generate DTDs that are tailored to their particular needs. Publishers of scientific journals have developed their own DTDs, which they use in-house to mark-up journal articles as they are created and to store them on computers. Digital library projects, such as JSTOR and American Memory, use simple DTDs that are derived from the work of the Text Encoding Initiative.

The disadvantage of SGML's flexibility is the complexity of the software needed to process it. While a program to parse and render a simple DTD is not hard to write, it is a forbidding task to create a general-purpose package that can parse any DTD, combine information from any style sheet and render the document either on a computer screen or printer. The market for such software is quite small. Only one company has persevered and created a general package for rendering SGML. Even this package is not perfect; it does not- implement all of SGML, runs only en some types of computers, and uses its own private form of style sheets.

HTML

The web has stimulated the development of simplified versions of SGML. HTML, the mark-up language used by the web, can be considered an unorthodox DTD. In many ways, however, it diverges from the philosophy of SGML, because it mixes structural information with format. HTML may have begun life as structural mark-up, relying on browsers to determine how to format the text for display, but its subsequent development has added a large number of features that give the designer of web pages control over how their material appears when rendered for screen display or printing.

Features of HTML

HTML provides a variety of tags that are inserted into documents. Usually tags are in pairs; *e.g.*, the pair of tags below indicates that the enclosed text is a main heading. <h1> This is a main heading </hl> A few tags are self-contained and do not bracket any text. An example is <hr>, which indicates a horizontal rule. Elements are often embedded or nested within each other. For example, a list can contain many paragraphs and tables can contain other tables. The following examples are typical of the features provided by HTML. There are many more and several of these features have a wide selection of options. They illustrate how HTML combines structural mark-up with formatting and support for online applications.

Structural elements many of the tags in HTML are used to describe the structural elements of a document. They include the following <body>the body of the document<p>a paragraph<hl>, <h2>, ... , <h6>headings (six standard levels)<em>emphasis<u1>, <01>,< d1>lists (unordered, ordered, & definition)<table>a table-Formatting Other tags in HTML define the appearance of the document when it is rendered for display on a computer or printed. They include the following.
line break<i>italic<font>details about the font to be used<center>center text<pre>pre-formatted text-Online services A final group of HTML tags are designed for online applications. They include the following.<a>anchor (used with hyperlinks)<img>location of an image<form>an online form HTML has grown from its simple beginnings and is continuing to grow"

Depending on the viewpoint, these additions can be described as making i-IHv1L more powerful, or as adding complexity and inconvenience. Nobody would argue the great value of some additions, such as being able to embed images, through the <img> tag, which was introduced in

Mosaic. The value of other additions is a matter of opinion. Simple formatting commands, such as <center> introduced by Netscape, can do little harm, but other features have added a great deal of complexity. Perhaps the most notable are the use of tables and frames. These two additions, more than any other, have changed HTML from a simple mark-up language.

The tension between structural mark-up in HTML and formatting to control appearance has become a serious problem. Many creators of web pages want to control what the user sees. They have difficulty accepting that they do not determine the appearance of a document, as seen by the user, and use every opportunity that HTML provides to control the appearance. An unfortunate trend is for designers to use structural elements to manipulate the design; many web pages are laid out as a single huge table, so that the designer can control the margins seen by the user. Skilled designers construct elegant web pages using such tricks. Less skilled designers impose on the users pages that are awkward to use.

The worst abuses occur when a designer imposes a page layout that will not fit in the window size that the user chooses or over-rides a user preference, perhaps preventing a user with poor evesight from using a large type size. Almost all new features that have been added to HTML have come from the developers of browsers adding features, to enhance their products or to keep pace with their competitors. Some we're indeed improvements, but others were unnecessary. The World Wide Web Consortium and the Internet Engineering Task Force provide valuable coordination and attempt to provide standards, but the fundamental control of.

XML is a variant of SGML that attempts to bridge the gap between the simplicity of HTML .and the power of full SGML. Simplicity is the key to the success of HTML, but simplicity is also its weakness. Every time a new feature is added to HTML it becomes less elegant, harder to use, and less of a standard shared by; all browsers. SGML is the opposite. It is so flexible that almost any text description is possible, but the flexibility comes at the cost of complexity. Even after many years, only a few specialists are really comfortable with SGML and general purpose software is still scarce.

XML is a subset of SGML that has been designed explicitly for use with the web. The design is based on two important criteria. The first is that it is simple to write computer programs that manipulate XML. The second is that it builds on the familiar world of HTML, so that people and systems can migrate to XML with a minimum of pain.

The underlying Character set for XML is 16-bit Unicode, and in particular the UTF-8 stream encoding. This permits documents to be written in standard ASCII, but supports a wide range of languages and character sets. For convenience, some character entities are pre-defined, such as &It; and > for the less-than and greater-than symbols. XML does not specify particular methods for representing mathematics, but a there is a separate effort, MathML, tackling the problems of mathematics.

Since XML is a subset of SGML, every document is based on a DTD, but the DTD does not have to be specified explicitly. If the file contains previously undefined pairs of tags, which delimit some section of a document, the parser automatically adds them to the DTD. The developers of XML have worked hard to gain wide acceptance for their work. Their strategy follows the philosophy of the Internet mainstream. The design has been an open process hosted by the World Wide Web Consortium. From the start, members of the design team wrote demonstration software that they have distributed freely to interested parties. Leading corporations, notably Microsoft and Netscape, have lent their support. This deliberate building of consensus and support seems to have been successful, and XML looks likely to become widely adopted.

Style Sheets

Mark-Up languages describe the structure of a document. SGML and XML use tags to describe the semantics of a document and its component parts. It does not describe the appearance of a document. Thus, SGML tags might be used to identify a section of text as a chapter heading, but would not indicate that a chapter heading starts a new page and is printed with a specific font and alignment. A common need is to take a document that has SGML or XML mark-up and render it for according to a specific design specification. For example, a publisher who creates journal articles according to a DTD may wish to render them in two different ways: printed output for conventional publication, and a screen format for delivery over the Internet and display on a computer screen. The first will be rendered in a format that is input to a typesetting machine.

The process requires that the structural tags in the mark-up be translated into formats that can be displayed either in print or on the screen. This uses a style sheet. For example, a. DTD may define an element as a heading of level two, denoted by <h2> and </h2> tags. The style sheet may state that this should be displayed as 13 points Times Roman font, bold, left aligned. It will also specify important characteristics such as the appropriate line spacing and how to treat a heading that falls near the bottom of the page. A style sheet provides detailed instructions for how to render every conceivable valid document that has been marked-up according to a specific DTD.

In creating style sheets, the power of SGML is a disadvantage. Readers are accustomed to beautifully designed books. Much of this beauty comes from the skill of the craftsmen who carry out the composition and page layout. Much of their work is art. The human eye is very sensitive; the details of how statistical tables are formatted, or the layout and pagination of an art book have never been reduced to mechanical rules. Style sheets can easily be very complex, yet still fail to be satisfactory when rendering complex documents.

Since SGML is a general framework, people have been working on the general problem of specifying style sheets for any DTD. This work is called Document Style Semantics and Specification Language (DSSSL). The developers of DSSSL are faced with a forbidding task. To date, DSSSL rendering programs have been written for some simple DTDs, but the general task appears too ambitious. It is much easier to create a satisfactory style sheet for a single DTD, used in a well-understood context. Many books and journals are printed from SGML markup, with special-purpose style sheets, and the results can be excellent. With HTML, there has been no formal concept of style sheets. The mark-up combines structural elements, such as various types of list, with formatting tags, such as those that specify bold or italic fonts. The tags provide general guidance about appearance, which individual browsers interpret and adapt to the computer display in use. The appearance that the user sees comes from a combination of the mark-up provided by the designer of a web page, the formatting conventions built into a browser, and options chosen by the user. Authors of HTML documents wishing for greater control can embed various forms of scripts, applets, and plugins.

The CSS (Cascading Style Sheets) and XLS (Extensible Style Language) (XSL), methods are important methods for providing style sheets for HTML and XML. The developers of XML have realized that the greatest challenge to be faced by XML before it becomes widely accepted is how to control the appearance of documents and have been supportive of both CSS and XSL. It is still too early to know what will succeed, but the combination is promising. These methods have the important concept of laying down precise rules for the action to take when the styles specified by the designer and the user disagree.

Cascading Style Sheets (CSS) and Extensible Style Language (XSL)

Mark-up languages describe the structural elements of a document. Style sheets specify how the elements appear when rendered on a computer display or printed on paper. Cascading Style Sheets (CSS) were developed for use with HTML mark-up. The Extensible Style Language (XSL) is an extension for XML mark-up. Just as XML is a simplified version of full SGML that provides a simple conversion from HTML, XSL is derived from DSSSL and any CSS style sheet can be converted to XSL by a purely mechanical process.

Currently, XSL is only a specification, but there is every hope that, as XML becomes widely adopted, XSL will become equally important. Rules in CSS a rule defines styles to be applied to selected elements of a document. Here is a simple rule: h1 {colour: blue} This rule states that for elements "h1 ", which is the HTML tag for top-level headings, the property "colour" should have the value "blue". More formally, each rule consists of a selector, which selects certain elements of the document, and a declaration, enclosed in braces, which states a style to be applied to those elements. The declaration has two parts, a property and a value, separated by a colon. A CSS style sheet is a list of rules. Various conventions are provided to simplify the writing of rule.

Inheritance

The mark-up for an HTML document defines a structure which can be represented as a hierarchy. Thus headings, paragraphs, and lists are elements of the HTML body; list items are elements within lists; lists can be nested within each other. The rules in CSS style sheets also inherit from each other. If no rule explicitly selects an element, it inherits the rules for the elements higher in the hierarchy. For example, consider the pair of rules: body I font-family: serif} h1, h2 {font-family: sans-serif} Headings h1 and h2 are elements of the HTML body, but have an explicit rule; they will be displayed with a sans-serif font. In this example, there is no explicit rule for paragraphs or lists. Therefore they inherit the styles that apply to body, which is higher up the hierarchy, and will be displayed with a serif typeface.

Cascading Style sheets must be associated with an HTML page. The designer has several options, including embedding the style at the head of a page, or providing a link to an external file that contains the style sheet. Every browser has its own style sheet, which may be modified by the user, and a user may have a private style sheet. Since several style sheets may apply to the same page, conflicts can occur, where rules conflict. A series of mechanisms have been developed to handle these situations, based on some simple principles. The most fundamental principle is that, when rules conflict, one is selected and the others are ignored. The most controversial convention is that when the designer s rule conflicts directly with the user's, the designer s has precedence. A user who wishes to over-ride thus rule can mark a rule with the flag "important", but this is awkward. However, it does permit special style sheets to be developed, for instance for users who have poor eyesight and wish to specify large font sizes. Page-description languages.

Since creators and readers both give high priority to the appearance of documents, it is natural to have methods that specify the appearance of a document directly, without going via structural mark-up. The methods differ greatly in details, but the underlying objective is the same, to render textual materials with the same graphic quality and control as the best documents printed by traditional methods. This is not easy. Few things in life are as pleasant to use as a well-printed book. Over the years, typography, page layout, paper manufacturing, and book binding have been refined to a high level of usability. Early text formatting methods were designed for printed output, but display on computer screens has become equally important. This section looks at three page-description languages: TeX, Postscript, and PDF. These three languages have different objectives and address them differently, but they are all practical, pragmatic approaches that perform well in production systems.

TeX

TeX is the earliest. It was developed by Donald Knuth and is aimed at high-quality printing, with a special emphasis on mathematics. The problems of encoding mathematics are complex. In addition to the numerous special characters, the notation relies on complex expressions that are not naturally represented as a single sequence of characters. TeX provides rules for encoding mathematics as a sequence of ASCII characters for input, storage, and manipulation by computer, with tags to indicate the format for display.

Most users make use of one of two TeX packages, plain TeX or LaTex. These packages define a set of formatting tags that cover the majority of situations that are normally encountered in typesetting. Closely allied with TeX is a system for designing fonts called Metafont. Knuth has taken great pains to produce versions of his standard font for a wide range of computer systems. TeX remains unsurpassed for the preparation of printed mathematical papers. It is widely used by authors and journals in mathematics, physics, and related fields.

Postscript

Postscript was the first product of the Adobe corporation, which spun off from Xerox in 1984. Postscript is a programming language, to create graphical output for printing. Few people ever write programs in Postscript, but many computers have printer routines that will take text or graphics and create an equivalent Postscript program. The program can then be sent to a printer controller that executes the Postscript program and creates control sequences to drive the printer.

Explicit support for fonts is one of Postscript's strengths. Much of the early success of the Apple Macintosh computer came from the combination of bitmapped designs on the screen with Postscript printers that provided a quality of output previously available only on very expensive computers. With both laser printing and screen display, characters are built up from small dots. Simple laser printers use 300 dots per inch and typesetting machines may have a resolution of 1,200 dots per inch or more, but most computer screens are about 75 dots per inch. The fonts that appear attractive on a computer screen are not quite the same as the ones used for printing, and the displays of text on a screen must be fitted to the coarse resolution. Usually, the operating system functions that display text on a screen are different from the Postscript commands used for printing.

Although Postscript is primarily a graphical output language, which had its initial impact representing computer output to laser printers, Postscript programs are used in other applications, as a format to store and exchange representations of any text or graphical output. Postscript is not ideal for this purpose, since the language has many variations and the programs make assumptions about the capabilities of the computer that they will be executed on. PDF, which built on Adobe's experience with Postscript, is a better format for storing page images in a portable format that is independent of any particular computer.

Portable Document Format (PDF)

The most popular page description language in use today is Adobe's Portable Document Format (PDF). Adobe has built on its experience with Postscript to create a powerful format and a set of tools to create, store, and display documents in it. PDF is an important format. It is' also interesting as an example of how a corporation can create a standard, make it available to the world, and yet still generate good business. PDF is a file format used to represent a document that is independent of applications and computer system. A PDF document consists of pages, each made up of text, graphics, and images, with supporting data.

PDF is an evolution of the Postscript programming language, which was also created by Adobe. One way to generate PDF is by diverting a stream of data that would usually go to a printer and storing it as a PDF file. Alternatively, the file can be converted from Postscript or other formats. The file can then be stored, transmitted over a network, displayed on a computer, or printed. Technical reasons for PDF's success Technically, PDF has many strengths. When viewed on a computer screen, most PDF documents are very legible while retaining the design characteristics of print.

If the computer that is displaying a PDF document does not have the fonts that were used to generate it, font descriptors enable the PDF viewer to generate an artificial font that is usually close to the original. The electronic additions are simple to use and provide many of the features that users want. They include hyperlinks, either within the document or to external URLs. The viewers provide a tool for searching for words within the text, though searching across documents is a problem. Annotations are provided. Printer support is excellent. There is even a method that creators can use to prevent users from printing or otherwise using a document in ways that are not approved. PDF is not perfect. It has problems distinguishing between certain types of file, or working with unusual fonts, but overall it has become a important format for online documents. Business reasons for PDF's success after a hesitant introduction, Adobe has been shrewd in its marketing of PDF. The company provides excellent PDF viewers for almost every known type of computer; they are freely available over the Internet. Adobe makes its money from a family of products that are used by people who create PDF files, not from the users of these files. Adobe owns the copyright in the PDF specification, but, to promote its use as an interchange format, gives broad permissions to anyone to create PDF files, to write applications that produce PDF output, and to write software that reads and processes PDF files. Potentially, competitors could create products that undercut those that Adobe sells, but the company accepts that risk. PDF is widely used in commercial document management systems, but some digital libraries have been reluctant to use PDF.

One reason is technical. PDF is best suited for representing documents that were generated from computer originals. PDF can also store bit-mapped images, and Adobe provides optical character recognition software to create PDF files, but many of PDF's advantages are lost when the used to store image files. The file sizes can be unpleasantly large and much of the flexibility that digital libraries require is lost.

In addition, some digital libraries and archives reject PDF because the format is proprietary to a single company. There is a fear that the decision to use PDF in a digital library IS more vulnerable to future events than using a format blessed by one of the standards bodies. This reasoning appears misguided. PDF had its first success with corporate America, which welcomes well-supported, commercial products. The academic and scholarly community can accept that a format maintained by a corporation may be more stable in the long term than official standards that are not backed by good products and a wide user base.

●●

11

Preservation of Digital Information

One important area where the digital library can extend the services it provides beyond that of the traditional library is in integrating and highlighting user contributions. With the exception of especially unique or noteworthy contributions, the traditional library is rarely eager to receive resource contributions outside of its usual channels, as the effort needed to catalog and integrate outside contributions into a physical library is substantial. Digital libraries, on the other hand, are more often willing to receive contributions. It has been demonstrated that a combination of minimal submission data and basic verification procedures can result in high-quality digital library contributions with low rejection rates.

Such contributions enhance the value of the digital library by increasing its size and diversity and the process of cataloging and integrating contributed resources into a digital library often requires less effort. However, the aspects that make digital libraries built from user contributions valuable-diversity of content, potential for large growth-also create potential drawbacks. For example, search and browse facilities enable users to find resources based on features such as author, subject, and keywords, but as a digital library grows, finding specific resources of interest among the entire collection can become more difficult. At the same time, the prominence of a given contributor's contributions becomes diminished as the library grows. One way to help users find resources of interest in a digital library while ensuring that contributors receive recognition is to borrow a concept that has long been part of traditional libraries: the special collection. By defining and making available virtual collections believe the digital library can extend the special collection model and-at a modest cost-provide benefits to both its users and contributors that will encourage its own growth and viability. Traditional libraries often contain, in addition to their main holdings, special collections.

The special treatment might be due to the rare or delicate nature of the materials, or because the library wants to highlight the materials in some way. In contrast to traditional libraries, the special or sub-collections of digital libraries can be much more fluid. Where the holdings of a traditional library are physically constrained to a single space and a single ordering, resources in a digital library can be distributed across many servers, can be owned by different organisations, and can be displayed in many different orderings and arrangements. This fluid nature makes defining collections and sub-collections in the digital environment less straightforward.

Adhering closely to the traditional library definition, one could consider a digital library collection to be all those resources that reside on a single server, or alternatively, all those that can be accessed though a given library's interface, even if they are physically distributed. As suggested in, however, even a broad definition of a collection in the context of digital libraries can be ambiguous. It can, for example, be influenced by the point of view of those making the definition. The people responsible for managing resources stored in separate databases might think of each as a distinct collection, while an end user with access to them all is more likely to consider them a single collection. Defining sub-collections can be even more flexible as there are many possible factors that can suggest how sub-collections can be formed. A sub-collection can be defined by including all those resources that share a topic or other significant attribute, those contributed by a specific organisation, or those used for a specific purpose. These sub-collection examples are instances of collections that cannot be easily replicated in traditional libraries. They are made possible by exploiting advantages the digital environment inherently provides: objects can exist in multiple collections, collections with the same objects grouped in different ways call co-exist, collections can be created dynamically and exist for varying amounts of time.

Although it is common for traditional libraries to create and maintain special collections, many digital libraries do not attempt to provide a similar service. Most digital libraries do create the most basic of virtual collections-the result set dynamically created from a search request or category browsing-but rarely do they explicitly create and promote the sort of virtual collections described above. Doing so, however, can benefit both the users of the digital library and those who contribute resources to it. A digital library that contains virtual collections helps its users in several ways. A new user who may be intimidated by a digital library's search interface or the number of results returned by a query might be better introduced to the digital library through the more easily exploreable partitioned set of resources in a virtual collection.

A directory of the virtual collections contained by a digital library, can provide a good introduction and overview of the library's contents to new or. casual users. Associating resources with virtual collections enables those resources to be found more easily, either by browsing the contents of a highlighted virtual collection or through standard search and browse interfaces. Looking at the use of the digital library from a "work-oriented perspective", other benefits to the user stem from a more productive use of time. In it is suggested that sub-collections can facilitate work by isolating a group of related content and enabling a user to focus on those resources. Defining virtual collections makes it easier for users to find and work with such groupings of related content, or by a "related resources" link based on virtual collection associations and tied to specific resources. Additionally, the virtual collection description might include links to related information outside the digital library, thus guiding users to more materials for their work.

Contributors

In most cases those who contribute resources to digital libraries are not directly compensated, yet digital libraries often depend largely on contributions for the content they provide. It is, therefore, in the best interests of the digital library to find ways to encourage new and repeat contributions. Virtual collections can benefit contributors in several ways. First, they provide an alternative distribution outlet. Contributors often have collections in which they have invested effort in creating and would like to see used more widely. Because a digital library will generally have a much larger base of regular users than the contributor, contributing the collection gives the contributor's resources more exposure.

By grouping a contributor's resources through a virtual collection the digital library helps maintain the resources' association with the contributor and in effect provides publicity and recognition to contributors. By explicitly highlighting virtual collections and the people and organisations that contributed them, a digital library can increase the visibility of contributors. As a result, contributors are likely to benefit from more traffic to their own web sites, and can point people to their contributions at hosting digital library. Virtual collections can not only help improve the "brand" of a set of resources and support their distribution, but can also offer basic infrastructure services. In some cases, contributing resources enables the contributor to share resources without the overhead of storing and managing them, while retaining an association with them. If a contributor owns a large number of resources, this is a significant benefit itself, and one that has been taken advantage of by several Open Video Project contributors. Finally, if the digital library shares information about resource usage, either directly to its contributors or as is increasingly common, through most recommended or top10 lists, the contributor can gauge the relative demand of his contributions.

Implementing Virtual Collections

The benefits of virtual collections do not come without a price, of course. For a digital library to be able to easily create and remove virtual collections, to associate resources with different virtual collections in a flexible way, and to help users find and use the virtual collections, the library must have a structured approach to representing these collections. Moreover, to make creating such collections practical, this approach should also strive to minimise the costs associated with creating virtual collections. In the remainder of this matter describe an approach to implementing virtual collections based on work in creating collections for two different digital libraries.

Contextual Metadata

Metadata is a key element of any library, traditional or digital. Metadata is used by libraries to describe and organise item-level resources and by users to search and browse the library. Collection-level metadata performs a similar function for collections and is used in traditional libraries for discovery across collections. Work on collection-level metadata from several fields including archives, museums, libraries, and the Internet is relevant to the design and implementation of virtual collections. As outlined in, each field defines collections differently and has different standards governing collection description. The past few years have seen a movement to create a standard for collection description that is informed by, yet transcends, the fields from which it is derived. Work in the UK and the US has resulted in the formulation of goals for collection-level metadata and. the definition and development of schemas to describe collections. Based on work with the eLib working group on Collection Level Descriptions, the RIDING Clump Project created a searchable database of collection descriptions to provide information about what was available in its libraries.

The purpose of its scheme was to describe any type of collection-physical or virtual, networked or otherwise. RIDING collection metadata should allow users to discover, locate and access collections, search across multiple collections and allow software to provide services based on user preferences. The Research Support Libraries Programme (RSLP) builds upon the RIDING goals above by requiring that collection metadata allow the refinement of distributed searching approaches based on the characteristics of collections.

The Alexandria Digital Library (ADL) is a research digital library focused on geo-referenced geo-spatial information. The goal of the ADL is to create a single model that supports the four roles ADL identified for collection metadata: collection registration, network discovery, user documentation, and management. Several themes emerge from this the requirements.

- It highlights the importance of establishing standardised collectionlevel metadata schemas that can effectively describe and manage a diverse set of collections and their metadata.

- It argues that the schemas must support a number of functional library services that enable users to access collections and items, to search for materials, and to comprehend and use them effectively.

One challenge to creating collection-level metadata noted in the literature is the potentially high cost of production. Metadata can be automatically-generated or human-created with the latter clearly imposing more significant costs in terms of human effort and time. In the context of collections, describes two types of roughly corresponding metadata: inherent metadata, or information that can be extracted from the resource objects themselves, such as total number of objects or total file-size of the collection; and contextual metadata, or metadata which involves human judgment to create, such as a textual description of a collection of resources.

There are significant advantages to utilising inherent metadata as much as possible. Because it can be generated automatically, inherent metadata has minimal costs associated with its creation and maintenance and can be updated on a regular, automated schedule. In contrast, human-created metadata is time-consuming, error-prone, costly to create, and more likely to be inconsistent. A person assigned to create metadata may only perform this task on an occasional, as-needed basis, and it may be a lower priority task than others for which that person is also responsible. Inconsistencies in metadata assigned to resources can arise due to variations in a given cataloger's judgment over time and because different catalogers may make varied judgements in cataloging resources. There are drawbacks to relying solely on inherent metadata to define virtual collections, however. A risk in complete automation is the loss of many of the benefits of creating a virtual collection. Contextual metadata is important because it enables us to give some character and cohesiveness to the virtual collection. A collection is likely to be more than an accretion of all it contains; it has been gathered for a purpose.

The use of contextual metadata and human judgement in selecting resources to be included in a virtual collection has other benefits. Virtual collections can be described "in terms of expected use in addition to being characterised by the terms they actually contain". Resources can be more carefully chosen for inclusion in a virtual collection, with consideration of expected use, resulting in a more concise collection of high-quality resources that is easier to for the user to search or browse. It is important to recognise, however, that a collection-level schema that relies heavily on contextual metadata is relatively costly to implement and thus less likely to be maintained in the long term.

A more viable approach is to define a schema for virtual collections that balances the costs and benefits of each type of metadata. In short, a cost-effective-schema should include useful inherent metadata, supplemented by contextual metadata that captures human judgments of a collection's nature and the selection of criteria for inclusion in the collection.

Intellectual Property in Digital Library

The educational community encompasses a broad range of public and private institutions whose primary missions include research, education, and the preservation of our scientific and cultural heritage. In the process of carrying out their missions, these institutions, which include research universities, colleges, university presses, libraries, scholarly societies, museums, and archives, among many others, are both creators and consumers of scholarly communication. These institutions participate in the full spectrum of activities regulated by the laws governing copyright and must be sensitive to the balance of interests embodied in them. While a degree of consensus has been reached concerning the rights of creators, copyright holders, and users of information in the print environment, new proposals for the copy rights of digital works are threatening to disrupt the balance between the rights of owners and public access in the electronic world.

As they revolutionise the means by which information is recorded, disseminated, accessed, and stored digital technologies are eliminating the technical limits that have supplemented the legal framework of balance between ownership and public dissemination: Unlimited technological capacity to disseminate transmission in ways that can violate the rights of copyright holders confronts equally unlimited technological capacity to prevent works from being used in ways contemplated by law. Carried to its logical extreme~ either trend would destroy the balance, with results that would likely undermine core educational functions as well as radically transform the information marketplace. The educational community is heavily invested in scholarly communication. This process includes such functions as exchange of cutting-edge discoveries and works-in-progress among scholars, scientists, curators; publication of new and synthetic works for the broad scholarly community; dissemination of new and existing knowledge to students through teaching; establishment of repositories to enable handing knowledge down from generation to generation; and transmission of knowledge beyond the educational community to the public. It requires the ability to cite and quote the work of others, regardless of format.

Scholarly communication involves individuals, academic departments and research units, libraries, archives, university presses, museums, commercial publishers, external research sponsors, academic and industrial software developers, and others. Because it carries information that ranges from complex graphical and sound data to plain text, and must reach an audience that ranges from Nobel scientists to freshmen in remedial courses to citizens visiting a local museum, scholarly communication must include the full range of content and take place in all media. It must flow back and forth between all of its participants and be capable of moving rapidly enough to contribute to the evolution of understanding and knowledge. It must be disseminated through an economically viable system, and it must not be overwhelmed by a permissions system so burdensome that it makes rapid movement impossible. Scholarly communication is based on an ethic of authorship that both compels publication and condemns plagiarism. It demand" accurate attribution and respect for the integrity of works while asserting the importance of evaluating and interrogating sources for cumulative advance of knowledge. By promoting trust between authors, owners, and users, adherence to this ethic facilitates the rapid and broad dissemination of information. Educational institutions have developed organisational structures that insulate faculty, curators, and students—the core, but not the only participants in scholarly communication—from direct dependence on economic returns from specific intellectual properties. The institutions, however, function as both owners and consumers of the intellectual properties that circulate in the process of scholarly communication. As such, some of these institutions, such as museums, university presses, and scholarly societies, depend on the revenue from copyright ownership to support their educational, dissemination, and preservation missions. New knowledge cannot be created without extensive reference to work already done by others and to the accumulated records of human and natural phenomena or can the accumulated collective knowledge of a society be transmitted intact to succeeding generations without its preservation and organisation. Libraries, museums, and archives play crucial roles as custodians of knowledge and must continue to do so in order to carry out core educational missions. Faced with an exponential increase in the rate at which documentation is growing, libraries, museums, and archives increasingly seek to exploit the unprecedented storage capacities and facility for more effective access strategies of digital media. Moreover, the increased data creation and storage capacities generate new pressures on systems for preservation, organisation, and access. Although the functionalities of digital technologies will continue to give rise to practices and relationships that bear little resemblance to those surrounding print, neither novel arrangements nor enhanced capabilities should obscure the fundamental continuity of purpose underlying preservation and organisation.

The requirements of the academic mission and the accumulation of a cultural heritage do not cease when information and documentation cease to have commercial value and pass out of the marketplace. Hence, relations among copyright holders, educational institutions, and the law must reflect the needs of the future as well as the present and should acknowledge the added value to society of preservation and of well-ordered systems for navigating information.

Working on the frontiers of technological, economic, and legal knowledge, the educational community seeks opportunities for experimentation with new institutional arrangements for managing the dissemination and preservation of knowledge contained in copyrighted and public-domain works. It also seeks a legislative and economic environment that fosters collaboration and a search for consensus rather than confrontation and litigation. In preparation for the ongoing legislative debates on intellectual property in the digital environment.

Faced with the strong interests of the infotainment industry to maintain tight control of intellectual property in a global marketplace, the educational community may strengthen its more balanced position by speaking as one voice guided by the principles. The following principles are based on the "University of California Copyright Legislation and Scholarly Communication Basic Principles," Working Draft, December 2, 1996.

DIGITAL PRESERVATION REQUIREMENTS

In order to preserve digital materials on a scale commensurate with mass storage capabilities and in formats that are accessible and usable, it is necessary to articulate some basic requirements. There are two ways to examine digital preservation requirements: from the perspective of users of digital materials and from the view of libraries, archives, and other custodians who assume responsibility for their maintenance, preservation, and distribution. Libraries and archives will not accomplish their preservation missions if they do not satisfy the requirements of their users by preserving materials in formats that enable the types of analyses that users wish to perform. At the same time, libraries and archives are unlikely to be able to satisfy all requirements of all potential users primarily due to resource constraints. By making explicit preservation requirements from both the users' and custodians' perspectives, libraries and archives will be better able to integrate digital preservation into overall planning and resource allocation. The potential uses of digital materials are varied, unpredictable, and almost endless. Any generalisations, even if restricted to one community of users such as humanities scholars, run the risk of overlooking and understating potential user needs. Precise requirements for presentation and analytical tools vary among disciplines, yet some basic requirements are likely to transcend fields and disciplines. The ability to establish the authenticity and integrity of a source is critical to users, whether it is generated by an individual, created in the conduct of institutional business, or produced through a formal publication process.

Mechanisms that will enable users to establish authenticity require archives and libraries to store much more than the content of digital documents. Attributes such as formal document structures, metadata that document the maintenance and use history of the document, time and date stamps, and a series of references among documents are essential for determining authenticity and for understanding the provenance of sources and placing them in a larger context. Networking and access to digital sources will change all dimensions the scholarly work process, including identifying sources, communicating with colleagues, interpreting and analysing data, disseminating research findings, and teaching. If their projections are correct, digital preservation programmes must support a high degree of integration of source material into analytical processes by coupling research sources with the tools necessary to analyse them; by maintaining linkages between research results and the sources on which they are based; and by providing a means to incorporate primary sources into teaching. Users will seek documents that are easily retrieved and manipulated, transmittable, and transportable from a repository to the sites of research, presentation, and teaching. It seems safe to assume that humanities scholars will need the capability to search through and select relevant sources from large bodies of heterogenous materials, to compare sources to each other, and to view specific documents at high levels of granularity.

Digital preservation will add little value to the research process if it serves only as an alternative form of storage from which analog replicas are produced for use with conventional analytical methods. Preserving digital materials in formats that are reliable and usable, however, will require long-term maintenance of structural characteristics, descriptive metadata, and display, computational, and analytical capabilities that are very demanding of both mass storage and software for retrieval and interpretation. Digital preservation requirements may be expressed differently by archives, libraries, and other types of repositories that are struggling to meet escalating user expectations with limited financial and technical resources.

Storage systems should be capable of handling digital information in a wide variety of formats, including text, data, graphics, video, and sound. Digital storage is not only an alternative means for storing print formats because many types of digital objects do not have print equivalents and cannot be preserved in non-digital formats. Ideally, storage media will have a long life expectancy, a high degree of disaster resistance, sufficient durability to withstand regular use, and very large storage capacities.

Conversion from analog to digital formats and migration to new generations of technology will be rapid, accurate, and inexpensive enough to permit very large scale transfers of heterogeneous materials. Storage space requirements will be minimal and not demand highly sensitive environmental controls.

Current Methods for Preserving Digital Materials

Most librarians and archivists have accepted the basic wisdom for now at least—that digital preservation depends upon copying, not on the survival of the physical media. But copying, also referred to as "refreshing" or "migration" is more complex than simply transferring a stream of bits from old to new media or from one generation of systems to the next. Complex and expensive transformations of digital objects often are necessary to preserve digital materials so that they remain authentic representations of the original versions and useful sources for analysis and research.

Current methods for preserving digital materials do not fully support achieving these objectives. When faced with the responsibility for preserving digital materials, archives and libraries face a series of complex and difficult choices based on the format of the original materials, the anticipated uses for it, and the technical and financial resources available to invest in preservation initiatives. Probably the most commonly used preservation strategy is to transfer digital information from less stable magnetic and optical media by printing page images on paper or microfilm. It seems ironic that just as libraries and archives are discovering digital conversion as a cost-effective preservation method for certain deteriorating materials, much information that begins its life in electronic form is printed on paper or microfilm for safe, secure long-term storage.

Yet, high-quality acid neutral paper can last a century or longer while archival quality microfilm is projected to last 300 years or more. Paper and microfilm have the additional advantage of requiring no special hardware or software for retrieval or viewing. Perhaps this explains why in many digital conversion projects, the digital images serve as a complement to rather than a replacement for the original hard copy materials.

Digital information can be transferred across successive generations of technology in a "software-independent" format as ASCII text files or as flat files with simple, uniform structures. Several data archives hold large collections of numerical data that were captured on punch cards in the 1950s or 1960s, migrated to two or three different magnetic tape formats, and now reside on optical media. As new media and storage formats were introduced, the data were migrated without any significant change in their logical structure. This approach has the distinct advantage of being universal and easy to implement. It is a cost-effective strategy for preserving digital information in those cases where retaining the content is paramount, but display, indexing, and computational characteristics are not critical.

As long as the preservation community lacks more robust and cost-effective migration strategies, printing to paper or film and preserving flat files will remain the methods of last resort for many institutions and for certain formats of digital information. Libraries and archives with large, complex, and diverse collections of digital materials are only beginning to test strategies that normalise various types of holdings by converting digital records from the great multiplicity of formats into a smaller, more manageable number of standard formats.

A repository might accept textual documents only in one or a few commonly available commercial word processing formats or require that documents conform to standards like SGML. Databases might be stored in one or a few common formats or converted to a SQL (Structured Query Language) compliant format, while image files might conform to the tagged image file format (TIFF) with standard compression algorithms. This approach has the advantage of preserving more of the display, dissemination, and computational characteristics of the original materials, while reducing the large variety of customised transformations that would otherwise be necessary to migrate material to future generations of technology. The strategy rests on the assumption that software products which are either compliant. with widely adopted standards or are widely dispersed in the marketplace are less volatile than the software market as a whole. Most common commercial products today provide utilities for backward compatibility and for swapping documents, databases, and more complex objects between software systems. Although this strategy simplifies migration and may lower digital preservation costs by reducing the amount of customised reformatting needed as technology changes, it does not eliminate the need for regular migration of digital materials.

Software and standards both continue to evolve and even repositories with structurally homogeneous holdings can expect to be required to migrate their digital materials periodically. Current methods fall far short of what is required to preserve digital materials. All current preservation methods involve trade-offs between what is desirable from the standpoint of functionality, dependability, and cost and what is possible and affordable with current technologies and methods. Consequently, most repositories are coping by employing interim and less than desirable strategies, if they are addressing digital preservation issues at all. Migration strategies that involve reformatting of digital materials to a simple standard format usually eliminate the structure of documents and relationships imbedded in databases. Computation capabilities, graphic display, indexing, and other features often are lost, thus limiting future analytical potential. Normalisation to standard formats is not always technically feasible and it usually is quite costly. Archives and libraries must also contend with entirely new forms of electronically-enabled discourse and new forms of artistic and cultural expression that do not have predecessors in the analog world. No current preservation method is adequate for preserving dynamic data objects from complex systems. There are no established conceptual models or technical processes for preserving multimedia works, interactive hyper-media, on-line dialogues, or many of the new electronic forms being created today.

The archival requirements tc preserve content, context, and structure and to maintain the capability to display, link, and manipulate digital objects only heighten their software dependency. The preservation community is only beginning to explore possible alternatives to storing digital information in "software-independent" form. Rothenberg proposed an approach for maintaining the content of digital materials intact without losing the ability to retrieve meaning-rich sources. He recommended retaining the original document in its original format encapsulated in a virtual "envelope" that contains software instructions for retrieval, display, and processing of the message in the envelope. The envelopes would contain contextual information and the transformational history of each object. Execution of the instructions would rely on an archive of hardware and software emulators or on instructions in the envelope with specifications to construct emulators. Important research is underway to define standards for data interchange that can. support electronic commerce and satisfy business requirements in a variety of environments. A major research project at" the University of Pittsburgh is defining metadata requirements for evidence that will support the need for integrity, authenticity, reliability, and archiving through standards for "metadata encapsulated objects".

Archives, libraries, and other institutions with preservation responsibilities will benefit if systems are built to implement such metadata standards. Wide scale adoption of data and communication standards by the originators of digital information to support current business needs will also facilitate long-term preservation. Rapid implementation of electronic commerce depends on widespread development and adoption of standards for EDI (electronic data interchange) transaction sets under auspices of the ANSI X.12 committee, and many organisations are adopting standards for format and definitions to enable exchange, reuse, and sale of digital information and to reduce conversion and maintenance costs.

Standards initiatives that address business needs for the secure and reliable exchange of digital information among the current generation of systems will impose standardisation and non-nalisation of data that ultimately will facilitate migrations to new generations of technology. Yet to benefit fully from the synergy between business needs and preservation requirements we have to move beyond simply paying tip service to cultural heritage concerns and recognise that equally critical social goals, such as long-term genetic research, monitoring global environmental change, locating nuclear waste sites, and establishing property rights are also dependent on long-term access to reliable, electronic evidence.

Much remains to be done in research, development, and implementation before we can assume that even a small portion of our digital heritage will survive more than a few years. It is fair to say that the state of development in digital preservation remains largely experimental. Only a few libraries, archives, and other institutions have established digital preservation programmes, while most research and innovation comes from pilot projects and prototypes.

RESEARCH AND DEVELOPMENT AREAS

The current state of digital preservation suggests several fruitful areas for research and development. The major areas are: storage media, migration, conversion, and management tools. These four domains are often mutually dependent and ultimately must to be integrated into an infrastructure for digital preservation. Yet better solutions are necessary in all four areas before such integration can occur.

Base Storage Media

The limited life of magnetic and optical media pose a significant problem, although this is not the primary limiting factor for digital preservation. Recent research on the longevity of magnetic media indicate a useful life span of 10 to 30 years if they are handled and stored properly. Some optical disk technologies promise life spans of up to 100 years. Most authorities argue that enhanced media longevity is of little value because current media outlast the software and devices needed to retrieve recorded information. Nevertheless, improvements in the stability, capacity, and longevity of the base storage media are needed to drastically reduce the vulnerability of digital materials to loss and alteration and to lower storage costs.

Ample research and experience provide evidence of what can go wrong with magnetic media as a result of binder degradation, magnetic particle instabilities, -and substrate deformation. Optical media are susceptible to damage from high humidity, rapid and extreme temperature fluctuations, and contamination from airborne particulate matter. To prevent these problems, it is imperative to store magnetic and optical media under strict environmental controls that are not always available, affordable, or convenient. Even modest improvements which produce storage media with larger per unit storage capacities and greater tolerance to variations in temperature and humidity will lower preservation costs by lessening the need for strict environmental controls, reducing the frequency with which digital media must be "refreshed" through recopying, and decreasing the number of storage units that must be handled.

This raises the question, however, of whether research on incremental improvements in current storage technologies will benefit preservation in the long run or whether we should seek alternative approaches to digital storage that more adequately meet archival requirements. As a frame of reference it is worth remembering that microfilm, which is considered the only acceptable archival storage medium, lasts at least 300 years with minimal maintenance if stored properly. Last June, the Los Alatllos National Laboratory announced the invention of a High-Density Read-Only Memory (HD-ROM) technology that uses an ion beam to inscribe information on pins of stainless steel, iridium, or other materials. The HD-ROM is capable of storing 180 times more information than current CD-ROM technology at roughly one-half percent of CD-ROM costs. According to the release about this technology, the HD-ROM is impervious to material degradation and it requires no bit stream interpreter because the technology can describe in human-readable form all of the instructions needed to interpret the data (LANL Ion Beam Storage). Such an approach illustrates the potential for solutions built on entirely new storage technologies.

Migration of Digital Materials

Better methods for migration of digital materials to new generations of hardware and software are much needed for digital preservation regardless of breakthroughs in mass storage technologies. Planning for migration is difficult because there is limited experience with the types of migrations needed to maintain access to complex digital objects over extended periods of time. When a custodian assumes responsibility for preserving a digital object it may be difficult to predict when migration will be necessary, how much reformatting will be needed, and how much migration will cost.

There are no reliable or comprehensive data on costs associated with migrations, either for specific technologies and formats or for particular collections, and little research underway on methodologies that would reduce the costs and burdens of migration. The preservation community as a whole would benefit tremendously from the development of backward compatibility paths that would be included as a standard feature of all software.

Backward compatibility or migration paths would enable a new generation of software to "read" data from older systems without substantial reformatting and without loss of retrieval, display and computational capabilities. Although backward compatibility is increasingly common within software product lines, migration paths are not commonly provided between competing software products or for products that fail in the marketplace. Stewards of digital material have a range of options for preserving digital information. One might preserve an exact replica of a digital record with complete display, retrieval, and computational functionality, or a representation of the record with only partial computation capabilities, or a surrogate for the record such as an abstract, summary, or aggregation. Detail or background noise might be dropped out intentionally through successive generations of migration, and custodians might change the format or storage media. Enhancements are technologically possible through clean-up, mark-up, and linkage, or by adding indexing and other features. These technological possibilities in turn impose serious new responsibilities to present digital materials to users in a way that allows them to determine the authenticity of the information and its relationship to the original record.

There are few well developed methods for preserving and migrating software so that it might be used to recreate digital documents that have the "look and feel" of the original sources. Maintaining repositories of obsolete hardware and software has been discussed periodically, but usually dismissed out of hand as too expensive and not demonstrably feasible. This approach deserves more serious consideration as a strategy for maintaining continuing access to certain types of digital materials. Feasibility studies and cost/benefit analyses should be conducted to determine the technological, economic, and commercial feasibility of maintaining selected legacy software systems and performing specialised migrations or, alternatively, of building and maintaining software emulators.

Conversion Technologies

Faster, cheaper, and higher resolution conversion technologies are another critical element needed to make digital preservation feasible on a large scale. Most archivists and librarians accept the fact that we live in a hybrid environment where paper, microfilm, video, and magnetic and optical media need to interoperate in a more integrated and transparent manner. The vast majority of primary sources today still reside on paper and/or microfilm with little chance that we will see the mass conversion of existing archival and library holdings to digital formats. Research and planning for digital preservation must recognise that we will be dealing with conversion for a long time and that investments in improving capture rates, accuracy, resolution, and verification will have long-term benefits. Moreover, improvements in conversion technologies may support hybrid solutions to preservation and access problems by permitting repositories to store certain formats of digital material on stable media, such as microfilm, with on demand conversion to digital form for analysis and reuse. Efforts to capture and store descriptive mark-up on film for subsequent conversion are hampered by unacceptable error rates in OCR technology and cumbersome conversion processes.

Development of Management Tools

A fourth area for research is in the development of management tools for digital libraries and archives that integrate descriptive control and maintenance with storage technologies. Dynamic digital objects, such as those found in hypertext systems, pose special management problems for both current and future retrieval and reuse. The boundaries of hypertext sources, like those found on the World Wide Web today, are difficult to ascertain because no single party or institution controls changes in the nodes and links that make hypertext objects live and highly responsive information resources.

A high degree of volatility accompanies these objects because the contents of nodes change, the sites where information resources are stored change, and the links between nodes change, move, and vanish. Some recent tools, such as the MOMspider (Multi- Owner Maintenance Spider) and Web:Lookout are capable of traversing a portion of the Web and noting maintenance problems such as broken links, moved documents, modified documents, and objects that have exceeded their expiration dates. While tools such as these are useful for current maintenance, they do not address long-term preservation concerns. If further developed to address preservation problems, tools such as these have the potential to serve as filters, identify similar or identical objects, and monitor for maintenance problems. Research and development of tools that would imbed more intelligence about the preservation status of digital material into the objects themselves would make monitoring and maintenance of large digital collections more automatic.

Recommended procedures for monitoring physical deterioration of magnetic tape, for example, involve reading a small sample of tapes periodically to determine whether any data losses have occurred. The potential exists to build monitoring and reporting mechanisms into digital objects, storage systems, and network architectures that could support self- reporting of physical status and initiate automatic maintenance procedures. Despite differences, some lessons from traditional preservation are transferable to the digital environment.

In order to avoid commitments that far exceed available resources and costly rescue and restoration efforts, preservation must become an integral part of the planning, design, and resource allocation for digital libraries and archives. Integration of preservation requirements and methods with access and maintenance systems is essential to fully and efficiently support the processes of migration, regeneration, and documentation of the life of digital objects. Planning for preservation must become an integral part of the design and management of digital libraries and archives.

PURPOSE OF PRESERVATION

Preservation is a response to the threat of destruction. Some individual ultimately must initiate the response when the threat has been recognised, and the scale of the reaction may be in proportion to the value that is placed on the object under threat. Their reaction incurs a cost which will continue to be incurred, while the threat appears to remain. Funds will be drawn upon, and resources will be mobilised, that have been held in reserve explicitly for the purpose of preservation. Other stakeholders are drawn into the preservation activity as time passes.

In the world of digital material, the old rules do not apply so clearly. The cost and effort required to preserve candidate digital material may not be proportionate to the value of the material, nor are they related directly to the urgency created by the threat. Whereas before benign neglect of printed paper-based material was a viable course of action, and a delayed reaction could in itself be an act of preservation. With digital material, decisions are required, supported by authorised expenditure, to enable resources to be deployed quickly in order to counter the threat of irreversible loss.

The resources may involve substantial capital investment as well as specialist labour, both available in the near term only at a premium. Because so much of a digital item is connected to its immediate technical regime, the preservation specialist is concerned not to leave out any information that will later prove to be valuable. Only what is sufficient and necessary should be carried forward. The preserved material, held as though in a sealed capsule, must be accompanied by material that moves forward technologically in step with the changing world, changing its format and style, while still being able to fulfil its purpose.

Unlike the existing national archives of printed material, the value of the digital material may not be directly proportionate to its age or cost of production. Digital material may need to be treated exactly the same, whatever its provenance. All technology consists mainly of electronic storage used for different purposes, having different orders of size, security, and cost. The first major factor affecting the approach to the preservation of digital items is the type of material. For example, textual documents are possibly the simplest items to preserve, they are well-scoped, containing all the information relating to document within the file, when it is presented for preservation. Complexity remains low if they use a standard mark-up language. The complexity rating rises when a document lipks to other objects, outside itself, or when essential extra functionality for document formatting is introduced, or the document contains a macro, or the document is intended to work in a networked environment and contains HTML linkages. The risk is that some of these features may not be reproducible, or inaccurately, in the future. Either way the evidential nature of the record is diminished, potentially catastrophically. At present, when such documents are retrieved, these functions are usually lost, and the unformatted text is displayed or "default" templates are used.

Therefore, by proliferation, the facilities will become embedded and supported in more and more products, irrespective of vendor. The material and the format become bound together, similar to a book. From the perspective of preservation and future access, the resources that maintain the usefulness of the material have been "donated" by the software vendors, although from self-interest. Technology Watch will monitor their continued willingness to donate the resources without change and without major change.

Most software developers aim to make their products able to import and export objects into many different formats. The translation from one into the other is not fool-proof but it serves the purpose of exchangeability. With preservation of evidence in mind, the future decoding of these formats will be critical. Exchangeability between current software products is not a sufficient mechanism to provide permanence. Formats become someone else's problem when the item to be preserved is held within a capsule, such as Microsoft Office or Lotus Notes, from which it can be redisplayed.

The translation or display is the responsibility of the enveloping software. The envelope will evolve over time, but the translation techniques will be preserved. Word Version 6 will always be associated with a Word Version 6 "launch" or "view" software module. In the same way, other formats which are standard at the time of capture provide the least risk path for preservation. Documents in a non-current, non-standard formats cannot be stored in their native format, unless a "launch" or "view" mechanism can be stored in a capsule with them.

With text-based documents, the rules of evidence do not require the archive to retain the original data with its full format characteristics. It is necessary instead to provide supporting evidence that the text could not have been amended during the time the item was in the archive. The most complex to guarantee preservation at present are the graphics formats. They are continuously evolving, and the evolution has still some time to run. Each software company adapts standards to suit their product, to limit the problems of upward compatibility, and to enforce customer loyalty.

A "launch" or "view" facility will have to be stored with them, or the graphic objects will have to be stored in a nonproprietary format, TIFF or BMP. As an recent example of the transitory nature of some of these graphics "standards", the popular GIF format, a common element on the Compuserve network, is now hardly used. This is a direct result of CompuServe being forced to stop using it as a result of copyright infringement law suit, successfully brought against them. GIF has now been replaced by a similar, but different format, invented by CompuServe. The net effect is that after a short period of time the old GIF will not be supported, under the terms of the settlement. Some stored CompuServe message attachments may therefore become garbled or inaccessible.

Overall, apart from the effects of the software market's internecine warfare, the main division of formats for the future are lossless formats and lossy formats. The degree of loss in lossy formats is only of concern to the preservation environment if the uncompressed object cannot serve the purpose for which it was preserved, for example, as evidence, supported by a adequate copy or facsimile of an original. In the last 50 years, the diversity of media on which data has been stored has not diminished, but increased. Despite the diversity, the most durable of media remains the tape. The original tape storage mechanisms have changed size, recording density, encoding, capacity, speed and reliability, so that they are no longer recognisable. After tape, the disk is the most durable, but the disk has changed more. radically than the tape. Optical, magneto-optical, magnetic and solid state devices now compete to hold commercial data.

The two technologies combine portability, reliability, speed of access and a greater capacity. They score highly in the "Capture" and "Storage" categories of the archive, because of their longevity, portability and lack of susceptibility to damage. All other devices do not score as highly. In the last 50 years, the computer marketplace has seen every combination of personal, workgroup, divisional and corporate computing promoted as the answer to business problems. Each new machine range has adopted to make a step change in functionality in order to outdo the competition and protect its customer base.

About 25 years ago, IBM halted its FS (Future Systems) programme because it had established through market surveys that it would lose half its customer base if it introduced a radical new technology that required everyone to change their programs and files. This same fear of losing market share still dominates the Operating System platform. "Transparency to the user" is declared for every major change in order to allay fears of another costly transition.

Convergence is therefore in progress over a wide range of hardware platforms via the operating system and its "open" file structures and encoding techniques. This is of great advantage to an archive. The hardware platform is not material as long as the archive media has an operating system-independent file recording and encoding structure. In the same way compatibility of recording material is taken for granted today for CD, audio cassette tapes and videotapes, but it was not always so. Recent product developments are soon to disrupt the status quo again, both in the home and in the office.

Hardware emulation has usually been preferred in order to provide speed and compatibility. Joint hardware and software emulation has been used. At the present day, software emulation dominates, being programmable even at the chip level. In an archive, it may be necessary to handle some emulations, but this can only be tenable in the short term, while both the emulated and the host emulator are current in technology terms. Obsolescence for the host environment will bring double jeopardy for the emulated environment. Archiving of an emulation and its dependants should be considered only for the near term, and in the advent of destructive forces. The major issue arising from running a long term preservation service is customer confidence. When stakeholders entrust unique and possibly priceless material to the archive is a greater commitment than that made by most businesses. The central six functions, stretching from Capture through to Access I Retrieval, are the core of the activity. The overall planning, reporting and administration are essential functions required to run the archive facility.

The archive is the goal for all the preserved material and the associated contextual data. How it is managed and run operationally will have an effect on the whole preservation process: efficient procedures during archive will not only reduce costs during Capture, but also further back up the business chain of activities, possibly improving the efficiency of the creators themselves. By increasing the confidence in the security of the archive and the integrity of the items, stakeholders may consider changing the way they work. By managing the central process as a value chain, from Capture to Retrieval, improvements can be made in the way staff work together, controlling costs, improving service levels, and raising quality levels.

The concept of project management will be very beneficial in managing all the resources more efficiently and controlling the changing technology environment so that the monthly operating schedule can be delivered on time, to budget. The archive needs a forward view of where change will strike it next. A six-monthly review is sufficient for planning purposes. The archive will have all the requirements of a small business to manage its assets, draw on local expertise and report back to branch management on the day-to-day practicalities and trends.

Storage Management is the key component in every management process, at some stage the data must be stored, retrieved, updated. When a technology prediction is linked to a database of existing archived items, the scale of the forecast and the potential impact, can give a manager some idea as to how to react and when to time the reaction. When change is unavoidable, the most up-to-date technology may not be the most attractive. Instead, a less leading edge implementation may allow one to miss out a conversion, because it has less risk of failure and may be more adaptable. With the preservation of digital material we are preserving far more than. any other society before has attempted to store. Technology Preservation is generally seen as not being feasible, as a computer processing environment is almost impossible to preserve indefinitely as a working museum artefact. Experience in the UK and audit work has shown that it is prohibitively expensive, even when the systems it was supporting were very valuable.

Equally the specialised variants of preservation demand and capture could create a cost-effective though non-standard model for long term preservation. The long term preservation of digital material is a subject which lacks many of the attributes of the well-established skills and knowledge of parchment, papyrus, paper and film-based preservation techniques. Therefore an open-minded collaborative approach will be essential if the digital library and the digital archive are to be as successful and as valuable as our current Collections and their priceless holdings.

Digital material requires a greater degree of positive effort to preserve its meaning and context than most non-digital artefacts. Four levels of context are considered to be necessary, represented by different types of metadata. Understanding the practical issues of preservation allows a balanced programme of preservation work to be planned. Scarce resources can be focused on ensuring the permanence of the digital material and while maintaining a cost effective environment for the long term. The framework identifies ten types of stakeholder, who affect the way the digital material is preserved and managed in the archive. Traditionally the creator, owner and user are seen as the main stakeholders. With the long term digital archive, the number of stakeholders increases significantly. The interplay of the stakeholders will determine when and where the archive is established, how the archive and its contents are used in the future, and how successful in the long term an archive for digital material can be. The management objective is that the archive environment must be kept current in technology terms in order to perm it unconstrained, secure access to all items in the store. Within that environment, the underlying technology is being altered by step changes in the configurations, and the technology will never remain the same from one to the next. The preserved material will reside within an environment which is in a continuous state of transition. Balancing enforced change with continued assured access is necessary in order to provide a stable operating environment.

Non-digital material, such as printed books, papyri and paintings usually carry within themselves sufficient physical and contextual information which allows them to be interpreted without a great deal of assistance. The context can sometimes be provided by the script, the language, the media, the style, and the signature. The item itself, because of its structure, may often act as part of the item's historical record.. Alterations, additions and editor's annotations may be present as part of the item. Even a palimpsest or an over-painted cartoon can provide extra evidence for the item's provenance. The type of contextual information for digital materials is similar, but usually the digital record is two dimensional, requiring the history to be explicitly stated as the evidence for it cannot be deduced.

Digital material is different also because the means of accessing, displaying and interpreting the physical record may no longer be operative because of technical obsolescence. Current technology allows the creation of a "bound" document, for example, using Windows '95 and Office '97 technology. The scale of the binding is under the control of the author, starting from association of external objects with a document to importing the objects and embedding them within the document. The objects can be any Microsoft Office-based product output. Macros can be used to enhance and extend this function further. As long as the capsule of information that is created is not affected by in-built technological obsolescence, the approach should viable over the long term. Similar principles apply to Lotus Notes-based applications. By linking the document to an environment, owned and managed by an international de facto standards maker, one ensures as best as one can, long term accessibility of the capsule. Even if Microsoft and IBM were to be broken up, the new owners of the patents and copyrights would be sufficiently powerful to maintain upward and downward compatibility path for the capsule and its hidden components. Currently most major office software providers provide a very wide range of "launch", conversion or import/export facilities, in order to keep their clients reassured and loyal, and to attract new users, who are in the process of switching products. Creating a capsule helps maintain the association of the context with the preserved item. A capsule does not in itself preserve the integrity of the contextual records unless another level or security is used. The "evidence" could be secured by the use of PGP or public-private key encryption. The capsule would then be locked, and could not be tampered with. Access would continue as usual with the public key.

The media and the environment need the attention of the preservationist. There is an obvious difference between working to ensure no loss occurs, and working with the knowledge that loss will undoubtedly occur whatever precautions are taken. The difference emphasises the different ways in which we manage the items in the archive and the archive environment itself. Additionally there may be some value in preserving the packaging of the digital material, similar to the dust-jackets of 1920's Legal Deposit material or an example of a CD, equivalent to an amphora exhibited as part of a museum's exhibition. A locked capsule and the original medium carrying the digital material need not be treated as unique items, as long as the technology which they rely on is extant. With technology we are in a much better position to understand the interplay of the resources involved. Preservation of the technology environment is within our capability. It is distinct from the complexities of preservation of digital material which we cannot see and cannot inspect except by the intervention of technology.

The stakeholders may be different people, or a combination of individuals and organisations. The Creators, Owners and Providers are the major stakeholders, recognised as being essential for cooperating with the Libraries and contributing to the holdings in the archive. Often at least one of these parties will have a financial interest through the copyright on the material. It is this interest that some archivists hope may encourage funding to be made available in order to manage and maintain a digital archive in the long term. The Regulators have set the scene with legislation to preserve ownership for a limited period of time, to ensure a national collection of material is established and to preserve items that are in the public interest. The situation changes with the plan for long term preservation.

The Regulators may therefore have a role in extending the legislation to make anyone who uses an archived item to contribute to its preservation. The fee would be collected by the Provider, a re-publishing fee. The original Providers of the designated archive material are very likely not to be the Providers of the copy from the Archive. Recently preservationists have identified a new Stakeholder: the Interferers. These individuals and organisations are frequently the antithesis of the current Regulators. New regulations are sometimes subsequently formed because of these pressure groups. At other times they are seen as simply a nuisance, obstructing the course of good preservation practice, taking a narrow perspective on minor issues. Their impact is usually to delay new measures and to initiate a review of current procedures.

Interferers can be put to good effect by judicious lobbying. Technology is an Interferer. The development of new media is driven by the potential revenue from accessing data, communicating information and developing commercially profitable knowledge bases. Storage is seen as a temporary issue, only a small proportion of the business event information is finally stored. The emphasis is on processing the data, in new and inventive ways, displaying the information as fast as possible anywhere in the world, linking various knowledge bases dynamically, and capturing more and more diverse data items to feed into the system.

●●

Index